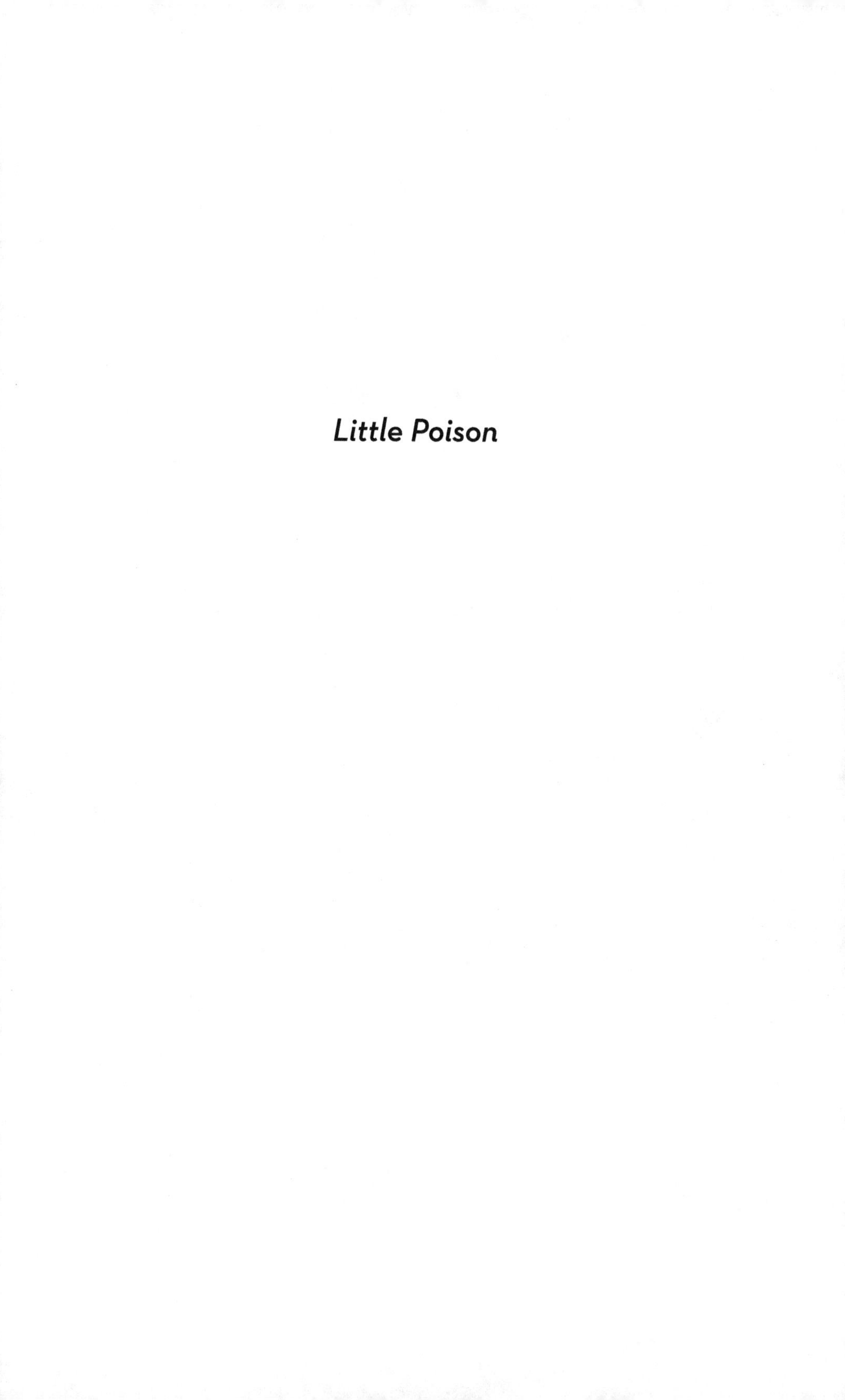

Little Poison

LITTLE POISON

Paul Runyan, Sam Snead, and a Long-Shot Upset at the 1938 PGA Championship

JOHN DECHANT

University of Nebraska Press
LINCOLN

The University of Nebraska Press is part of a land-grant institution with campuses and programs on the past, present, and future homelands of the Pawnee, Ponca, Otoe-Missouria, Omaha, Dakota, Lakota, Kaw, Cheyenne, and Arapaho Peoples, as well as those of the relocated Ho-Chunk, Sac and Fox, and Iowa Peoples.

Library of Congress Cataloging-in-Publication Data
Names: Dechant, John, 1983– author.
Title: Little Poison: Paul Runyan, Sam Snead, and a long-shot upset at the 1938 PGA championship / John Dechant.
Description: Lincoln: University of Nebraska Press, 2023. | Includes bibliographical references.
Identifiers: LCCN 2022034824
ISBN 9781496231420 (hardback)
ISBN 9781496235930 (epub)
ISBN 9781496235947 (pdf)
Subjects: LCSH: Runyan, Paul, 1908–2002. | Snead, Sam, 1912–2002. | PGA Championship (1938) | Golfers—United States—Biography.
Classification: LCC GV964.R86 D43 2023 | DDC 796.352092/2—dc23/eng/20220722
LC record available at https://lccn.loc.gov/2022034824

Designed and set in Sabon Next LT Pro by L. Auten.

For TVD

Contents

Illustrations

Prologue

In the beginning, he was just a kid trying to find his way onto a golf club, one across the road from his father's dairy farm. Then, in his tenth decade alive, there he was again, now an old man—a very old man—trying to get onto a golf club.

Not just any club. The most famous of its kind, Augusta National, known the world over for its annual Masters Tournament, a celebration of not just championship golf but also everything that's perfect about this former plant nursery, which golf legend Bobby Jones had first laid eyes on shortly after his Grand Slam conquest of 1930: the breathtaking reveal one gets when driving down Magnolia Lane, the flawless azaleas, the annual champions dinner, the nearly commercial-free television presentation, the meticulous course conditions (fawned over by club golfers and downplayed by golf course superintendents everywhere who each April, like clockwork, have to listen to a chorus of members asking, "Why can't our course look like that?"), the neatly packaged pimento cheese sandwiches, and the throwback pricing of other crowd-pleasing foodstuffs like chicken biscuits and Georgia pecan caramel popcorn. And on, and on. The place had become as famous for such hoopla and creature comforts as it had for its entire reason for being—golf.

Paul Runyan, ninety, described by one journalist that April day in 1999 as a "peanut of a man," accompanied by his second wife and carrying his own thirty-pound golf bag, had shelled out $10 for a shuttle ride from his hotel only to get dropped off at the wrong gate outside Augusta National, on the side of Washington Road.

Runyan now faced a half-mile walk to the famed Augusta clubhouse.

His journey to Augusta that early spring had been less than surefire.

Months before, after deciding he'd like to play as an honorary invitee in the Par-3 Contest, annually held on the Wednesday before the Masters begins, Runyan picked up the telephone and tried to let someone at Augusta National know he'd be coming. Problem. He couldn't get a live body to take his call. "Telephonic devices," as Runyan called them, were his kryptonite, and the voice on the machine asking him to press 1 for this and 2 for that and so on only confused him.

Didn't matter. He and his wife would head for Augusta National anyway. It would be Runyan's first trip there in four years. His very first trip came in 1934, during the first of FDR's several terms as president. That year he had played in the first Masters ever contested, then known as the Augusta National Invitation Tournament. It was played in March back then. He scored a featured pairing that year with no less than Bobby Jones, the man who founded the place. Now, in 1999, Runyan was back in Augusta, Jones was long dead, and Bill Clinton, a native Arkansan like Runyan, held the highest office in the land.

As Runyan and his wife walked toward the clubhouse that April morning, fate intervened. A car pulled over. Not just any car but one occupied by Sam Snead's manager and caddie. They recognized the man in the black sweater and gray wool golf slacks as Runyan and offered him a lift, which he accepted. It was 9:00 a.m., and the sun was starting to warm up this southern patch of golf heaven in a hurry. Runyan was a seven-year survivor of heart bypass and just a month removed from carotid artery surgery, performed to prevent a stroke. A car ride sounded like a good idea. That it came from two members of Snead's posse was more perfect. That's history winking at you.

Contest organizers found a spot for Runyan in the Par-3 Contest. It was an ideal spot, paired with former Masters champions Tom Watson and Ben Crenshaw, known as two of professional golf's finest gentlemen and biggest history buffs. And they found him a caddie, an Augusta regular named Rick Flinchum.

At 1:12 p.m. Runyan made it to the first tee of the 1,060-yard short course at Augusta National and shook hands with Watson and Crenshaw. Arnold Palmer made a special trip over from the putting green and hugged Runyan, smiling like he was embracing his own uncle at Thanksgiving. Then, wearing a white Callaway bucket hat, Runyan was announced to the crowd that had gathered around the tee. And off they went.

Runyan played the Augusta par-three course that day. Every hole. Not his best, but he played. He shot a nine-over-par 36, making four pars, two bogeys, two double bogeys, and one triple. As the group neared completion of the round and walked along a narrow path toward the ninth green that snaked around Ike's Pond, Ben Crenshaw made sure to take the inside route, acting as a human barrier just in case Runyan lost his balance and started to fall toward the pond.

"I grabbed him by the arm, and my caddie Carl Jackson and I both said that we better get him going the right way," Crenshaw remembered.

As for Runyan's game, Crenshaw could still picture a once-great player, trapped in the body of an old man. "No question, the vestiges were there," he recalled. "You could see in the way he put his hands on the club and the way that he swung, the way he handled the club. You could tell. It was there."

Playing in the group behind Runyan that day was Tiger Woods, two years removed from his first Masters victory, and he applauded from the eighth green when Runyan's second attempt found the green at the ninth. Woods had played a few groups behind Runyan the year before in a pretournament event at the PGA Championship at Sahalee Country Club near Seattle.

And in the group ahead was Sam Snead, eighty-six, winner of seven major championships and then the all-time leader in PGA Tour victories (eighty-two). Two decades later, Woods and Snead would become linked as Woods threatened to wrestle away the all-time wins record. Snead, on that sunny day in 1999, was sixty-one years removed from the greatest drubbing he ever took on a golf course in serious competition.

It had come directly at the hands of that peanut of a man, Paul Runyan.

PART 1

Hot Springs Boys

1

Something in the Water

Four thousand four hundred years. Scientists say that's the age of the water that emerges from the ground of the thermal springs in Hot Springs, Arkansas. The phenomenon is not easily or perhaps even entirely understood. Rocks called chert and novaculite, formed in deep ocean environments during the Carboniferous period, were folded and faulted as the earth's plates shifted, creating cracks that allowed water to seep into the ground when it rained on the Ouachita Mountains. The rainwater that seeped through, descending some eight thousand feet, started to warm as the earth's temperature increased with depth, a concept known as geothermal gradient. Then the folds and faults of the rocks created a path for the water to rapidly ascend, emerging through the Hot Springs sandstone at a temperature of 147 degrees Fahrenheit. One million gallons of thermal water flowed from the springs every day.

Was there something in the water? You better believe it.

THE CENSUS TAKER who visited Hot Springs Township, Arkansas, on January 21, 1920, likely had no idea of the serendipity that he was recording on the Garland County census form. But what person, whose job was to dispassionately interview people and update their basic information, could be expected to connect the dots that linked neighbors by deeper relationships like master and apprentice, friend, and mentor?

Jimmy Norton, forty-three, and his wife, Dela, thirty-eight, inhabited dwelling number 177 listed on that form. Norton hailed from Scotland and was employed as the manager of a local golf club, the census indicated. Make that *the* local golf club. And let's not stall over census jargon like "manager." Norton was the golf pro, plain and simple. On line 64 of that same census form, the line directly above Norton's, was the name Paul S. Runyan. Just eleven years old, Paul was the second son of Walter S. Runyan, thirty-eight, and his wife, Mamie, thirty-six. He had been born on July 12, 1908, but the census won't give you that, or any, birthdate. Nor will it give you the exact place of his birth, which was 19 Baker Street in Hot Springs. At that address stood a house, not a hospital.

According to the federal census, the Runyans in 1920 rented their home, and Walter (whose brother, according to family legend, was a moonshiner) worked as a dairy farmer. Any hopes he had about passing along the trade were about to dwindle. Around that time, young Paul decided that dairy farming would not be in his future. It was a fine enough occupation for his father, Paul thought, but the boy had been bitten by the golf bug, and Jimmy Norton—call him the golf pro next door—took a liking to Paul and offered to help.

Help with what? For starters, Norton provided Paul access to the game. The Runyans lived right across the road from the Hot Springs Golf and Country Club, yet the worlds of a dairy farming family and a typical Hot Springs golfer, who was usually a vacationer with enough disposable income to spend a few days or weeks soaking in the warm, supposedly curative spring water sheltered by the east-west-oriented Ouachita Mountains, were rungs apart on the socioeconomic ladder.

Paul started out as a caddie. Even though he considered himself the best caddie in the yard, he had a hard time getting bags because he was small. People worried he couldn't keep up, so on many occasions he caddied for Jimmy Norton. He fought a similar battle in the schoolyard. As an undersized kid, he became an easy target of bullies. He had his share of minor scrapes—nothing too serious—that toughened him up and taught him how to stick up for himself.

Hot Springs loopers were forbidden to play the course, even in the summer, which was the off-season in Hot Springs. The penalty for breach of this rule was termination. But Runyan was made an apprentice to Norton, which allowed him the opportunity to sneak in four holes each day on his way to school and five holes on the way back. The Runyan farmhouse was located about four hundred yards from the Hot Springs clubhouse, and Paul's country school sat adjacent to the fifth green. Paul and his older brother, Elmo, would get pulled aside by the school's headmaster during the morning recess and over the lunch hour for a quick rundown of their afternoon lessons. In exchange, they were allowed to leave school early to report for work at the club.

Picture them, the Runyan boys, leaving school early, bound for the golf course, already with four holes under their belt from the morning commute. Young Paul, dairy farming averse, his older brother at his side, and his father's disfavor on his mind, supremely confident, full of conviction, was embarking on another afternoon as a golf professional-in-training under the watchful eye of a transplanted Scot, his neighbor from dwelling number 177. Perhaps the boys carried their clubs. Or maybe they stored them at the clubhouse. Did they even have their own clubs at that age? It doesn't matter. Wait, yes it does. Everything about the game he loved mattered to the boy. Maybe it wasn't that Norton *offered* to help but that he simply had no way to tell the kid no. You can imagine what the other kids at school must have thought, seeing those lucky Runyans blaze through the afternoon curriculum over lunch so they could leave early for another afternoon at the golf club. It was like watching Tom Sawyer and Huckleberry Finn play hooky every afternoon—with the teacher's blessing. It sounds like a bizarre kind of work-study arrangement for adolescents, but when one of those kids was a golf-crazed aspiring professional, it was the perfect apprenticeship. Could Paul even keep the smile off his face each morning at school—feigning interest in reading, writing, and arithmetic—as his mind wandered toward his afternoon delight?

The money was good, too. Paul was paid 35 cents per half hour to shag balls while Norton gave lessons. The boy became proficient at using his catcher's mitt to snag balls on the fly and save himself some running around. Gratuity was usually 50 cents, sometimes as high as $1. And that came on top of what he made caddying; typically, as all caddies would attest, the better a golfer played, the better the tip. As a youngster, Paul was able to regularly bring home $45 a week to his mother. Other caddies were satisfied once they had collected $5. During especially good weeks, Paul's take-home pay shot up to $80, sometimes $90. As he put it, he had "more money to spend than any kid in Hot Springs." Still, golf rubbed his father the wrong way. Walter whipped his son several times for deserting the dairy farm for the golf course, Paul said. In the Runyan household, whippings were serious business. His son's loathing of dairy farming bothered Walter only a little. It was the boy's choice of alternative vocation that got under his skin. Golf, he insisted, was not real work.

On the subject of his golf obsession, Paul was unafraid of his father. Looking him directly in the eye, he told the old man, "Dad, you can whip me if you want, but it won't do you any good, because I'm going over to the golf course, and I'm going to become a golf professional."

The elder Runyan was no fool, even if the boy's words stung. It became hard to ignore his son's weekly haul of $45.

Pinpointing precisely when Paul and Walter had their come-to-Jesus moment over golf is difficult, but it likely happened in 1921. That was the year when the "small, but eager" caddie decided to make golf his future. Small but eager: those were his own words. That was one of two major decisions he made in 1921. The other pertained to the manner in which he played the game. Despite his love for golf, the game did not come naturally. It was a struggle right from the start. Other caddies were better players at first. The Vanoy brothers, described as "strong, sturdy farm boys," were two of his regular playing companions from the caddie pen, and both could hit the golf ball well past Runyan's longest drives. In order to compete, he had two options: go home and milk more cows to get stronger under the watchful eye of his father or get really good (or "clever," as he put it) at hitting short shots. Runyan opted for the latter.

It was a choice made out of necessity, he claimed. It began a lifelong love affair with golf's short game, and it would go a long way toward determining his future success as a player.

IT ALL BEGAN because a town wanted golf.

The Hot Springs Golf Club had been organized in January 1898, just five years after the Chicago Golf Club became the first eighteen-hole course in the United States and four years after the formation of the United States Golf Association. Things got moving fast. The Arkansas course was plotted that same month, and it opened for play on March

8. This initial routing consisted of nine holes, measuring 188, 202, 356, 370, 295, 263, 240, 256, and 295 yards. Those distances would make it a short course in modern times, at least in terms of yardage, but in 1898 it was plenty long.

Its geological natural wonder made Hot Springs a resort city. A baseball city. A hotel city. And folks with a financial interest in those hotels needed entertainment for their guests. After all, you can only spend so many hours a day soaking in a hot bath before your skin starts to take on the wrinkled appearance of a raisin. Enter golf, a new-to-the-country stick-and-ball game, fresh off a steamship from Scotland, with its strange rules and customs that offered just the sort of outdoor recreation the local innkeepers had in mind. Visitors to the golf club could pay a daily fee of 50 cents for use of the course. Or they could choose to pay by the week ($2) or month ($5).

This arrangement lasted barely more than a decade before the community truly got serious about golf. On April 17, 1909, the Hot Springs Golf and Country Club Association was formed. A board of directors was elected. Stock in the club was sold. And an option to purchase and build on 240 acres of land a mile and a half south of the city was taken at a cost of $15,000. By golly, Hot Springs, Arkansas, was going to have itself a proper golf club.

Yet for all their enthusiasm, the club's stockholders knew little about what they were doing. The first club president, Martin A. Eisele, whose signature was on the club's stock certificates, confessed as much, stating that "none of us had any previous experience to go on." The group estimated that a golf course could be built, and a clubhouse could be constructed, for a total of $20,000, though it's unclear, and was even then to Eisele, how they arrived at such a figure.

Off they went.

"The magnitude of this undertaking was, I confess, not fully appreciated by me when I assumed control of it, and I doubt whether many of our stockholders really knew just how great an undertaking this has been," Eisele wrote later in 1909. "To convert 150 acres of practically forest into a golf course within a year is a problem of some magnitude and involved the utilization of both energy and money, coupled with competent and intelligent direction."

On May 15, 1909, work began to prepare the densely wooded grounds for golf. Like much of Garland County and the nearby Ouachita Mountains, the terrain was rugged and heavily forested. Small trees and vines were cut down, and the low-hanging limbs of large trees were trimmed to create space, presumably for course routing and airflow. The club tabbed William Anderson of the St. Louis Golf and Country Club, considered by club members to be "one of the leading experts in the country," to lay out the course. According to Eisele, Anderson liked the site and suggested that with the proper care and budget Hot Springs could have one of the best golf courses in the country.

The sultry Arkansas summer made it a difficult time to build a golf course. With air temperatures ascending toward triple digits and an off-the-beaten-path job site that made it tricky to hire competent labor, the working conditions proved challenging. While many of his colleagues—likely other club stockholders—fled Hot Springs that summer for cooler climates to the north, Eisele stuck around to supervise the work.

Eisele may well have been the hero of the project. A druggist by trade, he had come to Hot Springs in 1887 and soon took ownership of a series of pharmacies. In 1907 he partnered briefly with Charles Walgreen in the Live and Let Live Drug Store. After a year, Walgreen sold his interest to Eisele and returned to Chicago, where he founded what would later become one of the most successful and recognizable drugstore chains in the world—Walgreens.

Eisele was in his early fifties during the construction of the Hot Springs Golf and Country Club. Despite his advancing age, he seemed well suited to the role of construction supervisor. From 1900 to 1907 he had served as superintendent of the Hot Springs Reservation. In 1832 President Andrew Jackson had designated Hot Springs as the first federal reservation of land for recreational use, and in 1921, five years after the establishment of the National Park Service, Hot Springs became a national park, joining the likes of existing parks such as Yellowstone and Yosemite.

After William Anderson completed his initial routing of the golf course, crews came in to cut down the remaining trees, pull the stumps, and burn the wood. Then the ground was leveled, plowed, harrowed, graded, raked (by hand), and rolled. It was a hot, dry summer, and the ground was hard. Finally, the course was seeded. Meanwhile, construction of the clubhouse was under way. After careful consideration, the club selected a site that was elevated and would look attractive on approach. Problem: the land was not theirs. That meant they had to purchase an additional six acres. Expenses continued to mount, and organizers had to borrow more money. Eisele remained undaunted.

A formal opening of the golf course had been targeted for the fall of 1910, and it was reported that President William Howard Taft, an avid golfer, would be on hand to hit a ceremonial tee shot. However, Taft's visit, at least in a ceremonial capacity, never came to fruition.

By all reports, the early years of the Hot Springs Golf and Country Club were a success. In March 1912, New York-based industrialist and philanthropist Andrew Carnegie, a vacationer to the Hot Springs area, visited the course and declared that it stacked up against any in the country. Members thought the same, but it was nice hearing it from an outsider.

Over the summer of 1912, the course was seeded with Bermuda grass. With each passing year, it became more evident that the grand vision was working. Visitors came from all over the country to play the course. Members paid their dues faithfully, and some even requested additional stock in the club. In 1916 the Arkansas State Golf Association brought its first state tournament to Hot Springs, contested over four days in April.

Then there strode into town one Willie Park Jr., whose talents were the final touch that the club needed to become an elite golf destination. The tweed-wearing, mustached Scotsman had won two Open Championships in the 1880s and already had numerous renowned golf course designs to his credit in Europe and the United States, including Kilspindie Golf Club, Sunningdale, and New Haven Country Club. Despite the praise that had been heaped on many of his course designs, Park kept a relatively low profile in Hot Springs. Described as a man with an "international reputation," Park's yearlong revisions to the course were plainly recounted as wonderful improvements. But those improvements—paired with the desirable Hot Springs winter weather—worked. The course was frequently overcrowded that year. The clubhouse was enlarged, locker rooms were added, and new showers were installed. Play doubled in November 1919 compared to the same month a year earlier. The club received letters from golfers around the country, expressing interest in playing the course during their time in Arkansas. Golf was so popular in Hot Springs, plans for a second eighteen-hole golf course were already in the works.

This all had to be music to the ears of Jimmy Norton when he showed up in Hot Springs. Not only would Norton work as the club professional, but the booming golf scene allowed him the resources to hire additional help. That help would eventually include his dairy farming neighbor's kid, Paul Runyan. The boy had played a little baseball and had dabbled in boxing, at least until his knuckles started to hurt, but he would have dragged those knuckles across broken glass for the chance to apprentice under Norton at the golf club.

Even Babe Ruth himself fancied all that Hot Springs had to offer, golf included. Ever since 1886, when Cap Anson brought his Chicago White Stockings to Hot Springs to prepare for the upcoming baseball season, the city had grown into a spring-training hotspot. Besides the comfortable weather, the owners and players enjoyed the first-class hotels, mountain trails, hot mineral baths, and active nightlife. Perhaps none enjoyed it more than the Great Bambino, who became something of an adopted son to the people of Hot Springs. The Babe liked to hike the mountains, gamble at the casinos, and play golf (when he wasn't hitting massive home runs, such as the 573-foot blast that rose over the right-center-field fence on March 17, 1918, from Whittington Park and landed inside the Arkansas Alligator Farm). Babe and his baseball training companions frequently would play for a box of cigars. It seemed that whenever the Babe teed it up, a decent-sized gallery turned up to watch him play.

Ruth took his time in Hot Springs seriously, even if it sounded more like a vacation than a training session. Three weeks of baths (taken in uncomfortably hot water, followed by a steam treatment, a half-hour sweat, and a cold shower), rubdowns, and casual rounds of golf topped off with cigars became routine for the big slugger every winter.

The Babe was sometimes a guest at the Majestic Hotel, regarded as one of the South's most famous hotels. Located at the intersection of

Park and Central Avenues, on the north end of Bathhouse Row, the Majestic—through an agreement with the federal government—had since 1886 been offering its guests thermal water from Hot Springs National Park in the hotel's therapeutic baths. Besides attracting the Babe and other baseball regulars, the Majestic later became popular with underworld figures such as Al Capone and Frank Costello. Why? Maybe because New York gangster Owney Madden set up shop in the city and maintained his spot there until his death in the 1960s. His association with the city made it a fashionable hangout for his racketeering comrades, who probably appreciated the security of staying in their hotels to receive a thermal bath over the risk of leaving the hotel and being in plain sight. Or maybe, but less likely, they just wanted to rub shoulders with professional athletes like Ruth.

And who knows how, exactly, Walter Runyan, Paul's father, got hooked up with the Majestic Hotel by managing its dairy farm. It's doubtful he yearned to catch a glimpse of the Major Leaguers, and it's even more doubtful that he had any ties to organized crime. He was a man in need of a steady income to take care of his family. When the boys were little he had worked as a fireman and a truck driver for a laundry, but he set his sights on something with more long-term potential. Little, if anything, is known about the precise nature of Walter's agreement with the Majestic, but what is known is that he was ill for several years when his boys were young. Mamie Runyan confirmed the presence of an illness to a newspaper reporter in 1934 for a profile about Paul, noting that her two boys had had to learn to fend for themselves at an early age. Walter's illness—once reported as a case of tuberculosis that sent him into the state sanitarium for five years and prompted Paul to seek out safe activities outdoors—limited him physically and thus stunted the output of his dairy farm.

The Majestic paid Walter $120 per month to manage the farm, but as his boys grew up and started to handle more of the labor, he asked for $250 per month. Management denied the raise, so Walter quit and went off on his own—with his two boys at his side—at the farm across the street from the golf club.

Paul's tale is not that of the wayward son, at least not in any classic sense. It's true that at an early age the boy decided he wanted to be a golfer, not a dairy farmer. Yet all indications are that he was, particularly as a boy, every bit the farmhand that his father needed for his enterprise to survive. He gathered wood for the stove and helped milk cows morning and night, and his brother Elmo—whose given name was Elmo Dickson and who sometimes went by "Dick"—worked right alongside him. They would rise each morning at 4:00 (3:00 in the summer) to milk the cows, cool the milk, then deliver it by horse and wagon. Eventually they bought a Ford to speed up the delivery process. Sadly, nothing could speed up the time it took customers to pay their bills. Between the farm work, the caddying, and his studies, young Paul Runyan's days were filled from dawn until dusk. His father recognized this fact, too.

"Paul was a good kid," Walter Runyan told the same reporter who interviewed Mamie in 1934. "He never smoked a cigarette. He never told me a lie."

Walter's insertion of "me" into that sentence uncloaks the dynamic between father and son. It's as if he's telling the reporter to distrust any supposed tension between him and his son, almost confessing that his lifelong disdain for golf had been overblown. There were worse boyhood diversions than caddying. Smoking cigarettes, for one.

Once, when the boys were young, they asked their father if they could go fishing. When they returned with wet hair, Walter asked if they had gone swimming instead. Dick wanted to fib their way out of it, but Paul wouldn't let him.

"Yes, Dad, we did go swimming," Paul said.

"What do you think I ought to do to you for disobeying?" Walter asked.

"I think we ought to be whipped," Paul said.

"About how hard?"

"About ten licks."

"That is exactly what I am going to give you."

Paul received ten licks, and his brother received twenty.

After the evening milking was done at the Runyan dairy farm, Paul would leave for the golf course, carrying a pail filled with golf balls. He would hit ball after ball into the setting Arkansas sun until the pail was empty, then pick them up one by one. If there was any daylight remaining, he would repeat the routine until darkness.

When the South Central Open first came to Hot Springs Country Club, Runyan was tempted to qualify for a spot in the field. Jimmy Norton preached patience and told Runyan to caddie for one of the professionals instead. He set him up to carry Macdonald Smith's bag. Smith was one of the best players in golf and, like Norton, a native Scot. Runyan took one look at the woods in Smith's bag and wondered how his player ever got them airborne. Then he watched him hit his brassie so high that it looked like it was going up through an elevator. It was a shot Runyan had never seen before and one that demonstrated how skillful elite professionals truly were.

As Runyan grew up and matured as a player, Norton let him take on more responsibilities as an apprentice, including club making and golf instruction. On the practice tee, Runyan became like a cash machine for Norton. As Runyan remembered, the lessons he gave put $500 to $700 a week into the till. He was paid a salary of $75 or $80 a week, so the extra money belonged to Norton and the club. The same went for the money he made on club repairs and cleaning. Sporting an attitude that was perhaps indicative of the era, Runyan was fine with the arrangement and simply grateful for the opportunity.

"I felt I was fortunate," he told veteran golf journalist Al Barkow for his 1986 oral history *Gettin' to the Dance Floor*, which includes one of the most detailed and insightful profiles of Runyan anywhere—exactly what you'd expect from an author as accomplished as Barkow, who in 2005 received the PGA Lifetime Achievement Award in Journalism.

"I was learning a profession and getting paid for it," Runyan said. "How much better can you do than that?"

As for Runyan's own game, his technique, particularly in the short game, was developed through circumstance and his own ingenuity. That's because the putting surfaces at Hot Springs Golf and Country Club in those early days were made of sand. To anyone unfamiliar with this footnote in the history of golf course architecture, it may come as a shock that many golf courses of yesteryear, in certain areas of the country (the Great Plains, for example, where reliable irrigation was impossible, or the South, where turf was unable to tolerate the summer heat and humidity), had putting greens that were made of sand. These surfaces were constructed by hulling out a parcel of ground and installing a hard base, such as slate or clay, then topping it with sand and applying a layer of oil, often clean motor oil or vegetable oil. In some cases, the sand greens were watered instead of oiled. The greens at Hot Springs, Runyan said, were made from a thin layer of oiled sand over a base of firm clay, and "of table-like smoothness," according to a report in the *Hot Springs Sentinel-Record* in 1924. The famed Pinehurst No. 2 course, now an anchor course for the U.S. Open, also began with sand greens and stayed that way for many years.

Why sand? Money, of course. Sand greens could be built and maintained at a lower cost than grass greens. Besides saving money, some courses opted for sand greens due to unfavorable climates and insufficient irrigation. The downside? Even the smoothest sand greens roll at a much slower pace than grass greens. And the oil, which would latch onto your pants, socks, golf ball, and hands (and eventually grips), could make you filthy.

Most sand-green courses are now gone, but some remain, scattered here and there, especially in states such as Kansas, Colorado, Missouri, and Nebraska. Canada, too. If you come upon one of these layouts today, say in La Crosse, Kansas, or Dannebrog, Nebraska, you'll pay a tiny fee to play the course, and immediately you'll notice the most distinguished accessory to these small, brown patches of sand etched into the landscape as putting surfaces: the rakes and the drags. In order to putt, each green has its own rake with a blunt side to drag a smooth path onto the green so a player can putt toward the hole. After finishing the hole, the green is then raked with the conventional side of the rake before the next group plays up to the green.

As Runyan honed his chipping and pitching techniques, he became frustrated by well-struck shots that would land in a pocket of sand on the green, often created by the tines of the rake, a missed footprint, or sometimes just a soft spot in the sand. These shots would stop dead in their tracks, without any rollout, creating a small sand crater around the ball. Other times, similarly struck shots would dodge the sand pockets and run through the back of the green. It could be maddening. Thus, he learned what any golfer who has ever played a significant amount of golf on sand greens eventually figures out: low-flying shots provide the most control of the golf ball. Low shots carried more forward momentum and were capable of powering through the pockets of sand, yet the overall distance the ball traveled was more predictable for the player. Developing good touch was made easier, and the vagaries of the sand green were mostly eliminated from the equation. Runyan started playing his chip shots, sometimes from as far as thirty or forty feet off the green, with a low-lofted club and a putting stroke. He developed this style over a six- to eight-month period during his caddying days and continued refining it. He employed a mostly wrist-free stroke powered by his shoulder joints, which caused the ball to come out gently knuckling, with minimal backspin, allowing it to "walk through" the sand.

What was the significance of young Paul Runyan crafting his short-game technique on sand greens? Oiled sand and finely manicured grass are worlds apart in composition. One is soft, uneven, resistant. Full of tiny rocks. The other is smooth, predictable, firm underfoot.

Another question, this time more direct: did learning the short game on sand greens ultimately contribute to Paul Runyan's success as a chipper, pitcher, and putter? The answer almost certainly is yes. His short-game technique was mostly self-taught, born out of necessity. And it worked.

But how could something that seemed to be such an apparent disadvantage—learning to control a golf ball's flight and roll on an entirely different playing surface—ultimately work in favor of the earnest farm boy from Arkansas? Let's count the ways. First, back up a bit, to the fairway. Eyeing a sand green from any significant distance—say between fifty and two hundred yards—is a daunting proposition. Most sand greens, when compared to typical grass putting surfaces, are much smaller, often 50 to 70 percent. The sand greens at Hot Springs were sixty to seventy-five feet wide, or about twenty to twenty-five yards. That's a narrow target, and while it's true that a ball landing on the green with anything other than a head-high, flat trajectory would stop dead in its tracks, balls landing just short of a sand putting surface would often take one large bounce over the green, missing it entirely. In Runyan's case, most of the balls landing short of the green would get snagged by the catcher's mitt that was the course's sticky and coarse Bermuda grass. Accurate shots of the proper distance were a must if you wanted to putt for birdie.

Having navigated his ball onto the green, a successful sand-green putter accepts the necessity of stroking putts with true, end-over-end roll. If the putter head contacts the ball with a descending blow, the ball will dig into the sand and come up woefully short, even on the smoothest of greens. Such a misstep can often go unnoticed on grass greens, even to a trained eye. And while sand greens are much slower putting surfaces than grass, putting on sand guarantees the old adage, "Never up, never in." That is, putts that don't reach the hole have no chance of dropping. The same is true on grass, but not *as* true. A little extra pop in the stroke is needed on sand to guarantee enough forward momentum for the ball to reach the hole. That heavier hit, and a few additional putts holed over the course of eighteen holes or a seventy-two-hole championship, can make the difference between winning and losing.

Then, of course, there's chipping. Runyan crafted a chipping technique that was an extension of his putting. He kept the ball low to the ground, which he used as a friend. He preferred using low-lofted irons, elevating the heel of the club off the ground, with the shaft nearly perpendicular to the turf. He adopted a unique split-hand grip, his palms facing upward in opposition. If you ask a golf historian or a well-informed instructor to explain the defining trait of Paul Runyan's golf game, that person would almost certainly direct the conversation toward his chipping technique. It came about, the little man said, out of necessity. There on the golf course across the road from his father's dairy farm in Arkansas. On the Bermuda grass and the oiled sand greens.

And it all began because a town wanted golf.

2

Six Hundred Balls a Day

The ascent of a young player—it's a bit like climbing a mountain. At times it seems impossible, out of reach. Trimming seven shots a round so you can go from good to great. Good luck.

The successes—however minor—and the failures—however disastrous—are public, played out in front of discerning galleries. In tournament golf, you eat what you kill. Many times, you simply don't eat. Meanwhile, the young player continues working behind the scenes, in darkness, on obscure workbenches like Concordia Country Club, often through the relentless heat and humidity of an Arkansas summer, sometimes in between lessons or other duties in the golf shop.

The young player is never truly alone, even if it seems that way. There are always ride-along companions, and Paul Runyan had his fair share. It's quite an interesting cast of characters if you get right down to it. As a caddie in Hot Springs, he shared the fairways with Emerson Carey, the salt tycoon and property owner from Kansas, not then knowing that his future in-laws would share geographic ties with Carey. In his twenties, Runyan chased daylight with Harry Tenenbaum, the golf-obsessed son of a Little Rock junkyard owner. Later he counted on the kindness of famed aviator and sportsman Logan A. "Jack" Vilas, who opened his wallet to pass along professional opportunities for the young pro. Somehow, they all pale in comparison to a traveling gambler known as Titanic, who, to be clear, was no companion.

It was never easy. Traveling a thousand miles by train to North Dakota. Spending all day on the practice tee giving lessons to beginners and women twice his age. Owing financiers during the Great Depression. Rat-holing money in order to get married. The six hundred balls a day might have been the easy part.

He must have loved it. How else could he have scaled the mountain?

"TEACH THE LADIES."

That was Jimmy Norton's advice-cum-order for his young golf apprentice Paul Runyan.

"And grow a mustache."

A mustache? Was Norton so concerned about the young lad's social prospects that he felt the need to grease the skids with grooming advice? Maybe, but the suggestion was more practical than vain. Norton knew the value of optics, and he realized that for his baby-faced protégé to be taken seriously as a golf instructor, the youth needed to look a little less baby-faced. With blond hair, straight teeth, and little wrinkles that formed between his eyes and upper cheekbones when he flashed his wide smile, Runyan the teenager (he barely looked it) took Norton's advice and grew some hair above his upper lip. He once described it as a "ragged, brilliantly red wisp that made me look like I was out on bail from the funny papers." How long it took him to cultivate such a facial accessory is unknown, but it wouldn't last. As for the ladies, Norton owned little in the way of patience to teach the finer points of the game to the fairer sex, especially beginners, so he delegated that responsibility. And if lightning should happen to strike, well, then good for the boy. Thanks be to the mustache.

Lightning *would* strike, but not immediately, and not in Hot Springs.

At seventeen, Paul Runyan left Arkansas for the great unknown of Fargo, North Dakota, a thousand miles to the north, where he accompanied Jimmy Norton for a job at Fargo Country Club, located in the valley along the western bank of the Red River. The club had become the state's first golf club in 1898, and in 1916 it purchased an additional eighty acres on the edge of Fargo. By 1923 FCC would become North Dakota's first eighteen-hole golf course.

References to Runyan's job responsibilities in Fargo are scant and usually described as somewhere between those of a caddie master and an assistant professional. That's not entirely accurate, according to Fargo businessman Roger Reierson, who met Runyan in 1995 while working as the communications manager for the U.S. Junior Amateur Championship, held in Fargo. Reierson explained: "They've had that job title wrong in some of the things that have been written about him. He actually was the assistant club maker. He worked out of the caddie shack and made golf clubs."

Paul Runyan: assistant club maker. Otherwise, very little is known of his time in Fargo, other than the fact that he was there. Today, FCC proudly claims Runyan on its website, touting his time there "in the early 1920s." But that's about it. However, he's hardly forgotten.

"The club and its members enjoy the connection to Mr. Runyan, although brief," said Mark W. Johnson, head golf professional in 2020. "Mr. Runyan is remembered here each year with our annual Runyan Cup par-three event. In addition, Mr. Runyan came back to speak at the USGA Junior Championship held here in 1995."

Runyan's time in Fargo was brief, a résumé builder. By acquiring on-the-job-training in club making, he had checked off another box in his education as a golfer. Then it was back home. It begs the question: if he had traveled so far for the job, why did he leave Fargo so soon?

"One word—winter," Reierson speculated.

You can picture the restless Arkansas farm boy taking one look at a North Dakota snowfall, the bone-chilling wind whipping across his adolescent face, mustached or not, and checking the train schedule for the next available ride home. Actually, he had planned to return to Arkansas anyway. That was home. That's where his family lived, his mentor lived, and Norton had arranged for the Fargo job to coincide with the off-season in Hot Springs. And, for a golf professional, the southern climate made a lot more sense than a start-up club less than two hundred miles from the Canadian border.

Back in Arkansas, Runyan resumed his old job in the golf shop at the Hot Springs Country Club. In February 1926 the club hosted the annual South Central Open, and on the eve of the tournament "Wild Bill" Mehlhorn, the cowboy hat–wearing pro with a balky putting stroke and a toothbrush mustache who'd finished runner-up to Walter Hagen at the previous year's PGA Championship, breezed into the golf shop carrying a set of hickory-shafted George Nicoll golf clubs and demanded to speak with someone who knew anything about club repair.

"Well, Mr. Mehlhorn, I'm the assistant club maker," Runyan said. "Can I help you?"

"You know how to lay heads off?" Mehlhorn asked.

"Yes, sir," Runyan said.

"I want you to lay the heads off on these shafts as far as you can lay them off. Then I want you to lay them off some more."

Essentially, Mehlhorn was asking to have the shafts filed down so the neck of the club would sit behind the club's straight edge, effectively reducing the offset.

"Mr. Mehlhorn, if I go too far, it's subject to breaking. You'll snap the heads off as fast as we can do it," Runyan warned.

"Well, if you've got any skills, you'll do it the way I want it done."

Runyan promised he would try. Mehlhorn said he needed the clubs back the following morning. Runyan looked at the clock and saw that it was three o'clock. He had to hurry.

Runyan spent nearly an hour with each club in the set. After sundown he relied on lamplight to illuminate high spots on the hickory shafts that needed to be filed down. It was tedious work, which lasted until eleven thirty that night. He finished the job with a new set of grips.

Mehlhorn arrived the next morning to critique Runyan's work. He grabbed each club and studied it carefully. As the seconds ticked by, Runyan became nervous that one of the clubheads might snap right off the shaft.

"I'll be damned," Mehlhorn finally said, breaking the silence. "Come to a place and get a snotty-nosed little kid, and he's the first guy I've ever seen that knows how to offset irons."

Runyan let out a sigh of relief.

"What do I owe you?" Mehlhorn asked.

"That's $1.80," Runyan said.

Mehlhorn paid his tab and tipped Runyan an extra $5 Then he went out and won the tournament with his newly adjusted golf clubs, defeating Bobby Cruickshank in a playoff. The clubs held up beautifully.

A FEW MONTHS later, shortly before his eighteenth birthday, Runyan found a job in Little Rock, fifty-five miles to the north and east of Hot Springs. He was hired as the golf professional at Concordia Country Club, a nine-hole club for the small Jewish community, located west of downtown. For a teenage golf pro who aspired to play the game at the highest level, the circumstances at Concordia presented a special opportunity. By Runyan's count the club had just forty members, most of them engaged in business and whose only opportunities to play golf came on Wednesday afternoons and Sundays.

"The rest of the time I practiced," he told Al Barkow. "On average I would hit six hundred balls a day, although a lot of them were short pitches and chips, because I recognized early that I had to be very good at the short game or I wasn't going to go anywhere."

At Concordia, Runyan's most frequent practice companion was Harry Tenenbaum, the son of Little Rock junkyard owner Abraham Tenenbaum, a Russian immigrant who had arrived in Little Rock in the 1880s driving a wagon full of scrap metal. Tenenbaum scratched and clawed for survival for a few years, and by 1890 he had enough money saved to rent a small warehouse for his scrap dealing. A sign outside his business read, "A. TENENBAUM COMPANY: BUYER OF HIDES, FURS, WOOL, BEESWAX, BURLAP BAGS, SCRAP IRON AND METALS." The scrap business was a serious trade in Little Rock. The Tenenbaums dealt with people from all walks of life, including farmers, butchers, and smelter operators. The once-small concern kept growing, and by 1900 Abraham's nephew Julius had joined the company. Tenenbaum Recycling Group (TRG) would one day become Arkansas's largest recycler and processor of scrap metal. It was a true immigrant success story that spanned more than a century.

Son Harry Tenenbaum lived a life deserving of its own book, or at least a cartoon strip. He was born August 6, 1902, in Little Rock, and by the early 1920s he had joined his father in the junk business, although he would not make it his life's work. Harry made news in Arkansas in the late summer of 1921—unfortunately for all the wrong reasons. Sort of. The *Arkansas Gazette* explained the situation in a story on Sunday, August 21, 1921, under the headline "Seek to Annul Secret Wedding." The story told how young Harry had been married that July in secret—well, partial secret—and his new mother-in-law was intent on dissolving the union. The bride in question was Bernice Cohen of St. Louis, whose father, Leon J. Cohen, had made a fortune during World War I as a successful junk dealer, just like Abraham Tenenbaum.

Mr. Cohen had been killed by a train in 1917 and left behind a sizable estate valued at more than $840,000. With that kind of money involved, it's easy to see why Mrs. Cohen would be protective of her daughter. The Little Rock rabbi who married the couple asserted that the union was entirely legal. Abraham Tenenbaum, meanwhile, rooted for his son and hoped Mrs. Cohen would simply drop her complaint.

Somehow, some way, the Tenenbaums got their wish. The couple stayed married and eventually moved to St. Louis, where Harry worked as a stockbroker. They had two children: a son, known as L. Jay, and a daughter, Joy. Harry Tenenbaum, as was his habit, stayed in the news. He became a well-known businessman and civic leader in St. Louis, where he was an executive of the Peltason-Tenenbaum Investment Company and president of the Signal Hill Telecasting Corporation, which operated TV station KTVI. His name was all over the newspapers in 1960 after he was accused of bribing commissioners of the Federal Communications Commission by sending them turkeys over the holidays. That headache, too, would somehow disappear, and when Harry died in 1964 he would leave behind an estate valued at $3 million.

But he was more devoted to golf than business in the 1920s, when he buddied up with Paul Runyan. In his early days as a married man and father, Tenenbaum was a prolific club golfer. Runyan was not just his pal but his instructor, too. In 1927 Tenenbaum won Concordia's club championship, defeating Philip Pfeifer two up in the tournament's exciting thirty-six-hole championship match. Tenenbaum and Pfeifer were co-medalists again in the 1928 club championship, with Tenenbaum getting the better of the action in the championship match. Tenenbaum and Runyan got along well and played golf together often, regularly bagging thirty-six holes a day and sometimes seventy-two holes, even on the hottest of Arkansas summer days. They were a fast-playing twosome that could zip around Concordia's nine-hole layout in just fifty minutes. On April 14, 1929, they were playing partners for an especially rare circumstance. On the sixth hole, a par three measuring 150 yards, Tenenbaum watched as Runyan hit a four-iron onto the green. Then Tenenbaum reached for his mashie (a club akin to a five-iron)—ignoring a suggestion from Runyan to take one more club—and hit a towering shot with a slight wind at its back that flew straight into the cup for a hole in one. On the green, Runyan, after conceding to his friend and pupil that he had mistakenly suggested too much club, holed his putt for a birdie. Runyan had the last laugh that day. He made six birdies, including the final two holes, and just one bogey to shoot a five-under-par 67, which tied his own course record, set the previous summer.

The constant play and practice on the mostly deserted Concordia Country Club, often in the company of Harry Tenenbaum, started paying off for Paul Runyan. Local Arkansas club professionals held a weekly game on rotating courses: Little Rock Country Club one week, Shrine Country Club the next week, then Willow Beach, and so on. In one of those weekly games, held in the fall of 1928 at Sylvan Hills Country Club, the six pros in attendance started the back nine fast, combining to make five birdies in the first five holes, capped off by Runyan's hole in one on the par-three eleventh, his second hole in one since moving to Little Rock. Runyan's 73 that day was one stroke shy of the course record held by Willow Beach professional Julius Ackerbloom.

In those days, there was no Arkansas section of the Professional Golfers' Association. Thus, Runyan and other area club pros were unable to play in a qualifying tournament for the PGA Championship. However, in 1927 the *Arkansas Gazette* reported that an effort was under way, spearheaded by local pros, to organize such a chapter. Still, Runyan found other avenues to test his competitive mettle. There were some small-time successes, like winning the Arkansas Open in 1926, a feat he would repeat in 1928 and 1929. In February 1926, he played in the South Central Open, held on the friendly turf of the Hot Springs Country Club, which seemed like the perfect battleground for the seventeen-year-old to find out where his game stood against the country's best golfers. The answer: he had a long way to go. It was the golfing equivalent of a boot kick in the teeth. His opening two rounds of 76-76 placed him in a tie for twenty-eighth place, fourteen shots behind halfway leader Harry Cooper. Runyan would finish the event with disappointing scores of 86-76 to shoot 314, twenty-nine strokes behind Bill Mehlhorn, whose play was aided by Runyan's skill at the workbench, and five shots behind his mentor, Jimmy Norton.

In 1927 Runyan entered the Western Open, held at Chicago's Willie Park–designed Olympia Fields. The *Chicago Tribune* described the field of 270 competitors that year as a "Who's Who" of golf, absent only Bobby Jones. Runyan opened with a 78, six strokes behind leader Tommy Armour, and rallied on the second day to shoot 76 and make the cut, but he still fell seventeen shots behind halfway leader Walter Hagen. However, scores of 82-78 on Saturday's thirty-six-hole finale left Runyan thirty-three shots behind Hagen, the eventual winner. Runyan beat just five players who made the cut. His totals of 314 in each event, while respectable, were far from what he needed to be a serious contender. The Western Open was a big-time golf event, where spectators had to shell out a couple of bucks to watch in person. To compete with the game's best, Runyan would have to find a way to trim roughly seven to eight strokes off his score—per round. It was a tall, almost impossible order.

TOURNAMENT GOLF IS a pressure cooker that, over time, can harden a player's nerves. Four-round marathons, where every foul ball must be played and every putt, by rule, has to be holed, have a way of separating the contenders from the pretenders. There's a unique tension that accompanies the duress of competition, and some players simply can't handle it. But there's another way to get accustomed to intense pressure on the golf course: open your wallet and play for your own money, or find someone to stake you and try playing with their money on the line.

One bright summer day in 1928, the telephone rang at Willow Beach Golf Club, located on an oxbow lake eight miles outside Little Rock, near a railroad line. The call was answered by nineteen-year-old Ernest "Dutch" Harrison, a young assistant pro working for Julius Ackerbloom at the club. On the other end of the line was a force of nature the likes of which has never been seen before or since.

"Kid, this is Ti Thompson," the man said. "Could we have a game?"

The man on the telephone was in town on business, he explained, and Harrison agreed to a round of golf. Harrison didn't realize his playing partner was sizing him up. After their round, the man invited

Harrison over to an apartment he was renting, where they ate a fried chicken dinner cooked by the landlady.

The man's real name was Alvin C. Thomas, and "Ti" was short for Titanic. He had been born in Missouri in 1892, the son of a gambling father he never really knew. His stepfather and grandfather taught him to play cards and handle himself outdoors, and as a teenager he landed a job in a traveling medicine show where he learned the life of a hustler. He could pitch horseshoes, shoot pool (and sometimes people), and fling playing cards with unmatched precision, one by one, through a transom and into a hallway until the whole deck had vanished—a feat he spent hours practicing to make it look as casual and natural as tossing a newspaper onto a front porch. Thompson once made $500 by winning a bet that he could jump across a pool table without touching it. He was tall and thin, remembered by those who knew him for his blue eyes and beautiful hands—skilled appendages that had made him a living in countless, unimaginable ways.

For such a keen player, he discovered golf relatively late in life, supposedly at age thirty to pass the time between all-night poker games in San Francisco. Titanic was a quick study. He taught himself to play left-handed and right-handed, and he leveraged that ambidexterity against unsuspecting marks to tilt the odds in his favor.

When Titanic Thompson showed up in Little Rock in the summer of 1928, he was not there to sightsee. As he told young Dutch Harrison, he was in town on business, and business meant gambling, hustling, and high stakes. Over the fried chicken meal in his rented apartment, Thompson explained to Harrison that he was arranging a golf match against two of Arkansas's best club professionals: twenty-year-old Paul Runyan and Harrison's boss, Julius Ackerbloom. Thompson claimed that he'd be staking his side in the match. Two Little Rock businessmen were putting up $3,000 on behalf of Runyan and Ackerbloom. After some side bets, the pot would grow to $4,000—serious money in 1928.

"If we won, I would receive $400," Harrison recalled for the author of his 1991 biography, *Mr. Dutch*. "'Course I knew he had a shadowy reputation—an' he sure had the sharpest, most penetratin' eyes I've ever seen. Them eyes jus' bored a hole right through ya."

Intimidated by his steel-eyed host? Sedated by a food coma from the afterglow of delicious southern fried chicken? Yes and yes. Whatever his reasons, Dutch Harrison agreed to play as Thompson's partner against Runyan and Ackerbloom.

On the morning of the match, Thompson cornered Harrison in the Willow Beach parking lot, backed him up against a car, and stuck his .45 revolver (with adhesive tape on the butt end of the grip) into his partner's belly. Titanic said he had heard that some folks had approached Dutch about throwing the match. "Who bought you off?" he demanded.

Who knows whether Thompson had really heard such rumors or was just testing the young man? And who knows whether that .45 was even loaded? Dutch insisted that nobody had bought him off. But those penetrating blue eyes. The uncomfortable prod of a revolver in the belly. It took considerable guts to face a man like that. It *sure* as hell took some guts to partner with him.

"C'mon, boy, let's go play," Thompson ordered.

Thompson had earned a reputation for manipulating odds in the craziest ways possible. He was known to lose a couple of early bets, usually just amounting to a few hundred dollars, before pressing the stakes and winning big. Harrison had heard a story of Thompson once betting someone $2,000 that he could throw a pumpkin onto the roof of a three-story building. According to Dutch, Thompson and his mark just happened to be standing near a sidewalk fruit stand with basketball-sized pumpkins, so he walked over to an adjacent fruit stand, picked up a softball-sized pumpkin, and threw it onto the building to win the bet. Once on the veranda of a Hot Springs hotel, Thompson bet well-known Chicago aviator and Hot Springs adopted son Jack Vilas—who became one of Paul Runyan's financial backers—that he could throw an English walnut from a batch he was shelling over an eight-story building. With $5,000 on the line, Thompson secretly swapped the walnut in his hand for a special one he had filled with lead and proceeded to toss it clear over the building, winning the bet.

Runyan knew of Titanic Thompson's reputation, so it was little surprise when the gambler approached him on the driving range that morning at Willow Beach. He wasn't there to make small talk, but the fiery hustler who had threatened Dutch Harrison in the parking lot now sounded more like a politician begging for a vote. In a voice loud enough to be heard by the dozens of people milling about, Thompson told Runyan that he'd give him half his purse if Runyan failed to win any holes that afternoon. Runyan knew better than to hitch himself to Titanic Thompson, so he passed on the offer. However, enough people had overheard their conversation, and Runyan became worried. If his play was less than stellar, the crowd would assume he was in cahoots with Thompson. Talk about pressure. Thompson knew every trick in the book.

As the match got under way, it seemed as though the whole town of Little Rock had turned up to watch. Sitting on the same location where the Union Army had crossed the Arkansas River to occupy Little Rock during the Civil War, Willow Beach Golf Club was the perfect setting for a big-time money match—out of town and away from polite society but near the train tracks for spectators who wanted to come out to watch. A flood the previous year had damaged the clubhouse and a bridge on the course, but the silt deposits left behind were viewed as beneficial to the turf.

Before the first tee ball was struck, Thompson convinced Runyan and Ackerbloom to give his side a stroke if he agreed to play left-handed. For all the stories about Titanic Thompson that the two young Arkansas club pros *had* heard, the ones claiming that he played just as well or better as a lefty had apparently gone over their heads. They agreed to his terms.

The only thing that saved the Arkansas club pros that afternoon was Runyan's steady play. And Ackerbloom's putting touch. Despite feeling scared to death, Runyan made five birdies. With a performance like that, nobody in Little Rock could accuse him of throwing the match. Years later, Runyan would admit that five birdies was only a partial output of what could have been a truly special round, if only he hadn't been so nervous.

The two sides came to the eighteenth hole, and Thompson and Harrison held a one-stroke lead. It was a short par four, and Ackerbloom drove onto the front of the green. Thompson was also a long hitter, and he belted his drive just short of the green, then stuck his approach stone dead for a sure birdie. To avoid losing the match and $4,000, Ackerbloom, who Harrison later said "wasn't much of a putter," would have to hole his eagle attempt from sixty feet. That's just what he did. Eagle beat birdie, and the match was halved.

In the aftermath, Runyan realized just how crooked and unscrupulous Titanic Thompson could be. Decades later, he confessed that the match could have ended his career before it ever really began.

The other lasting memory Runyan kept from that day was just how remarkable, how skillful, Titanic Thompson was in person. There was something he admired in the man, at least in the manner he played the game. For the rest of his life, he would tell tales of Titanic's astonishing feats on and off the golf course, with a twinkle in his eye and excitement in his voice.

Nobody would ever know how much money Titanic Thompson walked away with that day from side bets with unsuspecting Little Rockians, but after the match he took Dutch Harrison downtown and bought him a brightly colored, checkered suit. Harrison became Thompson's running mate for a while after the match in Little Rock, but that relationship was short-lived.

A few months later in 1928, Thompson's name started showing up in newspapers from coast to coast. He had been present for a late-night poker game that September on New York's West Side, and he was hardly the only shady character who was dealt cards. Arnold Rothstein, the underworld magnate and gambler who famously was alleged to have fixed the 1919 World Series, had a seat at the table that night, and when the game ended he had lost so badly that he had to write hundreds of thousands of dollars in IOUs, including a $30,000 note to Titanic Thompson. Rothstein failed to make good on his debts in a timely fashion, and in early November he was murdered by a gunman in New York's Park Central Hotel. The names of various professional gamblers showed up in the newspapers in connection with (or perhaps as suspects in) Rothstein's murder, including George McManus, Nate Raymond, Jimmie Meehan, and, as described by the *New York Daily News* on November 6, "a gambler from the middlewest, whose professional name is Titanic," who just hours before the murder had apparently met up with Rothstein at the Park Central to warn him to pay up. All kinds of theories were floated in the newspapers about what had happened and who had gunned down Rothstein. Thompson didn't seem to mind the attention. He even sneaked out to Yonkers and played a couple of money games at the Grassy Sprain Club against the club's pro, George McLean. Predictably, Thompson lost about $2,500 in the first contest, only to hit it big during the rematch, pocketing $13,000 that had been raised by a group of McLean's friends.

After intense police questioning, McManus was hit with murder charges and Thompson became a state's witness at the trial. McManus was an all right guy, Thompson said during cross-examination, and not the sort to seek revenge through murder. He must have been convincing on the witness stand. McManus was acquitted. Thompson walked away.

Titanic resumed his hustling ways for decades. He would be married to five women during his lifetime, and he was believed to have killed five men, although not Rothstein. He eventually settled down, a bit, and lived out his days in Texas, where he died in 1974.

One final point on Titanic: Why the nickname? Remember the pool table he jumped over without touching? That incident happened in 1912, when Thompson was just a young man, shortly after the RMS *Titanic* sank in the North Atlantic Ocean. After Thompson collected his winnings, someone asked his mark what the kid's name was. The man said, "It must be Titanic. He sinks everybody."

Well, not everybody.

ABOUT THAT LIGHTNING—it struck on and off the golf course. In the years 1929 through 1931, it seemed as though everything in Paul Runyan's life was happening with the sudden ferocity of an electrical storm. There was a beautiful girl, a new job, a significant golf victory, a wedding, another new job, and another significant victory. This all happened amid a stock market collapse and the beginnings of the Great Depression.

First the girl. Runyan was running ("sprinting," said pupil and friend Gene Littler) from the golf shop to the clubhouse one day at Concordia Country Club to take a telephone call when he swung open the clubhouse door at full speed, striking Joan Harris right in the face and knocking her flat on the floor. It's unknown what precisely he did or said in the next few moments, but shortly thereafter Joan and Paul would become an item, and in 1931 they would become husband and wife. It seems plausible that he gave up on the telephone call in order to tend to the girl. And who could blame him? Joan was cute, smart, stylish, and, most important, single.

Joan was the second daughter of Sam and Gertye Harris of Little Rock. The family was relatively new to Arkansas. Most of Joan's childhood had been spent living in Hutchinson, Kansas, where Sam worked for the Great American Life Insurance Company, which had opened a regional branch office there in 1916. He packed up the family and moved to Arkansas around 1923, when an opportunity came up to become a Great American field supervisor. Older daughter Jane, a 1922 graduate of the University of Kansas, stayed behind to marry John Schwinn, the managing editor of the *Hutchinson Gazette*.

After graduating from Little Rock High School, Joan, like her big sister, attended KU, where she joined the Alpha Delta Pi sorority. After college, she attended the Otis Art Institute in Los Angeles, an independent professional art school that had been founded in 1918, but she moved back to Arkansas to be near her parents, and her future husband's penchant for steamrolling through life at a breakneck pace would bring them together. Of that face-on encounter with the clubhouse door, you might say she was in the wrong place at the right time. Or vice versa.

Runyan gave Joan's father golf lessons, and when Sam Harris asked him to teach his daughter, Runyan immediately fell head over heels for the girl. "Every time I looked at her I was so dizzy from thinking how grand she was I didn't know what end of the club she was hitting the ball with," he wrote. Runyan would lie awake at night with two thoughts on his mind: winning golf tournaments and marrying Joan.

Before getting married, Runyan had to make plans for their future. Many of the country's successful golf professionals in those days set up shop along the Eastern Seaboard. That's where the money was. The ones who were truly good players would work all spring, summer, and fall at their northern clubs and then head south over the winter to play competitively in Florida, Georgia, and the Carolinas. Runyan arranged for a job at Forest Hill Field Club in Bloomfield, New Jersey, a club that had been founded in 1896 and boasted a golf course designed by A. W. Tillinghast. Runyan's boss at Forest Hill would be Craig Wood, an accomplished player who would later capture two major championships—the Masters and the U.S. Open—and would finish runner-up in the other two.

The Forest Hill job would be a big step up for the Arkansas farm boy. He thought as much, yet he held serious reservations about making good on his commitment. He privately worried that the club's members might not take him seriously, might think him too young for the job. After all, he was barely old enough to have a drink. And, apparently, he owed some money back in Arkansas. Making a go of it in professional golf—then and now—takes up-front capital investment. Over the winter of 1930, Runyan played some events on the West Coast—"the California tournaments," wrote journalist Miles Wolff—but left California with little to show for his efforts. His Forest Hill salary could help him pay down his debts, but he seemed concerned about abandoning his Arkansas backers under such circumstances. This was all weighing on his mind when he showed up at Pinehurst, North Carolina, in late March 1930 for the prestigious North and South Open golf championship.

How did he perform under such strain? He won the damn thing outright.

If Paul Runyan had a coming-out party in professional golf, it came at Pinehurst No. 2 in the spring of 1930. The North and South was a highly regarded event, and its outcome carried more weight and generated more newspaper ink than other run-of-the-mill contests held at less architecturally significant venues. It all started when New York advertising executive Frank Presbrey convinced Pinehurst owner and founder James Tufts to hold annual golf competitions to draw attention to his up-and-coming resort in the North Carolina sandhills. Tufts and his son Leonard began the North and South in 1901, and by the 1930s the event had found a comfortable spot on the golf calendar—late in March following the professional circuit's tour through Florida that lasted the month of February and a good chunk of March. According to golf writer Dan Jenkins, "The North and South was the Masters before there *was* a Masters and for many years before the Masters finally out-Southerned the North and South."

Pinehurst No. 2 was like the rarest of high school sweethearts, a once grand beauty that became lost to time—obscured or overgrown in the context of golf course maintenance—then stripped away and rediscovered much later in life, loved and appreciated all over again. The No. 2 course was still in its high school phase when Paul Runyan and 114 other golfers rolled into town in the spring of 1930, twenty-three years after Donald Ross came up with the initial design, and that spring the Presbrey-Tufts hype machine was in full flight. If Runyan had an advantage, it was that Pinehurst No. 2 in 1930 was a sand-green golf course, a combination sand-and-clay surface much like what he had grown up playing in Hot Springs. The Pinehurst greens would remain that way until 1934, when Ross developed a strain of Bermuda grass that could withstand cold weather. Three experimental greens that year proved his Bermuda's sustainability, and he converted all the greens to Bermuda in the 1935–36 season.

Playing with some leftover Wilson Why Nots from his stock at Concordia Country Club, Runyan grabbed the first-round lead with a one-over-par 72 that featured six birdies but fell off the pace with a second-round 77. Fortunately for Runyan, he picked a convenient day for a wayward round. Pinehurst, described by Associated Press sportswriter Dillon Graham as "stubborn" and "subtle," proved especially difficult in that second round, thanks in part to a cold breeze that swept through the grounds and kept the entire field from bettering par. At the halfway point, Henry Picard held the lead at 146, followed by Frank Walsh from Chicago and Tommy Armour from Detroit, who were at 147. Runyan sat in fourth place, tied with Whiffy Cox, three shots off the pace. He had played the first two rounds in relative obscurity, while the large galleries followed well-known, established players like Armour, Horton Smith, and Bobby Cruickshank. That was about to change.

Thirty-six holes would be played on the final day, and Runyan, wearing a blue beret angled confidently atop his head, came ready with his best stuff. "With a large crowd billowing about him and stampeding in his path, Paul Runyan, 21-year-old assistant professional from Bloomfield, New Jersey, today shot near perfect golf for two rounds to win the 28th annual North and South open golf tournament here," Graham wrote for the AP. Runyan's third-round 72 tied him for the lead, and he began the afternoon round by carding seven straight fours, en route to a front-nine 37. For the first time, it occurred to him that he was no longer playing for just a paycheck. He had a real chance to win.

At the turn, Johnny Dawson, a field representative for Spalding, handed Runyan a half dozen Spalding Dots, a much better golf ball than his Wilson Why Nots. "These were the first Dots I had ever seen, much less hit, and I was delighted," Runyan later wrote.

He came home in a flurry, shooting 33 on the back side for a final round 70 and a two-shot victory over Frank Walsh. For a while it seemed that Joe Turnesa, who was still on the course, would likely tie Runyan, and a playoff would be needed; pars on his final two holes would have done the trick, but Turnesa's bunker play doomed his chances. Defending champion and crowd favorite Horton Smith, playing with a nasty sunburn on his arms, finished eighth.

Miles Wolff described Runyan's play on the final day as spectacular. "With several thousand watching him, he putted for a par four on the final eighteenth with the nonchalance of an Englishman sipping tea," Wolff wrote. If only it had been that easy. After the round, Runyan admitted that his cool demeanor masked his nervousness. The large crowd heightened the tension, as did the knowledge that he was close to the lead throughout the final nine holes.

When it was all over and he was assured that he had won, Runyan's first thought was about the money he owed back home. Tournament purses in the early 1930s were noticeably affected by the dreadful state of the economy, but his $1,500 winner's check felt plenty abundant. After all, some fifteen million Americans—nearly a quarter of the workforce—were unemployed, thanks mostly to the Depression. The first-prize booty was just enough to make him "even with the world," Runyan explained to the press.

"Yes, sir," he told the assembled media after his round, "that's just what I'm going to do with that $1,500. I'm going to pay my debts."

About those debts—to whom did he owe the cash? It might have been some members from Concordia Country Club in Little Rock. In

Gettin' to the Dance Floor, Runyan described to Al Barkow the Concordia members helping him make a couple of partial tours to California and Texas.

Or could it have been his backer Jack Vilas, the famous flier who once got conned out of $5,000 by Titanic Thompson on the veranda of a Hot Springs hotel? Maybe, but there's no direct evidence of that.

Vilas was no insignificant character in Runyan's success. He was more than a benefactor. He was an inspiration. In 1913 Vilas became the first pilot to fly across Lake Michigan, doing so in an hour and forty minutes. After wintering in Hot Springs for roughly a decade, he moved his family there in 1917, when he was in his late twenties, and he must have been the envy of every boy in town. His exploits as an auto racer-cum-aviator who also liked to hunt, fish, trap, and swim were well chronicled in the local newspapers. Vilas was even known to referee boxing matches and had served a stint as an assistant chief of police in Hot Springs, during which he drew wide praise by nabbing the thieves who broke into the local high school and stole $1,400 from the vault, then the largest-known robbery in Hot Springs—a case he cracked inside of twenty-four hours. In 1929 Vilas wrote an autobiography for his children, a 235-page treat of a book that recounted numerous feats of derring-do from the first half of his life (like hunting alligators, which, he explains, can be a real joy if you have the right equipment and you know what you're doing: "The whole trick in alligator shooting is to get your alligator after you have killed him, as they always sink"). The fact that he was a standout golfer only cemented his legend in Runyan's mind. As a boy, Runyan had admired the way Vilas put his hands on the putter, particularly his reverse overlap grip, and began employing a similar technique in his own putting.

Back in chapter 1 there was a mention of the federal census from 1920. It showed that Runyan's neighbor from dwelling 177 was golf pro Jimmy Norton. On that same document, separated by twenty lines, was Vilas, Runyan's neighbor from dwelling 182. That house, which Vilas had built during the winter of 1916–17, was called Golfwoods Farm by the Vilas family, presumably because of its proximity to the golf course.

Vilas, on the surface, hardly seems like the type of guy who would hound a friend to pay up. He wasn't hurting for money. However, by 1930 Vilas's life was heading in a much different direction than it had been a decade prior. That January, a little more than two months before Runyan's Pinehurst triumph, the *Arkansas Gazette* reported that Vilas's wife, Susan Wharton Vilas, was suing for divorce, alleging cruel and barbarous treatment by her husband. It was reported that she was awarded $100,000 and sought custody of the couple's three children; later Jack Vilas was granted full legal custody. One of those children, daughter Ariel, was a precocious golf talent mentored by Jimmy Norton (in Runyan's absence, it turned out that Norton wasn't averse to teaching females, talented ones at least). Later that year, Mrs. Vilas filed suit again, this time for $500,000. The newspapers reported that she remained in Hot Springs immediately after the divorce, and Jack went back to Chicago. It was a sad ending to a relationship that began on moonlit nighttime dates, an aerial courtship filled with lovemaking among the clouds above the St. Lawrence River. Two years after the divorce, Jack's brother Royal, a financier and sportsman, shot and killed himself in front of a dresser mirror in the bedroom of his Chicago-area home.

"There was more tragedy, and he carried it with him, but it certainly did not define him," said Dr. Faith Vilas, Jack's granddaughter, a senior scientist at the nonprofit Planetary Science Institute, headquartered in Tucson, Arizona. Dr. Vilas's areas of professional expertise include asteroids, dwarf planets, and outer planet satellites, but she also has a keen interest in her grandfather and has been working on and off for many years on a book about his life. So passionate was her curiosity that in 2013 she re-created his flight across Lake Michigan, one hundred years to the day, knocking almost an hour off his time while aboard a Cessna 185 amphibious seaplane.

"He was quite a character," Vilas's granddaughter recalled. "Let me put it this way: as a [grandfather], he was great. But as my father said to me one time, and I don't remember the context of it, 'Your grandfather's the most selfish son of a bitch I've ever known, and any selfish bone you have in your body was inherited directly from him.'

"He was larger-than-life in many ways," she continued. "He had money. There's no question he had money. So to be a benefactor or to show someone favor like that would have been entirely within his personality and his reason. I would expect that."

Could Runyan have owed Vilas? He owed money to somebody, and he didn't shy away from it. Maybe.

It's also possible that the money he owed was actually a Runyan family debt back on the Arkansas dairy farm. Paul had been sending money home to help out whenever he could; by that point his father's health was a liability, and much of the operation fell onto his brother's shoulders. All that mattered to Runyan in the immediate aftermath of the North and South victory was that he could pay up and get on with his life—and his golf career.

That night, runner-up Frank Walsh wired Craig Wood, Runyan's soon-to-be boss in New Jersey. "Congratulations," he wrote. "After this keep unknown assistants at home."

Runyan sent his own telegram to his fiancée, Joan Harris, in Arkansas. His message at 6:25 p.m. on the night of his victory was so simple she probably wondered if it was a joke or if part of it was missing. He wired, "Jo honey I won, Paul."

HOW IMPORTANT WAS Runyan's win at Pinehurst? According to a clue hiding in plain sight, very important. In this case, plain sight is the internet, that incomparable finding aid at our fingertips that can yield so much assistance to a researcher, while at the same time churning up enough gobbledygook in its wake to render a person almost paralyzed by the question of which rabbit hole to go down—that is, to click on—next. It must have been a dull night at my house on New Year's Eve 2019, because shortly before 9:00 p.m. (my computer time-stamped the acquisition of what I'm about to explain) I came upon the image of a handwritten note Runyan had scribbled off on February 27, 1994, to a woman named Sharon. Scribbled is unfair to Runyan, whose handwriting was nothing if not elegant. But this note, written on his own stationery, which included the street address and telephone number of his then-residence in Pasadena, California, is straight to the point, without excess. Presumably, he's answering the question, "What was your greatest thrill in golf?" He appears to be responding to fan mail.

Sixty-four years removed from his triumph in the North Carolina sand hills, Runyan wrote Sharon that his greatest thrill in golf "was winning the North and South Open at Pinehurst in April of 1930."

His memory failed him slightly—he had clinched the victory on March 28—but that can be forgiven. Six decades should be enough to earn him a mulligan on the precise date. Still, it's a telling statement. Something special happened at Pinehurst that week in 1930. For Runyan, his victory carried deep meaning. He needed the money, but maybe what was more important was that he needed the validation. With his victory over a top-flight field on a well-respected golf course, that's just what he got: validation. At Pinehurst, Runyan proved something to the golf world and to himself. He belonged.

WITH HIS DEBTS paid off, Runyan left for New Jersey and his new job working for Craig Wood. His time there would last only a year, but it was an eventful stay. If the Forest Hill members had any concerns about the credentials of their youthful new assistant professional, those concerns were put to rest upon release of the May 1930 issue of *Golfers Magazine*, which sold for 20 cents a copy. Pictured on the blue-outlined cover was "North and South Open champion" Paul Runyan, photographed wearing a sweater, posing with his driver in a follow-through position, his ever-soft grip pressure cradling the club, and a relaxed smile on his face.

Runyan joined some esteemed company as a sports champion in 1930. Connie Mack and the Philadelphia Athletics captured the World Series, Notre Dame repeated as the national champion of college football, and Bobby Jones made history by becoming the first golfer to capture golf's Grand Slam, winning the U.S. Open and U.S. Amateur Championships and, across the Atlantic, the Open Championship and the British Amateur Championship in the same calendar year.

Runyan described Forest Hill as "a kind of hell-bent-for-leather place where nobody had much money but spent what they did have." During the depths of the Great Depression—"depths" is exactly how Runyan described this period in his own writing—a golfer at Forest Hill could still arrange a $5,000 Nassau. The members were hardly professional gamblers, just normal businessmen who enjoyed golf and got a rush out of playing for big money. Runyan could wager too, when he wanted to. Early on, he was banking $400 a month at Forest Hill, between his lessons and base salary. His side games with members, who, at least initially, paid off like slot machines, were even more lucrative. He made $700 gambling in his first month on the job. However, that quickly changed the following month, when he lost $1,100. That month began a vexing run of bad luck that surprised even his boss, Craig Wood. Match after match, Runyan kept losing to members—$30 here, $50 there. It kept adding up. For a young man saving up to get married, the losses must have caused a few sleepless nights.

"You've got to be the worst match-maker in the world," Wood joked.

"Craig, it's not true," Runyan said. "I'm playing them at full handicap, and I'm playing up to mine. But everybody I play with is going crazy, beating their own handicaps by a mile."

One day Runyan shot 63 to tie the Forest Hill course record and lost two of the three matches he had going. The bad luck reached a crescendo days later when he broke the course record and still lost money—to a fourteen-handicap player who shot a career round of 73. Eventually, Runyan learned that the safest bet was playing with his boss, Wood. At least he wouldn't have to give strokes.

That August he and Wood teed it up at Yountakah Country Club, and Runyan bet his boss that he could shoot the course record. It was no duel with Titanic Thompson, but this time Runyan had his own money on the line, and his 67 that day set the course record by three shots. He carried that momentum into the New Jersey State Open a week later at the Asbury Park Golf and Country Club. His six-under-par 66 in the opening round broke the Asbury Park course record, and it could have been even lower; he missed a six-foot putt on the last hole for 65. A second-round 74 put him two shots clear of Arthur Straub, who formerly held Runyan's assistant job at Forest Hill. Their mutual boss, Craig Wood, was seven strokes back at 147.

Under cloudy, threatening skies, playing in front of a sizable gallery of the state's best amateur golfers and numerous female admirers, Runyan vanquished the suspense on the final day, shooting rounds of 73-69 to win in a seven-shot runaway. Straub fell to third place, ten shots back, and Wood finished eighteen shots adrift of his assistant.

Runyan collected a $400 first-prize check and a medal from the New Jersey State Golf Association. Just as important, he was starting to gain notoriety in the professional golf ranks. References to his play in just about any newspaper would note that he was a North and South Open champion, proving that the win in the North Carolina sand hills was a special kind of currency in golf circles. Now he had another notable state golf title to go with it.

Witness the Associated Press's coverage of Runyan's engagement in February 1931: "Announcement was made today of the engagement of Paul Runyan, New Jersey Open and North and South Open golf champion, to Miss Joan Harris of Little Rock, Ark., daughter of Samuel Thomas Harris, president of an Arkansas bank." Another, lengthier engagement announcement dubbed him a "golf professional hero." In some ways, it had been a speedy ascent for the young pro from Arkansas, who just three and four years prior was stuck in golf gridlock, finishing four-round events twenty-five to thirty strokes behind the serious contenders.

Paul and Joan's engagement happened in St. Louis, where they met up and stayed with Runyan's old buddy from Little Rock, Harry Tenenbaum. On the train ride back to New Jersey, a man passed by Runyan on his way to the dining car. Runyan was minding his own business, probably working through the mental gymnastics of getting married and how he could stretch his $700 in savings (plus the $250 he had just pocketed playing golf in St. Louis) to start a life together with his new bride. The man stopped and turned around and asked, "Aren't you Paul Runyan?" Then he asked if he could sit for a chat, and after a few minutes the man invited Runyan to join him in the dining car. He was Gerald Rosenberger, a sports-crazed New Yorker who looked and talked like a well-connected man. They shared a meal and talked sports, then went their separate ways. It was a sort of first for Runyan—being noticed hundreds of miles from home, away from a golf course.

On Christmas Eve 1930, Runyan was in New Jersey, working his new job at Forest Hill and separated from Joan, who was back in Arkansas planning their wedding. He missed his new sweetie, so he sent Joan a holiday telegram. He wrote, "Darling, I wish you a heart full of joy and gladness on this day and for the years to come. My only regret is that I cannot be there to enjoy it with you. Love to all." When it came to Joan, Runyan knew his feelings immediately. There was no waffling. He had found his future, and he was intent on keeping her.

The run-up to Paul and Joan's wedding was idyllic for the bride-to-be. Considering the abrupt run-in at Concordia Country Club that had been their introduction, the social whirl seems well deserved. There was a bridal shower on March 13, eight days before the ceremony, and a bridge tea hosted by friends a day later. On March 17 there was another party, followed by bridge suppers on March 18 and 19. Then there was a dinner dance on March 20, the night before the wedding. Did Runyan even touch a club that whole time? It's hard to picture him stopping cold turkey, but where would he have found the daylight to squeeze in any golf?

The wedding at Joan's parents' house in Little Rock was attended only by relatives and intimate friends. The 4:00 p.m. ceremony was described in the *Arkansas Gazette* as "a beautiful afternoon wedding." The Reverend Paul W. Quillian of Winfield Methodist Church married the couple on an improvised altar before the fireplace in the living room of the Harris home. The bride wore a three-piece Lanvin designer dress in French blue, trimmed in fitch fur. She accessorized with a hat, tan shoes, and an orchid corsage. After the wedding, the couple and guests cut into a three-tiered wedding cake and washed it down with punch.

Then, almost abruptly, Mr. and Mrs. Paul Runyan hit the road. The groom had business in Pinehurst, North Carolina, the following week, where he would defend his title at the North and South Open. His new wife would be there for support, just in case lightning happened to strike twice.

3

Samuel Jackson

Hearing the legend of his upbringing was a little bit like listening to the lyrics of Chuck Berry's "Johnny B. Goode," about the boy from the woods and the evergreens who could play a guitar like nobody's business. It was as if Sam Snead came out of nowhere, and nowhere happened to be a small resort town in the Virginia mountains. And just like the hero of that song, Sam had a doting mother who thought the world of her boy. However, her vision for his future had nothing to do with seeing his name in lights. She wanted him to know how to take care of himself, so she taught him various life skills, like how to sew.

But a young man's mastery of needle and thread doesn't preclude a similar mastery of wild turkeys and bobcats and river trout. That's where the Snead lore really picks up steam. He was the boy from Virginia known for his athletic gifts and survival instincts. It was more than just lore; he had both those traits in spades. But that didn't stop the spawning of more lore. And his family? There was his legendary uncle who supposedly stood 7 feet 9 inches tall and wore a size 28 shoe. And his brother the inventor, who made his own radios and even developed a photoelectric dimmer for car lights. You cherry-pick characteristics from all these people and project them onto Sam, then you watch him wind up and hit a golf ball a country mile with the grace of a lion on the Serengeti, and you have storytelling gold. The golf press fell for this narrative hook, line, and sinker—and Snead was happy to oblige. That is, he played along with the country bumpkin routine and perhaps even found it advantageous at times.

He was burned more than once by people who should have had his best interests at heart. Sadly, their jealousy got in the way of good manners. Perhaps that's why he found it comfortable to play along. The less of your soul you put out on public display, the less you stand to lose. But even those people who sought to hold him back stood no chance. They could dull his confidence, his self-belief, sure. They could even slow his ascent, a little. But there's no stopping a train barreling down the tracks, and in the mid-1930s the Snead express was picking up steam, rolling through obscure stretches of railway such as the Middle Atlantic Golf Championship and the Cascades Open. He was running full throttle by 1936, and the rest of the golf world was in for a big surprise. Sam Snead was there to stay.

LIKE HIS FUTURE foil Paul Runyan, Sam Snead grew up in Hot Springs. That's Hot Springs, Virginia, not Arkansas.

But hot springs are hot springs, and the draw was much the same—warm water straight out of the ground, high in mineral content, paired with swanky accommodations and southern-style hospitality. Good for the soul. Even better for tourism.

For whatever societal differences may have existed between the two Hot Springs, one thing they shared in common was an ability to attract outsiders. Ten years before the United States declared its independence, Virginia frontiersman Thomas Bullitt surveyed land in what would become Bath County, and when he received his colonial land grant of three hundred acres, he built a lodge around the property's hot and warm springs. Thomas Jefferson, James Monroe, Alexander Hamilton, and George Washington were among the establishment's first guests. Dubbed the Homestead, this place was the first rendition of what later became known as the Omni Homestead Resort. It became Sam Snead's golf playground.

In the 1830s, physician Thomas Goode purchased the land from the Bullitt family and expanded the spa to cater to a larger audience of prospective visitors. The spa business continued until the last decade of the nineteenth century, when a group of investors that included J. P. Morgan bought the resort and rebuilt it. Naturally it became a desirable spot for well-heeled businesspeople and families to spend leisure time. These "ultra rich," who had the means to migrate with the seasons, found the area so desirable that by the Roaring Twenties some had begun buying land and building magnificent seasonal residences. Horseback trails, scenic automobile overlooks, and accommodations for hunters and anglers soon followed.

Just a few years before Thomas Bullitt's land grant, Sam Snead's ancestors also had received a large parcel of land from the king of England. That land grant was near the Homestead, and it was on that land where Snead grew up. Many of his ancestors would make the property's family graveyard their final resting place. Sam's father was a handyman, at one point working at the town's power plant and at another point working as an engineer at the Homestead hotel. The extended Snead kinfolk included an eclectic blend of athletes, inventors, musicians, and entertainers. One thing they were not was ultra rich. They weren't dirt poor, but there was never much money left over for extras.

The youngest of five boys, the future golfer received from his parents the name Samuel Jackson Snead. His middle name was a nod to Confederate general Stonewall Jackson, whom Sam's grandfather had known personally. Sam's mother was forty-seven years old when he was born in 1912, and she taught him to cook and sew when he was young. Her efforts to domesticate the boy took, mostly. Sam could tailor his clothes all his life, and when he was young his mother suspected that he'd make tailoring his life's work. He spent many hours at her sewing machine, adjusting the seat of his pants, making French cuffs, and performing other alterations. Perhaps he was influenced by the fancier clothes he saw worn by the wealthy out-of-towners who came to Hot Springs on holiday, and he felt a few minor tweaks to his own duds could enhance his image, even boost his self-confidence. Or maybe he simply liked clothes and working with fabric. However, the backwoods lifestyle of the Virginia mountains was impossible to escape and equally responsible for shaping the child's worldview. He trapped all manner of animals in the wintertime, including rabbits, wildcats, weasels, and skunks. Snead said he hunted turkeys each day on his way to school and once captured a bobcat with his bare hands. He even nabbed trout with his bare hands, using a technique he described this way: "Why, you jes' reach in with your hand and rub them along the belly, workin' up towards the hid. You work up softly like and then, pingo! You pinch that trout right back o' the gills."

Snead never shied away from discussing the hillbillies he grew up around, describing them as having crooked noses, lean facial features, and bad teeth, and he once explained to a golf journalist that those people were better left undisturbed.

"Above all, Sam was at home in the woods and the mountains: behind the natural athlete lies the natural backwoodsman, the 'ridge-runner' of the Appalachians," wrote the revered golf journalist Herbert Warren Wind.

In Wind's writing, it's clear that he was fascinated by Snead's country upbringing and his *Bonanza*-like insight into every tree, shrub, snake, and beast that grew or roamed on the vast "Ponderosa" that was the Snead homestead. "In Sam's neck of the woods the man who could bring in a wildcat alive was highly esteemed," Wind wrote in his *Golf Book*. "Sam brought in three."

Snead credited his uncle Ed for first introducing him to golf. Uncle Ed would show up on Sundays, grab his nephew by his ears or hair, and take him outside to pitch horseshoes—a game the boy always won, or so he claimed. Then Sam started fooling around with a jigger in the backyard, chipping balls into tomato cans set into the ground.

"Gimme that," Uncle Ed told him.

They stopped pitching horseshoes and started chipping golf balls.

"I beat him at that, too," Snead recalled. "Then one Sunday he came up with this bag of clubs, half left-handed, half right-handed, and he said, 'C'mon, damn you, we're going to the Goat.'"

The Goat was the nine-hole golf course at the Homestead Resort. The way Snead described it, you'd play six holes up the mountain and three holes off it. They played the Goat because they weren't allowed onto the resort's eighteen-hole courses.

Snead's clubs were sometimes more primitive than the mismatched contents of the bag from Uncle Ed. He would find hickory and dogwood sticks in the woods and use them to take cuts at rocks. Or so the legend goes.

At age seven, Snead started caddying. He and his brothers would often play together, and eventually they were allowed onto the "big courses" at the resort. When Sam landed a job working at the Homestead as a club maker, he had it made.

Snead described his employment this way: "I put wooden shafts on the heads. The shafts were spliced then, there was no hosel. You fit the spliced end over the head, glued it, then wound it up. I had to trim those shafts down with a piece of steel or glass and be very careful because if you trimmed too much they got too whippy."

Snead became a high school jock, playing whatever sport was in season. He was a halfback on the school's football team and handled the squad's kicking and punting duties, supposedly carrying an average of more than forty yards in the latter. Standing 5 feet 11 inches tall, he was a fixture on the basketball team's starting five all four years. He was a pitcher on the baseball team (and on the town team) and starred as a hard-to-catch sprinter in track and field who could run the 100 in ten seconds flat. Herbert Warren Wind even reported that Snead would occasionally get dragged onto the tennis court as a mercenary by well-meaning fathers who wanted to use their Hot Springs vacation to teach their spoiled tennis-playing sons a thing or two about real competition. For each victory, Snead would receive 50 cents. It's unknown whether he pitied those boys or hated their well-to-do guts. Command performance matches like these were a means to an end. If that's what it took to scare up 50 cents, so be it. And there was the time when a Golden Gloves boxer making his way through Hot Springs asked around for a sparring partner. Who turned up? Samuel Jackson Snead. He knocked the guy out, too, in the second round. It turned out that Snead was a regular among the Hot Springs boys who boxed as entertainment for Homestead guests on Friday nights. At $50 per fight, win or lose, those were good paydays for a young man.

During his spare time as a high schooler, Snead worked a couple of jobs. He operated his uncle's restaurant for roughly a year and worked at a drugstore, where his shift ended at 11:00 p.m. When he got off, he'd walk the two and a quarter miles home alone, through the woods, where every little sound could be mistaken for a panther or bear or other dangerous creature.

With so many promising opportunities as an athlete, you'd think Snead would have been a shoo-in for a college athletic scholarship. There were offers, had he chosen to pursue baseball or football. A broken left hand during his senior football season prompted Snead to begin swinging a golf club regularly, in part because he thought it would help increase the hand's flexibility so he could knit well. That's right: golf became rehab for knitting. As a golfer, he had unquestioned ability, but college teams were rare in those days and scholarships even rarer. Snead's high school coach, Harold Bell, recommended that four years spent working in the golf business would put the aspiring pro closer to a professional career than a college degree, so Sam opted to stay close to home and work at the Homestead.

There, Snead learned the business side of golf from club pros Freddie Gleim and Nelson Long. Snead described Gleim as "the most apt man I ever knew in running a pro shop." Even in the pouring rain, Gleim would have a full lesson book, thanks to a shed on the property where he would take his pupils to hit balls under cover.

Snead's big break came one day in the early 1930s when Gleim and Long were out playing golf and he was left running the golf shop. A "big-busted woman," as he described her, came into the shop hoping to arrange a golf lesson. When Snead explained that both teaching pros were taking a little time for themselves, she asked him, "Couldn't you give me a lesson?" Snead struggled to find a believable excuse before another employee spoke up and told Snead that he'd watch the shop for as long as the lesson lasted. The only question remaining was whether Snead could negotiate a swing around the woman's busty physique.

"I didn't know whether she should swing over or under her bosom, but I knew a few tricks, like laying out the clubs for alignment, and I worked her," Snead recounted to Al Barkow. "Boy, she was sweating after I got through with her."

Snead's pupil turned out to be a woman with some real influence. After the lesson, she told him he should be managing a club of his own. Her comments were flattering, but for him they were wishful thinking, Snead figured. A couple of days later Toby Hanson, the resort's athletic director, pulled him into his office. Snead became nervous that he was in trouble.

"How'd you like to go over to the Cascades course as a pro?" Hanson asked. The woman, it turned out, had told Hanson all about the wonderful lesson she'd gotten from the twenty-year-old golf shop assistant.

The Cascades course had been without a golf pro since the stock market crash of 1929. From the point of view of resort management, employing young Sam Snead at the Cascades course was a low-risk move. He could pocket whatever money he took in for lessons, and the resort supplemented his arrangement with a sandwich and a glass of milk every day for lunch. During his downtime, Snead practiced. A lot.

"Oh, I beat sod," he remembered. "They said, 'Hey, you're beatin' all the grass off.'"

During his first two weeks on the job, Snead broke the course record twice. But all in all, the year was rough, thanks mostly to the Depression and the stalled economy. Few people were traveling, which meant activity at the resort was down. Business was so slow that Snead would rent out his own clubs, half the set at a time, for $1.50.

However, his constant assault on the Cascades sod—and the solitude it offered—paid dividends. Snead taught himself how to play and to hit different shots, fully unencumbered by too many mechanical thoughts. And what a master class he gave himself. Snead's swing, known for its apparent ease, with his supple upper-body extension away from the ball on the backswing and his pronounced sit-down move in the knees and hips that returned him to an unencumbered hitting position, was unmatched in its power and grace. Snead's oily hold on the club made it seem like the instrument in his hands and its intended target on the ground were an afterthought to moving his body into its rhythmic anatomical peak. If a golf ball should happen to get in the way of the clubhead on the way through, so be it, but it was bad news for the ball. Years later, legendary instructor Bob Toski would invite Snead to participate in *Golf Digest* instructional clinics, and Snead would show up and hit a variety of shots that students at the golf schools marveled at—high draws, low fades, piercing long irons, flighted short irons, you name it. Snead would hit a high draw on command, and someone in the gallery would ask him what parts of his set-up and anatomy he focused on before and during his swing to produce such great control on command. But those kinds of swing thoughts were too technical for the man who had taught himself to play in the quiet of a Virginia resort during the Depression. Snead would answer plainly, "I was thinkin' high draw."

THERE WAS LITTLE fanfare for Snead when he became a professional golfer. His old boss from the Homestead, Freddie Gleim, even harbored a little resentment, or so it seemed. Snead would ask Gleim to watch him hit a few balls, but Gleim would say, "You're a pro now, you ought to know." Maybe that was a blessing in disguise. Snead did all right figuring things out on his own.

"See, when I got that pro job at the Cascades and started shooting those low scores, he didn't like that at all," Snead said to Al Barkow for *Gettin' to the Dance Floor*, explaining Gleim's strange behavior. "He thought he was a good player, better than he actually was. He'd say, 'Oh, you think you're hot stuff now, huh?' It was just jealousy."

The Cascades, Snead's home course at the Homestead, hosted the 1934 Middle Atlantic Golf Championship, and Snead joined the field that July in Hot Springs, during the same week that John Dillinger was gunned down outside a Chicago theater. Snead played a partial practice round before the event with Chandler Harper, Virginia's amateur champion. He played those ten holes in two under par, only to watch Harper navigate the same stretch in four under. After their friendly tune-up, Snead told the local press that he was impressed with Harper's game, especially his iron play. Still, Snead held the course record at the Cascades, and that had to count for something as he looked toward the start of competition. A field of forty-three competitors teed it up at the Middle Atlantic Championship, and, ultimately, Snead would not raise the trophy. Nor would his practice partner Harper, the stroke play medalist, who made it as far as the semifinal match before losing to eventual champion Bobby Reigel. Snead took away from the experience an exposure to a strong field of golfers, albeit a small one. And, being the local pro, he garnered some attention from the press, which would make him more used to it the next time around.

In 1935 Snead, still mostly unknown as a golfer, traveled to Miami, Florida, to play in the Miami Biltmore Open. He took two and a half days to drive down from Hot Springs in a Model-A Ford. Driving through Georgia, it was not uncommon to encounter one-way wooden bridges that were as long as a short par four. Snead had to look ahead to make sure nobody was coming his way from the other end before proceeding onto the bridge. On other parts of the trip he'd encounter cattle sleeping in the road, making driving at night especially taxing. A bovine beast could blend in with the road, and a driver could easily miss the animal until he was right up on it. While Snead avoided run-ins with cows, his Model-A did its fair share of damage to wandering hogs and pigs along the way. Still, he made it to Florida.

In Miami, Snead carried in his bag a two-wood on loan from Freddie Gleim. By his recollection, he won between $150 and $200 in the tournament. (A check of the records revealed that Snead actually pocketed $108.33 in prize money for his 290 total, which was nine shots behind winner Horton Smith.) Gleim was also in the Miami field, and after the tournament he told Snead, "I've got to have that two-wood back." Snead explained that he was planning on going to Nassau to play in the Nassau-Colonial Open, but Gleim insisted he needed the club because he too was heading for Nassau and wanted the club in *his* bag. Snead returned the two-wood and, without a driving club, made plans to head home to Virginia. After Gleim left for Nassau, likely with most of the other players, who had boarded the ss *Northland*, Snead peaked into Gleim's locker to see if the two-wood had really made the cut. There it was, sitting alone in the locker. Gleim never wanted the two-wood for Nassau; the club was incidental. Snead concluded that his old boss was trying to eliminate him from the field. The strategy had worked.

That September, back in Hot Springs for the Cascades Open, Snead, now twenty-three, started fast with a first-round 68, the day's low score by five shots. A second-round 76 kept him in first place, three shots clear of the field and in great position to capture the winner's share of the $2,500 purse. After a third-round 71, he still led by three shots. Then his old boss Gleim butted in. To be fair, Gleim had been prompted by the president of the Homestead, Fay Ingalls, to interfere with Snead's thought process. Apparently, Ingalls and others at the Homestead, who collectively had a hunch Snead might be impossible to beat on his home course, never wanted him to play the tournament in the first place. They would have preferred that a bigger name, such as Bobby Cruickshank or Johnny Revolta, win the tournament and thus bring the hotel more publicity. Although you have to wonder what part of "Unheralded Local Pro Captures First Victory on Home

Course" was unattractive, publicity-wise. Surely the Homestead could have won favor with that story.

Just before the final round began, Gleim said to Snead, "How do you ever expect to be a pro with that left elbow coming out like that?" Snead liked to play a low-running hook with his three-wood, and he sometimes set up with the face a little shut to the target to promote the shot shape. By the second hole, Gleim's comment was on Snead's mind, and he started fidgeting with the position of his elbow. His shots quickly went awry. He made eight on the hole and shot 80 for the round, earning $275 while finishing four shots behind winner Billy Burke.

"Hell, I could shoot 80 around there with two clubs," Snead said regretfully years later.

While researching *Sam: The One and Only Sam Snead*, his biography of Snead, Al Barkow dug up a photo taken on the day of the final round of the 1935 Cascades Open. Snead is pictured walking down the first fairway, wearing a necktie and holding a driver in his right hand, and he wears a look of disappointment on his face that seems unfathomable for a young professional holding a three-shot lead, looking to win his first golf tournament. Barkow suspects the expression is reflective of what Snead was feeling inside, shattered that his mentor Gleim and the power brokers at the Homestead wanted him to fail. They got their wish that day.

Gleim's gamesmanship had gotten to him, and Snead decided immediately after the tournament that if anybody ever started to say something to try and get in his head, he would simply ignore it. Other players would have to best him with their golf clubs, not mind games.

A YEAR LATER—1936—SNEAD was back in Miami. He was still flying under the radar as a professional golfer but had positioned himself to make a splash when the time was right. He had signed an endorsement contract with the Dunlop Tire and Rubber Company. The deal paid him $500 a year and included a set of golf clubs and a dozen balls every month. While the Cascades debacle had ended poorly the previous fall, some good fortune had come from it. Shortly after the final round, Snead had been approached by Freddie Martin, the golf manager at the Greenbrier Hotel in West Virginia, who told Snead he could come give golf lessons at the Greenbrier, if he wanted. The offer came with a $45 monthly salary and room and board. Snead accepted almost immediately. It began a lifelong association between Snead and the Greenbrier.

Not surprisingly, Snead's departure got under the skin of Fay Ingalls. But after the stunt Ingalls had pulled before the final round at the Cascades, it seemed like a fitting turnabout.

There was also this story, relayed to Al Barkow by Snead's friend Lew Keller. Sometime in 1935 two guests at the Homestead invited Snead up to New York to play a match against amateur Tommy Tailer, an accomplished player from the right side of the tracks. One match turned into two—both played at the Meadowbrook Club on Long Island—and Snead prevailed against Tailer, albeit with considerable effort. When it was over, his New York backers paid him $10,000 for his work. It turned out they had been gambling on the match with much higher stakes than Snead ever realized. The trip and his surprise winnings provided him with some much-needed start-up money for his pro career.

The warm December weather in Miami in 1936 was a perfect respite from West Virginia, where temperatures struggled to reach 50 degrees. Snead tied for sixteenth place at the Miami Biltmore and won $100. Then it was on to Nassau, and this year nobody would stop him from boarding the boat. Perhaps someone should have. Snead joined Johnny Bulla and Bobby Dunkelberger aboard what Snead described as a "small freighter" about forty-five feet long. He figured it went about ten miles per hour, and the trip—which Snead recalled as two hundred miles—took one whole afternoon and night. For Snead and Bulla, it was a nightmare. They both became seasick. Meanwhile, Dunkelberger had no problems and ate everything in sight. This only infuriated Snead and Bulla. It also made their stomachs churn even more.

In Nassau, Snead tied for forty-first place. While there, he spoke with Henry Picard and Craig Wood about playing some events on the West Coast. Just a few weeks earlier, he had finished third in the Cascades Open, winning $300. Snead was feeling good about his golf game and his chances to cash, but he wanted another opinion. He was still awaiting his check from Dunlop Tire and trying to avoid a foolish financial decision. Picard warned him that he had better expect to reel off top-three finishes on the West Coast in order to pay for his travel and expenses.

Then Wood addressed Snead's situation bluntly. "You want to know whether you're going to stay home and teach or be a player?" he asked. That was it. *Am I good enough to make a living as a player? Or is it back to Virginia to fold sweaters and give lessons to busty women for a sandwich and a glass of milk?*

"Yes," Snead said.

Wood advised him to go out to the West Coast and try his luck. Why not? He even backed up his advice by promising Snead that he'd lend him enough money to get back home if the trip went bust.

"My goodness," Snead said, his way of thanking Wood for the vote of confidence and the financial cushion.

Snead's friend Leo Walper offered Snead a ride to the West Coast, as long as Sam paid for half the gas. But Walper was pulling a trailer. Snead figured that meant the trip would take at least a week and eat up most of his $300 savings in the process (who knows what happened to the $10,000 he supposedly banked from his two days in New York the previous year; Barkow suspects the tale of Snead's mere $300 in savings may have been exaggerated by Snead over the years in an effort to talk poorer than he really was).

Then Johnny Bulla said, "Hey, Jackson, I'll go." They agreed to drive out together in Bulla's 1936 Ford, splitting the costs. Snead had an uncle, George, who lived in Los Angeles and would put them up, as long as they agreed to share a bed. They stopped along the way in Greensboro and picked up a football-playing friend of Bulla's in search of a ride who agreed to pay for half the gas and oil, further reducing the expense. "When we got there, we wouldn't let him out of the car until his sister came down with the money," Snead said.

After all, this *was* the Great Depression.

Sam Snead was out on the West Coast, playing the odds with his professional future, and he was betting on himself. Still, he liked the idea of some insurance, even beyond what Craig Wood had offered, so he asked Johnny Bulla if he'd agree to split their tournament winnings. Maybe Bulla liked the way he was playing or simply had a strong independent streak, but he passed on the offer.

Welcome to California, young Mr. Snead, where it would be every man for himself.

PART 2

Little Poison

4

White Plains

For all the grueling train trips and lousy accommodations and penny pinching that accompanied the life of a professional golfer in the 1930s, that was only one slice of the pie. Those sacrifices for the sake of top-flight competition were about cementing your place in the game. They were about playing for trophies, fame, competition. Nowadays we'd say those efforts were about building a brand. Back then, it meant getting your name in the newspaper. The paychecks were nice supplemental income, but they were just that—supplemental. For many or perhaps most professionals, Paul Runyan included, your livelihood centered on the club where you were employed. Your bills were paid through sweat equity and long hours on the lesson tee, if your club even had one. You had to give playing lessons, sweet-talk members, humor their twerpy kids, sell equipment, and maintain a social presence at the club. It was a busy job but a necessary one if you wanted to provide for your family.

A good club was critical, and Paul Runyan found one in White Plains, New York, in the spring of 1931. It was an elite job, even if the club itself was relatively new. It would become Runyan's home for more than a decade. And the first thing he did? He made the conscious decision to turn the place into a training ground, even if nobody else knew it. While he was giving lessons for $4 an hour, part of his mind was on his own game, his own technique. He would practice whenever he could squeeze it in, and the rest of the time he would lay off the booze, the indulgent food, and other country club creature comforts that always seemed nearby. He made sure to stay Boy Scout–ready at all times, so whenever he and Joan boarded a train for a golf tournament, his body and mind were already primed for the crucible of competition. By never letting his guard down, Runyan felt he gained a significant physical and psychological advantage over other players.

And when success followed, be it a string of high finishes or even an unlikely win against a good field highlighted by the ever-confident Gene Sarazen, the critics tried to decipher how it was even possible. How, with his sway? With that jerky swing? And such a short hitter? Sure, the little guy could putt, but was it really that much of an advantage? What was the secret sauce? Watching Paul Runyan win a golf tournament was a bit like seeing a magician's act in person. You knew it wasn't really magic, but you couldn't quite figure out how he did it. You saw him pull the rabbit out of the hat, but you failed to witness the hundreds of hours spent in front of the mirror, perfecting the routine. Sure, you watched the final nine holes of a Runyan victory, but you missed the thousands of balls back in White Plains. And Forest Hill. And Concordia. And Hot Springs. And on the old man's dairy farm.

Of course it seemed improbable. You didn't know the half of it.

THERE WOULD BE no repeat victory for newly married Paul Runyan on the sand greens at Pinehurst in 1931. The defending North and South Open champion performed admirably, despite opening the tournament with a disappointing 76. His four-round total of 295 was good enough for eleventh place and a check for $90. Joan Runyan, still aglow from her recent wedding, followed the action from the gallery.

After Pinehurst, the Runyans headed immediately for Augusta, Georgia, where Paul would compete in the Southeastern Open. There, Runyan's play was sharper, especially in the early rounds. He started off strong with scores of 70-72 and contended throughout the event, finishing in second place, two shots behind Australian Joe Kirkwood. Runyan earned $750 for the high finish, but his payday and Kirkwood's triumph were overshadowed the following morning by news of the sudden death of beloved college football coach Knute Rockne, who perished along with five other passengers and two pilots when their California-bound airplane crashed in rural Kansas.

By the spring of 1931, Runyan's time at Forest Hill in New Jersey had come and gone. A year working under the tutelage of Craig Wood would prove invaluable, however, and Runyan would spend the rest of his life telling friends of his admiration for Wood. Strong of character, Wood was always well dressed, handsome, and well liked by members at his clubs.

A new opportunity presented itself at Metropolis Country Club in White Plains, New York, but first Runyan had to ace the interview. If he thought Forest Hill and its gambling-happy membership could make for an intimidating scene, he surely swallowed hard when he and Joan arrived at 865 Park Avenue, the residence of club member Gerald Rosenberger—the man who had recognized him on the train from St. Louis—to discuss the Metropolis job along with other members of the club's board of directors. "Everyone was there in black tie—they had had a dinner—and I was very impressed," Runyan recalled years later.

The whole thing had happened rather unexpectedly, as far as Runyan was concerned. Rosenberger had called up Forest Hill after the train bump-in and asked Runyan if he'd consider another job opportunity. Runyan told him he'd listen to any proposal. Thus the impressive black-tie, full-court press.

The tuxedo-wearing board members must have been equally impressed by the smooth-talking southerner and his attractive wife. Runyan was offered the job and a $7,500 guaranteed annual salary. Any additional earnings, presumably from lessons or his tournament winnings, would be his to keep. He would start the new job that April.

The only suspense came when, just forty-eight hours after Runyan said yes to Metropolis, Craig Wood announced he'd be leaving Forest Hill. The members at Forest Hill asked Runyan to reconsider. He liked Forest Hill and thought long and hard. He even figured he could make more money as the head professional at Forest Hill. But he was young and green, and he told himself that backing out of a signed agreement with another club would be a bad way to start a career. He told the folks at Forest Hill thanks, but he was already committed elsewhere. Over time, the decision to go to Metropolis would prove to be a wise move.

"It was a great break because Metropolis was the highest-grade establishment I have ever worked at," he told Al Barkow. "It was the way they ran it. Mr. Edmund Waterman ran the place like a czar. He was the president of the club the 14 years I was there, and he guided me into becoming a good golf professional. He said he wasn't going to tell me how to teach, but he did tell me how to run the business correctly, and how to comport myself."

Metropolis Country Club, at least by name, was relatively new when Runyan signed on. The club had been established in 1922, when members of the Metropolitan Club of New York City acquired a golf course from Century Country Club. The course originally had been designed by Herbert Strong but was expanded and redesigned when A. W. Tillinghast got his hands on it in 1929. While the club itself might have been a new creation, its members were familiar with the country club lifestyle. They knew that hiring a competent head professional was a top priority, and it became their next order of business. With Runyan, they had found their man.

Working for Edmund Waterman was a bit like trying to impress a junior high principal: if Runyan just practiced good manners and stayed in his own lane, the rest of the job came easy. Waterman insisted that Runyan never address a member using his (or her) first name until he was asked. Naturally, the first member to insist on such informality was Gerald Rosenberger, who had hired him. Within six months, almost everyone at the club, except its oldest members, had insisted that Runyan address them on a first-name basis. Runyan learned to be especially careful in his personal behaviors and habits. Metropolis had a membership of 1,600, and that meant numerous opportunities to socialize with folks who meant well in their encounters with him. A member could invite him to sit down for a drink, and a couple of those here or there would do no harm. But with dozens of those requests, day after day, Runyan could easily find himself drowning in a haze of martinis and highballs. Yet he realized that constantly saying no could be hurtful to members and ultimately jeopardize his job security. So Runyan made the conscious decision to become a teetotaler. That took minimal effort anyway, because he never drank and was already disciplined in his personal habits. He credited farm life for instilling in him the necessity to eat healthy and avoid vices. There were also his playing aspirations to consider. Because he was slightly built and a short hitter, Runyan convinced himself to train smarter than his competition. He believed that discipline could make up for his physical shortcomings. Just twenty-three years old, he started treating his body as his greatest asset. In that regard, he was strikingly forward thinking as a professional golfer. Knowing that his playing opportunities were irregular and a good portion of his time would be spent on the lesson tee with members, he committed to always being in training, like a boxer preparing for a big bout. He was careful about even the slightest distractions, like card games. If he stayed up late playing gin or bridge, he would notice the difference in how he felt the following day. However, a fine line existed between vigilance and hypercautiousness, especially with sleep. His failed attempt on the California circuit in 1929 was due in part, he believed, to going to bed too early. The fair-haired boy from Arkansas had decided that he'd hit the sack every night by 8:00 p.m. on the West Coast, but his body wasn't ready to sleep. He tossed and turned at night and showed up at the golf course barely able to move. That behavior, too, would have to be modified.

THAT FIRST SUMMER in New York, Joan returned to Arkansas to spend time with her parents while Paul was away from their White Plains apartment playing tournament golf. When he returned home, he realized just how much he missed his wife and began writing her daily letters. He tried to distract his mind by giving golf lessons, going to the movies, and dining with the Rosenbergers, but he couldn't shake the empty feeling of being a bachelor again. In Little Rock, Joan was busy catching up with old friends and spending time with her parents. She went shopping with her mother, went out to a dance one night, and answered endless questions from her old school chums about her new husband and their life together in New York. One day she went to Hot Springs for a visit with Paul's mother. Her letters to Paul indicate a similar empty feeling. In one of them, she wrote, "Gee, honey, I think about you so much and wonder what you are doing until I don't enjoy myself. I guess I never should have come down here until you could come with me!"

After a few days trading sobbing, almost desperate letters, Paul had had enough. He convinced Joan to come home early. Shortly after she returned, Paul, perhaps feeling a touch guilty, handwrote Gertye Harris a polite, heartfelt, sometimes even funny letter of apology on Metropolis Country Club stationery:

Aug. 11, 1931

Dear Mother Harris:

Please don't be angry with me if I seemed to rush Joan away from you.

I have become so attached to her that I really missed her very much. Our little apartment didn't seem at all the same with her away.

Of course I realize you are her mother and probably miss her terribly, but I really need her worse than you do now. I promise Mother Harris that as long as it is possible we will see you once or twice each year. We are looking forward to seeing you in California this winter.

Do you think Joan looks as though I had been treating her well? I love her so much and so much want to make her happy. If there are any suggestions you wish to make that might help me do so, I would welcome them.

I want you to know I will always be grateful to you and the Governor for all you have done for Joan and me.

Joan and I spent our day off this week at Lido on Long Island, where I played golf with Bobby Cruickshank and Mac Smith and Joan swam in the Atlantic with Mrs. Cruickshank and her little daughter. I enjoyed it a lot and I am sure she did too.

You must be sure to visit us next summer as I am sure we have many places of interest to show you. We have often wondered how you would like to go down Broadway with us dodging the elevated pillars and taxi cabs. It really is a great ride if you have good nerves. I promise if you will come up, I will try not to scare you to death.

I must close Mother Harris and get to work. Loads of love to you and the Governor.

Paul

ON THE COMPETITIVE circuit, Runyan's play heated up that fall. In late September he won the Westchester Open at Green Meadow Country

Club. The following week he was victorious at the 1931 Metropolitan PGA Championship at Rockville Country Club.

At Rockville, Runyan finished stroke play in second place behind Gene Sarazen, who fired steady, successive rounds of 71. Yet in the match-play finals it was Runyan who had the upper hand, taking down Sarazen 3 and 1 to claim the Metropolitan PGA title. With play described in newspapers as a "brilliant display of sub-par golf," Runyan took the fight to Sarazen immediately, shooting a morning round of 70 to gain a three-up advantage. In between rounds, rather than hanging around the clubhouse and worrying about holding on to his lead that afternoon, Runyan retired to the nearby house of a Rockville member, where he read the comics to pass the time. When he returned to the club after lunch, he sprinted out to a five-under-par 31 on the front side that nearly put the match out of Sarazen's reach. The Squire rallied over the final nine holes, but Runyan's birdie on the thirty-fifth hole closed out the match. Disgusted at the outcome, Sarazen flung his putter toward the hole after Runyan made the eighteen-footer to win.

The new Met champion's "brilliant display" that day included some classic Runyan recoveries that demoralized Sarazen. Runyan needed just twelve putts over his outward nine holes. There was a holed chip from the trees on the third hole that afternoon with Sarazen in close for birdie, a putt the Squire would subsequently miss. And later Runyan missed the green with three successive iron shots that all found greenside bunkers. However, his wedge and putter carried him, and he failed to lose any of those holes.

Runyan's win was popular among his peers. They found him kind and agreeable but had also grown tired of hearing Sarazen boast about his own play and complain about a lack of competition in the professional ranks. The golf scribes noticed this dynamic. That fall columnist Lou Niss wrote, "It is always a day for rejoicing when Sarazen takes it on the chin in a golf match, which is quite often considering the rating that Sarazen gives himself."

Runyan's friends and the members at Metropolis also took great joy in the win. Herbert Strong, the original course architect at Metropolis, wrote to Runyan that he couldn't remember a more enjoyable match than his defeat of Sarazen. Some of his old buddies from Hot Springs got together and wired to share their congratulations, too.

The victory was extra special for Runyan. The previous spring, Sarazen had been in Augusta, Georgia, when he was asked for his opinion of Runyan's golf game. "Just a fair golfer," Sarazen said. "His swing is too loose."

Runyan was more complimentary in his assessment of Sarazen, years later describing him as the only player who ever caused him to feel intimidated. In his prime, Runyan stood just 5 feet 6 inches tall and weighed all of 130 pounds; he had a hard time intimidating anyone. Like Runyan, Sarazen was a smaller man; unlike Runyan, he was a long hitter. Runyan picked up on Sarazen's arrogance and began noticing that Sarazen played his best golf when he was mad or keyed up. So Runyan kept quiet and resolved to suck the life out of his opponent through his own steady play. The strategy worked.

As for that supposedly loose swing, Sarazen's assessment of Runyan's technique was probably accurate. Runyan maneuvered the club in those days with a pronounced swaying motion away from the ball and a subsequent lunge back into impact. It lacked the elegance one would expect from a top-flight professional. Columnist Ralph Trost described Runyan as a player who made the most of his swing, which was hardly perfect and lacked physical power. "Paul Runyan gets the clubhead away low and with a stiff arm motion with the left arm in control," Trost wrote. "Then comes an upward jerk followed by a lopping downward swing with the finish another jerk."

Runyan seemed undaunted by these assessments of his game. His swing was self-taught, and he knew that fact better than anyone. Having spent countless days on the lesson tee with his members at Metropolis (and before that at Forest Hill and Concordia and Hot Springs), he had seen enough golf swings to know that looks were overrated. If his move put the club on the back of the ball, how it looked was irrelevant. The flight of the golf ball would be the ultimate evidence on which to judge his technique.

GERALD ROSENBERGER, ED Waterman, and the other power brokers at Metropolis Country Club must have grown sore from patting themselves on the back over the good play of their head golf professional in 1931. Generally speaking, a club pro's success in tournaments means good things for the club. Members want to sign up for more lessons. Enthusiasm to play with the pro is high. And the esteem that accompanies a reputed golf professional can help attract members and generally encourage activity at a club.

Take Jesse Jelenko, a Metropolis member whose golf scores were typically in the 90s. Jelenko was a hardworking dental alloy supplier who loved to unwind on the golf course. He and Runyan played together often; in fact, Runyan once stated that he had as much fun playing with Jelenko as anyone he ever played with, professional or amateur. Part of the reason was Jelenko's propensity to raise the stakes, sometimes even while in the act of swinging the club. He once clipped Runyan for upwards of $100 over the back nine at Metropolis by one-putting every green, including a forty-footer on the tenth hole and a sixty-footer on the fifteenth. Standing over the putt on fifteen, Jelenko asked the pro what sort of odds he'd give him.

"Mr. Jelenko," Runyan said, "it doesn't make any difference."

"Twenty to one?" Jelenko asked.

"You're screwing yourself," Runyan said. "I'll take it."

The putt dropped. Runyan could only laugh. And pay up.

After Runyan's first year at Metropolis, Gerald Rosenberger and Metropolis member Mannie Dias rounded up a group of thirty-five members to chip in $100 apiece to send Paul and Joan south over the winter so he could compete against the game's top professionals. (Runyan mistakenly remembered it as seventy members at $50 apiece, but a letter from Dias corrected the figure. Regardless, the total was the same.) The $3,500 came with a few strings attached. Both parties agreed that Runyan would send back any checks he won, and if there were any profits left over at the end of the tour, they would get split 50/50.

"I am quite sure that the holders of these units will get a great deal of pleasure out of it, and I am also quite sure that you will win enough money to more than defray your expenses, and I hope some profit besides," Dias wrote to Runyan that October.

That November, Paul and Joan set out on his first full seasonal golf tour. Their travels would take them—by train—from New York to

Florida to Southern California, then down through Arizona, Texas, Louisiana, and Florida again before their return to New York. An overnight train berth in those days cost about $8, but with your professional livelihood at stake, a good night's sleep was worth the extra cost.

In describing the touring lifestyle of the 1930s to Al Barkow, Runyan noted that there was so little money at stake, players didn't take themselves too seriously. To be more precise, they didn't get too wrapped up in the financial implications. "We fought like cats and dogs for the titles, but the money didn't seem to make that much difference," he explained. Amateur golf was still king in the eyes of most folks who paid attention, including those who wrote about it. Professionals were, for a time anyway, treated like second-class citizens, a group—with their endless side bets, exotic shoes, alpaca sweaters that they wore just to keep their shirts clean, and endless stories about what it was like to actually work in a golf shop—who were politely reminded to come and go through the back door, not the front.

Finding a full box of adequate golf balls was sometimes a chore. In the days before true quality control at the manufacturing plants, players and their caddies would test each golf ball carefully before putting it in the bag, checking for the proper compression. Players also sought out any sort freebie they could get their hands on—car rides, meals, opportunities to hunt or fish on golf course properties. One of the oldest tricks in the book, if you were in citrus country, was stuffing oranges by the handful into your golf bag to save on the food budget. Sometimes those oranges were cradled by dirty clothes that you had stuffed into your bag, just to have somewhere to put them.

And when a tournament ended "you loaded into somebody's Graham-Paige or Essex and drove until you threw a connecting rod," wrote Dan Jenkins. In Runyan's case, that car would one day be a six-wheel Buick (two extra wheels resided up inside the wheel wells) that he bought for a shade less than $1,000.

Most players carried mismatched sets of clubs that could be adjusted in the parking lot with the business end of a boot and an obliging piece of stone curb. They all knew how to play cards, shoot pool, and gamble whatever money they had. Some, like Frank Walsh, were keen pranksters. When he was the first to arrive at a hotel, Walsh would sneak into another player's hotel room and short-sheet the bed or leave behind a frog or some other unwanted souvenir.

Runyan, always serious by nature, grew to appreciate the different characters he encountered playing professional golf. He admired Al Watrous, who practiced tirelessly but enjoyed life's simpler pleasures, like the solitude of dining alone on the balcony of his hotel room. He latched onto Tommy Armour because he admired his intelligence; Runyan, of course, considered himself among the game's more intelligent players, but he lacked formal education. And he learned countless lessons from playing practice rounds with Horton Smith, who was businesslike in his approach to golf and always kept a watchful eye on Runyan's technique. In the event Runyan ever lost track with a particular part of his game, Smith could help decipher where he had gone astray.

Runyan and other players would often split expenses to stay afloat. In a city like Los Angeles, that could mean splitting cab fare from the Hollywood Plaza Hotel to Riviera Country Club, which hosted the Los Angeles Open. The sting of that $7.50 fare was a bit less prickly when it was divided by four, like Runyan did one morning with fellow players Frank Walsh, Cyril Walker, and Armour. Walker, who liked to sing and tell stories, kept the ride entertaining. The British-born Walker's play could also be entertaining but for all the wrong reasons. He was an especially slow golfer; at the 1929 LA Open, after refusing to comply with tournament organizers who insisted he speed up or let other groups play through, two police officers carried him off the golf course and told him never to come back. When the media found Walker that day, he conceded that he might be slow but that Armour was even slower.

Perhaps Runyan's contemporaries thought of *him* as a sort of character. His playing style was unique. So were his personal habits, like not drinking and fastidiously watching his diet. Few players took their personal health as seriously as Runyan in those days. He dressed for golf with a certain panache, often wearing spiked saddle golf shoes and all-white ensembles. He was commonly referred to as "dapper" and "impeccable." Some people might have mistaken that for flamboyance. For a man who was generally considered reserved, the way he dressed seemed to be his way of expressing himself. And there was dancing. Paul and Joan Runyan were known as one of golf's premier dancing couples. They both enjoyed music, and when the mood was right, a night out dancing was just what Paul needed to distract himself from the pressure of tournament golf. It sure relieved the tension better than an early bedtime followed by a restless night tossing and turning. Sometimes the Runyans would meet another couple for dinner at a local supper club and then go dancing before lights out at ten thirty or eleven o'clock. The Runyans were famous on tour for their interpretation of the rumba, while Walsh and his wife preferred the tango.

Runyan's tour that winter was characterized by steady play. He tied for eighth at the Arizona Open in January. A week later he shared the thirty-six-hole lead at the Texas Open. But the highlight that winter came in Tampa, Florida, in late February, when he captured the Gasparilla Open. Scoring was low that week at the Palma Ceia course—so low that a two-round total of 144 was needed just to advance into match play. Runyan fancied the low scoring and kept winning his matches. He knocked off Tony Manero to grab a berth in the finals, where he defeated Willie Macfarlane from Tuckahoe, New York, 3 and 1. The victory earned him $925 in gold—pirate gold, claimed the tournament hosts in Tampa.

After the Gasparilla victory, columnist Ralph Trost—who had described Runyan's swing as two jerks and a lopping downward swing—hailed Runyan's win, in spite of his physical shortcomings. Yet Trost's column is puzzling. Was it a veiled critique or brutally honest? He wrote that if you lined up a dozen of golf's most prominent professionals on a practice range and watched them hit balls, Runyan would be the least impressive. Trost was aghast that a swing full of jiggles and jerks could be so reliable under the pressure of tournament play. What was undeniable, Trost wrote, was Runyan's knack for great putting.

Somehow, some way, the whole of Runyan's play was greater than its parts. "When this slim, smiling, suave, blond-headed youngster from Arkansas first invaded New Jersey, the boys who didn't know of his Southern tournament record stamped him as one of those pleasant-faced agreeable lads who would never get anywhere," he wrote. "He didn't seem possessed of the nerve, the strength, or the courage."

Another Trost column a month later continued his fascination with Runyan's methods. Again, he heaped praise while also offering critique and dismay. He described Runyan as "soft-spoken" and "angelic-looking." But he went on to list the skills Runyan supposedly lacked, such as a steady foundation for his swing, a perfect pivot like Macdonald Smith's, or easy footwork like George Voigt's. And on and on. "But he can putt," Trost concluded. "Marvelously."

Clearly, Runyan had been underestimated.

Runyan earned $4,700 that winter. "I figured, pretty nice, made my winter expenses and lived quite well, didn't have to spend any of the pennies I saved during the summer, and got 50 percent of the purse money I won—another $2,200 or so," he said. Or so he thought.

When he and Joan returned to New York, the Metropolis members threw a dinner party in his honor. Paul and Joan were wined and dined, and nobody said a word about settling up the finances. Finally, the Runyans learned that the club had sweetened the deal. The Metropolis members agreed to let Paul keep their share of the profits and even threw in a $1,500 bonus. No strings attached. Perhaps they were buoyed with optimism by the sound of FDR's New Deal, which would start to take shape in the spring of 1933, but in the depths of the Depression, when a quarter of the American workforce was unemployed, such generosity is hard to fathom. The gesture meant so much to Runyan that he held on to the canceled $1,500 check for the rest of his life.

5

"I Don't Know How He Does It"

The sudden attention must have felt good, if only for a moment. Think about it. You're pitching equipment for the foremost name in sporting goods in the company of the iconic Bobby Jones, who, retired or not, was more than just a golfer. More than an attorney, or a club designer, or even a club founder. Jones was an American icon, a brand, a once-hotheaded southern sage whose every move was fawned over as if he were Clark Gable, Fred Astaire, or Jack Dempsey. Jones was a man who knew what it felt like to be thrown a ticker-tape parade in New York City, an honor he shared with princes and dukes, military leaders and aviation heroes—folks whose likenesses would get placed on postage stamps and currency. He was a man who could match his stride to the cadence of the latest brass band to break into "Dixie" every time he descended a flight of stairs to greet an admiring crowd.

How could Jones the attorney have ever lost a case? Everybody loved Bobby. And it seemed everybody found his sudden retirement aggravatingly fascinating, tabloid-worthy, a bit like the public obsession over author J. D. Salinger decades later. But Jones didn't totally disappear. He quit competitive golf, but he didn't quit being a voice for the game. And here was little Paul Runyan, son of a southern spa town, drafting in his wake, dropping by his law office in Atlanta to talk shop. Even padding Jones's wallet with a few bucks in friendly practice rounds, alongside Horton Smith and Ed Dudley. Striding down the fairways at Augusta in his starched plus fours and sweater vest, asking Bobby about the placement of bunkers or how in the hell he hit a four-wood so high and soft off a downslope that it could still hold the green. Oh, wait, it was a three-wood? You don't say, Bobby.

Surely, at some point, Runyan had to pinch himself and ask, "How did I get here?"

He got there by hitting his stride at the right time. Gobbling up tourna-

ments on the winter circuit. Winning by wide margins—sometimes eight or nine strokes. And he did it not by hitting the ball far—he hit it barely far enough—but by doing everything else better than his competition. He became a master of fairway woods, prompting Grantland Rice to dub him "Runyan of the five spoons." Hey, whatever you say, Mr. Rice, thanks for noticing. And to watch him putt, forget it. Even the immortal Jones had to shake his head and concede that the undersized pro from Arkansas by way of White Plains could devastate his competition through sheer volume of made putts. Want to make the hole larger? Go ahead, Mr. Sarazen, give it a try. See if you can stop him.

Someone gave him a handle: Little Poison. It's a moniker that sounds more like the name of a twenty-first-century hip-hop artist than a golfer. Experience will teach you that nicknames, whether flattering or scathing, usually reveal a truth about the person they're meant to label. Runyan predated hip-hop superstars by decades, but succumbing on the golf course to his brand of golf was particularly infuriating to opponents. He was golf's version of the Princeton offense. Don't you dare make a mistake—not one—otherwise Little Poison will be there, ready to make you pay.

WHEN SPALDING CAME calling, Paul Runyan was smart enough to listen.

A. G. Spalding and Brothers sporting goods branded itself as the company that had developed the first official baseball of the National and American Leagues (1876, 1889), the first baseball glove (1877), the first American football (1887), and the first basketball (1894). Spalding was a giant in the world of sporting goods, and around 1932 Runyan joined its ranks, to use and endorse its golf clubs.

The association was noteworthy because Spalding also had the world's most famous golfer, Bobby Jones, under contract. For the newly retired-from-serious-competition Jones, the Spalding deal (and his film agreement with Warner Brothers) presented an opportunity to cash in on his celebrity in ways he simply couldn't have done while competing as an amateur golfer. Spalding gave Jones a platform and eventually put his name on a product. He would match wits with Spalding's club maker J. Victor East to develop a matched set of irons, stamped with the signature of Robert T. Jones Jr., available to the masses in hickory and steel shafts. These new "Robt. T. Jones Jr."

models were "designed by Bobby—made by Spalding," according to some spicy Spalding ad copy from 1932. It's a pattern that's repeated in the golf equipment industry to this day. Those golfing masses—the incurable hackers, the midhandicap club golfers old and young, the scratch players, and even the supercompetitive amateurs—have always wanted to play the same equipment the pros play.

Spalding was a key player in the golf business. Certainly the Jones association helped the brand. During one twenty-year period in the 1910s, 1920s, and early 1930s, eighteen of twenty winners of the U.S. Open played a Spalding golf ball. In the 1930s, those balls retailed for anywhere from a quarter apiece for the Wizard golf ball up to 65 cents apiece for the Top Flite or Kro-Flite ball.

When Runyan captured the North and South Open at Pinehurst in the spring of 1930, he did so playing a set of Walter Hagen clubs. Runyan had a discerning eye for equipment, thanks in part to his days as an apprentice, when he was making and repairing clubs in Arkansas and North Dakota. He knew what he liked, and he knew what *he* needed to play his best golf. He also held Bobby Jones in high regard.

"When Jones first came with Spalding, Victor East was with them, of course," he told Jones historian Sidney Matthew in a 1993 interview that's now part of Matthew's expansive Jones collection on file at Atlanta's Emory University. "And Victor East was very smart. And Bobby was extremely smart. Bobby Jones probably had more to do with the improvement, particularly with the wooden clubs, of Spalding than Victor East did."

Runyan marveled at the shots Jones could play with his fairway woods, particularly off uneven lies and downslopes. Pair Jones's shotmaking skill with his degree in mechanical engineering from Georgia Tech, and you have someone uniquely qualified to influence golf club design.

Runyan's first encounter with Bobby Jones had come at Olympia Fields in Chicago back in 1928, when Runyan, then nineteen, made birdie on consecutive days at the eighth hole, each time with Jones watching the action from behind the green. "You kind of like this hole, don't you?" Jones asked him.

"Yes I do, Mr. Jones," the starstruck Runyan replied.

That was as far as their association went until 1930, when Jones and Runyan crossed paths at the Southeastern Open in Augusta, Georgia, an event that predated Jones's creation of Augusta National Golf Club and the Masters Tournament. The purse at Augusta in those days was typically somewhere between $3,500 and $5,000, Runyan recalled, and in 1930 the event was held on two golf courses: Augusta Country Club for the first two rounds and the Forest Hills–Ricker course for the final two rounds.

The *Atlanta Constitution* dubbed the event that week the Augusta Open, and it could just as well have been called the Bobby Jones Coronation Open, because that's what happened. Jones sprinted out to a wide lead (ten shots entering the final eighteen), and in the last round he came to the tee of the 192-yard sixteenth hole five under par for the round. The galleries had been growing in size all day, and they began to grow impatient as Jones waited on the tee for some twenty minutes due to a backup in the groups ahead. No matter, Jones just lay down on the grass and waited until the green cleared. But after a pulled iron shot into the woods and a three-putt, he made a triple-bogey six. He parred the seventeenth, then on the final hole hit a spectator with a tee shot that bounced into more trouble, eventually leading to a double bogey. He played the final three holes in five over par and still shot even par for the round and 284 for the tournament—thirteen shots ahead of the next-best finisher, Horton Smith, who shot 297. Yet it was Smith who took home first-place money. Jones was an amateur and could not accept it.

Runyan barely factored into the tournament that week at Augusta. Of course, he probably cared very little, still riding high off his victory at the North and South Open at Pinehurst the week before.

Runyan's friendship with Jones would continue to grow over the years and seemed strongest after Jones had mostly quit competitive golf. Spalding would sometimes invite Runyan to Rich's Department Store in Atlanta to lecture about golf while promoting the company's line of golf clubs, and Jones would always invite Runyan to his law office for a visit.

"And every time it inevitably got back to technical aspects of golf," Runyan later recalled.

When it came to proper technique and technical excellence, Runyan and Jones saw eye to eye. At least Runyan thought so. He had a hard time refuting anything Jones had to say about the golf swing. Years later, *Golf Digest* editors, upon hearing of Runyan's affinity for Jones, presented him with copies of the magazine's collection of Jones's writings on golf.

Runyan and Jones tightened their bond on the golf course through practice rounds—at least until Jones decided to hang up his spikes. Even late in his competitive career, Jones was a match for anyone, Runyan recalled.

"In the friendly $1 Nassau matches that are played from Monday to Thursday, Bobby Jones and Ed Dudley never lost a single eighteen-hole match to any of the two-man teams," he said with a touch of hyperbole. "I partnered with Horton Smith every time we played against him. We never won an eighteen holes. And it was largely Jones. Dudley was a magnificent player then, but the fact that they did these remarkable things was largely Bobby Jones's doing. Because he shot 66s, 67s, 68s time and time again."

Ultimately, Runyan's association with Spalding would last three decades. A few years passed before Victor East could please Runyan with a set of hand-forged clubs exactly as Runyan wanted, but in the meantime both sides found the association beneficial. Even though he was still relatively unknown in the very early 1930s, Runyan would prove himself as a dependable pitchman for Spalding. As a trade-off, Runyan had access to industry-leading clubs and balls—and to Bobby Jones.

THE YEAR 1933 was a Ryder Cup year for golf professionals from the United States and Great Britain and Ireland. The team competition would be played that June in Southport, England, with Walter Hagen serving as playing captain for the American squad. If finding a place on the Ryder Cup team was any motivation at all for Runyan in 1933, it certainly showed in his play. One *Los Angeles Times* reporter years later called Runyan the hottest golfer on tour between 1933 and 1935. He started fast in 1933, capturing the Agua Caliente Open in Mexico in January by two strokes over his practice round partner, Horton Smith.

That victory came with a $1,500 first-place check. Later that month, in between winter events, he and Joan swung through Hutchinson, Kansas, where Joan had grown up, to visit her family. Naturally, Paul spent his downtime in Hutchinson trying to stay tournament sharp on the golf course, where he and his father-in-law—whom he referred to as "the Governor"—played a round at Carey Lake (now known as Carey Park) with the club's head professional and a local newspaper reporter in front of a gallery of a dozen or so locals. A few days later, Runyan and the local pro teamed up in a friendly match against two club pros from nearby Wichita.

In early March Runyan partnered with Horton Smith to win the International Four-Ball Team Matches in Miami, Florida—an event that golf journalist Dan Jenkins once lumped into a group of tournaments (including the Goodall Round Robin, Westchester 108-Hole Open, Dapper Dan Open, and Vancouver Jubilee) that sounded more like a string of events on a billiards circuit. Smith's ball striking at the International Four-Ball was wild and Runyan missed his share of greens, but his chipping and pitching rarely put par in doubt as they cruised to the victory. Then, just days later, Runyan was victorious in the Florida All-Year-Round Open, played at the Miami Biltmore.

Runyan's $1,000 victory at the Miami Biltmore was noteworthy for its implementation of a rule change—the use of six-inch cups, supposedly at the request of Gene Sarazen. At nearly two inches larger in diameter than a typical golf hole, which is four and a quarter inches in diameter, the experiment raised the question of how valuable putting really was. If Sarazen thought that putting mattered too much and a larger cup would level the field on the greens, he was sorely mistaken. It's true, putting mattered. But larger cups were not the answer to negating the advantage gained by good putters. Runyan torched the field with rounds of 69-64-65-68 for a four-round total of eighteen-under-par 266 and a ten-stroke victory. He cruised around the golf course that final round, wearing a white tam-o'-shanter and saddle golf shoes, accompanied by a large gallery. More than a thousand fans, three deep in spots, surrounded the final green to see him close out the tournament.

"Runyan's rout of the field of nationally known golfers was consistent from every point," read page 8 of the *Miami Daily News* on Monday, March 6, 1933. The statistics support that statement. Runyan putted well, but his game at the Miami Biltmore was buoyed by more than just his putter. For the week, he hit fifty-five of seventy-two greens-in-regulation, the most of any player in the top ten finishers. He made twenty-three birdies, converting eight of nine birdie putts from inside six feet; five of fourteen attempts from six to fifteen feet; eight of twenty-eight attempts from fifteen to twenty-five feet; and two of eleven tries from more than twenty-five feet. And he never three-putted.

The unusually robust statistics compiled that week at the Miami Biltmore revealed even more. Out of eighteen players tracked, Runyan finished seventeenth in driving distance, routinely outdriven by Sarazen and Hagen by 25 to 30 yards. The *Miami News* reported those driving distance figures the day after the event. Hagen averaged 247.2 yards, Sarazen averaged an even 240, and Runyan averaged just 220.4 yards. Somehow, through strong approach play and timely putting, Runyan made sure none of that mattered. Ryder Cup captain Hagen finished in third place, twelve shots behind Runyan. And Sarazen, the brain behind the six-inch cup experiment, finished fifth, fifteen shots back. Still, Sarazen threw on a sweater and a bow tie and showed up at the trophy ceremony, standing alongside amateur Johnny Goodman, biting a smile while Runyan collected the $1,000 first prize from Judge T. E. Price of the Biltmore.

SHORTLY AFTER RUNYAN'S victory at the 1933 Florida All-Year-Round Open, golf columnist Ralph Trost penned an article in the *Brooklyn Daily Eagle* that highlighted Runyan's progressive attitude toward equipment—an attitude that predated his association with Spalding. Trost pointed out that Runyan was one of the first players in professional golf to adopt steel-shafted clubs. Only his jigger, which Trost described as "a golf club with the loft of an old-fashioned mashie but with a thinner blade," carried a hickory shaft. Runyan's jigger featured a slightly shortened shaft, which Trost speculated allowed Runyan to creep closer to the ball on chip shots. For the short-hitting Runyan, who was often strategizing how to place his ball in advantageous chipping positions on holes where he couldn't reach the green in regulation, a reliable chipping club was mandatory. But why hickory? Beyond habit, was there a reason? A mechanical advantage? Runyan once described to Sidney Matthew the differences between steel and hickory, explaining that steel-shafted clubs allowed strong hitters to unload into the golf ball with maximum force. "The vibratory cycle is fast enough to straighten out," he told Matthew. "But the hickory wasn't. You had to wait and make long, loose, languid swings to give the club time. Even the stiffest hickory shaft, its vibratory cycle might be even a little slow for Paul Runyan." Deciphering that statement, it seems Runyan was saying that hickory shafts had a little more subtlety, or play, than steel. And that was apparently a feel he sought while chipping around the green.

The details of Runyan's equipment were fascinating, but Trost's real find was the revelation of Runyan's nickname, which he alluded to in the article's opening line. He wrote, "Paul Runyan, otherwise 'Little Poison' as far as some of the big names in golf are concerned, is one of the players of steel." Later in the article, he called Runyan by the same moniker, writing, "The truth is that 'Little Poison' just naturally jiggered the boys right out of three big purses."

Little Poison. Who first coined the nickname? Another player? A writer, maybe Trost? Runyan himself?

According to Runyan, the credit went to golf writer Lawrence Robinson of the *New York World-Telegram*, who first used the nickname in 1931. Professional baseball had its own Little Poison in undersized outfielder Lloyd Waner, who debuted for the Pittsburgh Pirates in 1927 and played through the 1940s. Robinson knew this but didn't let it stop him. In Runyan's case, the nickname fit like a glove, and it would follow him for the rest of his life. Small in stature, long on grit, Paul Runyan was a ruthless competitor. To his adversaries on the golf course, Runyan's game was like poison—and there was no escaping it.

WITH MANY OF the game's top professionals in Miami for consecutive events in the spring of 1933, some important golf business was conducted behind the scenes between the International Four-Ball and the Florida All-Year-Round Open. With the Ryder Cup looming that summer, George Jacobus, president of the PGA, invited a handful of team members and PGA vice president Tom Boyd out to dinner at Auby's Lagoon, a popular Miami Beach nightclub, to discuss preparations for the event. Those players were Walter Hagen, Denny Shute, Craig Wood, Olin Dutra, Horton Smith, Tom Boyd, and Runyan. The evening concluded with plans being made for the team to travel together from New York to England on June 15, with the matches beginning on June 26. They also decided that the team would remain in England until after the Open Championship, which was being played at St. Andrews in Scotland in early July. Jacobus and Boyd were trying to organize some exhibition matches for the Ryder Cuppers between the two events, including a pair of matches near London.

The American Ryder Cup team that sailed to England in June 1933 was not immune to controversy. For anyone who's followed the biennial golf matches over the years, particularly in modern times, such controversy is typical of an American squad. In 1933 much of the noise centered on the selection process for determining which players were chosen for the team. A PGA selection committee was responsible for assembling the team, and the committee drew the ire of Gene Sarazen, who took issue with the omission of 1931 U.S. Open champion Billy Burke. Sarazen suggested publicly that he'd donate $100 of his stipend if other players would do the same to make room for Burke to travel to England. Scottish-born Tommy Armour, who often held opinions contrary to Sarazen, inserted himself into the public discourse, calling Burke's omission "one of the outstanding disgraces of golf."

Captain Hagen was less interested in the selection process than Sarazen. He told the press that he liked his team and that he was sure Burke had been given due consideration. PGA business administrator Albert Gates publicly stated that the selection process was fair and that Burke wasn't even the first man out among the players under consideration for the final spot. But the pressure continued to mount from Sarazen and other outspoken professional golfers, and at the last minute the PGA relented and placed Burke on the team. The decision was aided by Johnny Goodman's victory at the U.S. Open that summer in Chicago. Goodman's win allowed the PGA some wiggle room. Informally, they had reserved the final spot on the team for the national Open champion, provided he was an American professional and not already a team member. Goodman was an amateur and not eligible for the Ryder Cup. Thus, Burke got the nod.

More controversy loomed in the weeks that would follow the Ryder Cup. Team members would be staying in Europe for the Open Championship at St. Andrews, and some players had booked exhibition matches after the Open. These matches and subsequent travel plans threatened to interfere with their participation in the PGA Championship, held near Milwaukee, Wisconsin, in early August. Sarazen, Hagen, Shute, Joe Kirkwood, and Craig Wood threatened not to play in the PGA sectional tournaments used as qualification for the championship; it seemed they were trying to coax the PGA into rescheduling the tournament. PGA officials compromised by exempting all the Ryder Cuppers from qualifying.

Before leaving for England aboard the *Aquitania*, Runyan hosted the Ryder Cup team at Metropolis Golf Club in White Plains for a tune-up match against a squad of the New York metropolitan area's best amateur players. The Ryder Cuppers won four out of five foursomes matches that day, including an easy 5-and-4 romp by Runyan and Hagen over Max Marston and Jess Sweetser. The exhibition helped raise $1,500 for the PGA's unemployment fund, and the club kicked in $500. After a farewell dinner, the American players boarded the *Aquitania* and set sail for England.

At sea, the Ryder Cuppers received first-class treatment. The Runyans' C-deck stateroom had two beds, a full bath, wardrobe, dressing table, and sitting area. Fresh sea air was captured by an outside ventilator and filtered into each room. You could get a fine haircut, have your clothes pressed, watch a movie in the motion picture theater, and always find a tasty meal. The Runyans dined regularly with the Farrells as well as the Shutes and Dudleys. On the night of June 20, the players and their spouses were treated to an elaborate six-course dinner on board the ship.

The Southport and Ainsdale Golf Club in Southport, England, was the host site for the 1933 Ryder Cup. Situated near the coast along the Irish Sea immediately south of Royal Birkdale Golf Club, Southport and Ainsdale was thought of as a stern test with all the usual charms of links golf, such as intimidating sand dunes, abundant heather and gorse, and a cool breeze coming in off the Irish Sea.

Bright sunshine greeted both teams and seven thousand spectators on day one for the thirty-six-hole foursomes matches. Southport and Ainsdale's club professional, Percy Roberts, serving as starter, stirred up the crowd by barking out the contestants' names in a loud voice to welcome them to the tee. Runyan, twenty-four, the youngest player on either side, partnered with his old boss Craig Wood, and after the morning eighteen they stood all square with Syd Easterbrook and Bill Davies. Cloudy skies threatened that afternoon, but the rain never shook loose; neither did the Americans. Easterbrook and Davies held off Runyan and Wood one up, and Great Britain led overall, 2½ to 1½ points, at day's end.

The crowd was larger on day two for the eight singles matches. It was so large that some 250 stewards carrying long canes with red flags on top were needed to direct the crowds. Runyan was slotted in the fifth match, playing thirty-six-year-old Percy Allis, whose son Peter—the future Ryder Cupper and, more famously, legendary golf commentator—would have been just two years old at the time. The course was buzzing with energy, aided by the presence of the Prince of Wales, on hand to watch the afternoon play. Stately golf writer Bernard Darwin, grandson of the famed British naturalist Charles Darwin, called it "one of the most exciting days of golf and before the biggest crowd I ever saw on a golf course in my life." At the end of the morning round, Great Britain led three matches, the Americans led three matches, and two were all square. Runyan lost the last three holes of the morning round to go from two up to one down. In the afternoon, he found himself three down with six holes to play but staged a brave rally, winning the thirteenth, fourteenth, and fifteenth holes to get back to all square. However, it was Allis's day; the Sheffield-born Brit won the sixteenth to regain the advantage and then won the seventeenth to close out the back-and-forth match 2 and 1. Allis soaked in the spoils of victory, walking back to the clubhouse amid wild cheering from the hometown fans. The raucousness continued when Denny Shute missed a four-footer to lose on the final hole to Syd Easterbrook. With that, Great Britain recaptured the Ryder Cup by a final margin of 6½ to 5½ points. Billy Burke, the last-minute American selection, won a point in the only match he played at Southport and Ainsdale.

Afterward the Prince of Wales presented the Ryder Cup to the victorious British squad and its captain, J. H. Taylor. He thanked the American players and congratulated them on their play, then he pulled U.S. team captain Hagen aside and, according to Hagen's personal account, suggested it was time they shared an adult beverage. Hagen was gracious in defeat and called it "a great day for professional golf." Runyan, no doubt disappointed by the result of his first Ryder Cup, turned his attention toward the upcoming Open Championship at St. Andrews.

Runyan's first taste of the home of golf left him—like many players throughout the course of golf history, including Bobby Jones early in his career—wondering what all the fuss was about. The fairways were hard as a rock, the large crowds were barely manageable without gallery ropes, and the course seemed outdated to Runyan. "When I played [St. Andrews] first in 1933 there was not a single change made on any one of the original two courses in the last 140 years," Runyan recounted. "When I went there, it's the gospel truth, the hazards were catching good first shots that were intended to catch poor second shots."

St. Andrews that week played 6,572 yards, but the firm playing conditions caused it to play much shorter. Runyan's caddie was David Herd, a cousin of Scottish pro Sandy Herd, who had won the 1902 Open Championship at Hoylake. Runyan would continually ask his caddie where to aim his tee shots on each hole, and Herd's answers were confounding to Runyan, who was making his first tour around the Old Course.

"Over toward yonder steeple," Herd would tell Runyan to aim.

"He can't be right," Runyan would say to himself. Rather than follow Herd's advice precisely, Runyan would hedge and aim closer toward what looked like the fairway. After continually hitting what he thought were good shots, Runyan would hand his driver to Herd, who would be hanging his head.

"What's wrong, David?" Runyan would ask.

"You'll see," the caddie would say.

When the pair arrived at Runyan's ball, it was often stuck in a pot bunker that had been invisible from the tee. Runyan was dismayed. Pot bunkers at the Old Course usually called for a sideways blast just to get back into position, causing a player to lose almost a full stroke to the field. It was a poor recipe to get into contention. Still, Runyan, whose odds to win that week were pegged at 20-to-1, battled, shooting rounds of 76-77, but he missed the cut by one stroke. He left St. Andrews disappointed, and when Denny Shute redeemed his missed putt on the final green of the Ryder Cup to win the Open in a playoff over Craig Wood a few days later, Runyan kicked himself even harder. Shute had been steady—not spectacular—in his four consecutive rounds of 73, but steady proved good enough to win a major championship.

"If I had qualified, I might still have won," Runyan lamented.

The Runyans stayed in Europe for two full weeks after the Open, celebrating Paul's twenty-fifth birthday while abroad, before sailing from Le Havre, France, on July 20, aboard the SS *Washington*. They arrived at the port of New York a week later. Once he was back on home soil, a horde of anxious members at Metropolis Country Club awaited lessons from their head professional. Reportedly, Runyan gave on average a thousand lessons a season at a rate of $4 per hour—more lessons than any other touring professional.

At the PGA Championship, held outside Milwaukee in early August, Runyan made it as far as the quarterfinals before getting steamrolled by Willie Goggin, 6 and 5. Goggin was victorious in the next round, too, before falling to Gene Sarazen in the final match.

Runyan's 1933 season was far from over. In late December, he showed up in California as a crowd favorite at the Pasadena Open. The fans loved his playing style, but tournament organizers were just as taken by a letter he had written earlier that month to the Pasadena Junior Chamber of Commerce expressing his affinity for the tournament and his desire to win it. That's just what he did. His two-under-par total of 282 was good enough for a three-stroke victory over Macdonald Smith.

"This is certainly a wonderful Christmas gift for me," Runyan quipped as he accepted the winner's check for $1,000. Joan Runyan played to the crowd, grabbing the check and saying, "After all, it was my good cooking that enabled you to win."

Runyan's caddie that week at Brookside Park, a Pasadena local named Walter Crabb, also liked the size of that winner's check and was given a generous tip, according to the *Pasadena Post*.

That afternoon a telegram arrived for Runyan from his parents in Hot Springs, Arkansas. "Congratulations. Proud of you," they wrote. Ed Waterman also sent one, writing, "Heartiest congratulations and sincerest wishes for a very happy and prosperous new year to you and Mrs. Runyan from every member of the Metropolis Country Club."

GOLF WOULD CHANGE forever in 1934, and so would Paul Runyan's place in its history. He was arguably the game's best player. In the span of a month that spring, he notched two eight-stroke victories and a nine-shot conquest in seventy-two-hole stroke play events. The hot play continued throughout the season, and by late summer he would find golf immortality.

Looping back to Augusta, Georgia, Bobby Jones opened his dream enterprise, the Augusta National Golf Club, in January 1933 to much fanfare. Trains from across the country descended upon Georgia that month, and celebrities from all walks of life disembarked eagerly from them to catch a glimpse of Jones's pet project. The list of arrivals included sportswriter Grantland Rice, flying ace Elliott White Springs, author Charles Francis Coe, future USGA president Fielding Wallace, and financial journalist B. C. Forbes, who founded *Forbes* magazine. Jones spent the week before the club's opening in Augusta getting his licks in on the golf course, where he reportedly shot three or four rounds of three-under-par 69. On the evening of Saturday, January 14, a celebratory dinner was held at the Bon Air Vanderbilt hotel, and the orchestra started playing "Dixie" when Jones and his father walked into the room. Even a few years into retirement, Jones was still treated as a conquering hero, especially in Georgia.

The hype around the Augusta National Golf Club was building toward the following March, when the club would host the first Augusta National Invitation Tournament, informally known as the Masters—the same Masters that eventually supplanted Pinehurst's North and South as the South's marquee golf event. Not immediately, mind you, but the signs were there in year one, including, as Dan

Jenkins described decades later in *Sports Illustrated*, a golf course that "looked as opulent as a LaSalle with chrome horns," delicious southern food and drink, a preeminent host (Jones), "and so many southern colonels sitting under crawling wisteria that you were tempted to look up who won the Civil War."

When Paul Runyan set foot on the grounds of Augusta National for that first Masters in the spring of 1934, he had to be careful not to do anything to disrupt his rhythm. World-class golf was seeping out of him like water from a busted pipe, and he aimed to keep it that way. Three weeks before the Masters, Runyan won the St. Petersburg Open in Florida by three shots, then a week later he captured the West Coast Open in Belleair, Florida, by eight shots. His hot play at Belleair included a pair of 68s over the final thirty-six holes that iced the victory. The following week, he and Horton Smith came within a whisker of defending their title at the International Four-Ball at Miami Country Club but lost to Al Espinosa and Denny Shute on the thirty-sixth hole. Runyan saved his best golf for last in the run-up to Augusta, winning the Charleston Open a week later in South Carolina by nine shots. His eleven-under-par total included a final-round 65, establishing the competitive course record. He was playing better than anybody, and everyone knew it.

Runyan was impressed by the beauty of Jones's new club in Augusta—impressed but not stunned, having already encountered the charms of the city during his appearances at the Southeastern Open. "It was almost as beautiful as it is now," he told Sidney Matthew in 1993. "However, if you went over and played Forest Hills–Ricker at the same time, it had almost the same beauty. It didn't have quite as much floral beauty. But it had tree beauty just as much as Augusta National."

Runyan also felt that the nearby Augusta Country Club, at least in those early days of the Masters, played a few shots harder than the 6,700-yard Augusta National. That's not to say Jones's course was a pushover. Far from it. But it could be had, in spots. Take the tenth hole, which in 1934 was played as the opening hole, prior to the club reversing the first and second nines. Runyan called it a "set-up hole," where birdie was a real possibility if you played the hole as intended. By his recollection, the opening hole in 1934 played just 380 yards (a 1934 newspaper description of the hole listed it at 430). Even for Runyan, that meant he could reach the downhill hole with a driver and a six-iron, which had to come in with hook spin to counter the mounding and work toward the hole location. But the majority of the golf course posed a problem for Runyan and other short hitters. Even in its earliest days, the course favored length. Certain holes required a significant carry off the tee to find a flat spot in the fairway, and the farther from the tee you could carry the ball, the wider the landing areas. Runyan found that to be the case on thirteen of the fourteen driving holes. There were fairway bunkers that awaited errant shots around the 215-yard mark; if you could carry the ball 235 yards, they were no problem. But Runyan had no 235-yard carries in his arsenal. Not without a stiff breeze at his back.

There was significant pretournament buzz surrounding the 490-yard par-five fourth hole (now the iconic thirteenth), which Grantland Rice teased in a column just days before the start of play. Players had expressed "dark foreboding," Rice explained, about the hole "with its double guard of brook and ditch." Bobby Jones's practice companion Ed Dudley said, "I've never seen a hole where you can step into a 6 or a 7 so quickly." Runyan and Horton Smith finally got the better of Jones and Dudley in a friendly match that Tuesday, two days before the tournament began, both shooting one-under-par 71s, handily defeating the previously untouchable duo 6 and 5.

That was the golf course. Then there was the atmosphere, which Runyan described as being much like a clambake. In 1934 Bobby Jones and the club's organizers had little idea how impactful their golf course and the Masters Tournament would one day become. There was much anticipation but still a small start-up feel that first year, a bit like a long overdue family reunion. The club brought in countless gallons of corn whiskey, available to players and patrons alike as they passed through the clubhouse.

On the eve of play, a local hotel hosted a pretournament Calcutta. Why a hotel? "Because there wasn't room enough in the clubhouse then to cuss the cat without getting hair in your mouth," Runyan once explained with his typical southern colloquialisms. The room that night was crowded with sportswriters, players' friends, and bookies.

Fourteen members from Metropolis Country Club had come down to watch Runyan play, and he was worried that they'd bet too much money on him and add to the pressure. Whether he liked it or not, Runyan's stellar play over the previous year had made him the most attractive bet in the field—save Bobby Jones. This made him leery, and he pleaded with the Metropolis members to take it easy, so he didn't become better than a 6-to-1 bet to win. The bidding on Runyan stopped at $1,800, which seemed to satisfy him. As for Jones, he went for much more—that number has been debated for years by those aware of Augusta's first Calcutta, but Runyan remembered it as somewhere between $13,000 and $16,000—about three times the cost of the average American home in 1934.

When play got under way, Runyan, by virtue of being the leading money winner among the professionals, found himself paired with Jones for the first thirty-six holes. Hole-by-hole coverage of their play rivaled the twenty-first-century tracking of Tiger Woods's every move; it was a tribute to Jones's status as one of the country's most revered sportsmen, even in semiretirement. The *Atlanta Constitution*'s coverage of the event that week was akin to a presidential visit. The crowd at the golf course could feel it, too. By 3:00 p.m. the guards watching the front gate reported that they'd seen license plates from thirty of the forty-eight states and four from Canada come down the drive. Another observer reported seeing a car from Cuba with a Chilean tag on it.

Jones and Runyan began their round that Thursday morning at 10:35. Large crowds followed the twosome all day. Jones stirred the patrons with his second shot on the par-five fourth that rifled past the pin and settled just ten feet away, where he would two-putt for a birdie. But both players struggled with the cool breeze on the second nine. Runyan stumbled to an inward 39 and a score of 74, while Jones's short game abandoned him completely in his opening round 76.

Runyan steadied himself on day two with outward birdies at the fourth and reachable (even for Runyan) par-five sixth hole (now the fifteenth), en route to a 71. Jones's putter was no better that day, and he took thirty-eight putts while shooting 74. Poor putting in the company of Paul Runyan had to make Jones feel even worse about his effort on the greens. However, that failed to prevent a kind word about his playing companion. "Gosh, that Runyan can putt," Jones told the press while lamenting his own problems on the greens. "He didn't miss but one under 10 feet today."

Despite Jones's shaky putting, Runyan remained an admirer, calling Jones "one of the most superlative shotmakers the world has ever seen before or since," one whose only weakness was the putter. He had witnessed his fellow professionals, so resentful and unwilling to admit that Jones was better, shrink to nothing in his very presence. Runyan was determined to play *his* game—but you bet your sweet life he was paying close attention, hungry for any little tidbit he could learn by watching the country's most-famous golf-playing attorney up close.

Halfway through the first Masters, it was apparent to even the most loyal Bobby Jones supporters that his putting problem would be his undoing. Runyan sat just three shots back of halfway leader Horton Smith. And while they would not be paired together over the final two rounds, Runyan and Jones did what great players do, even when victory seems hard to fathom—they fought for every stroke like the future of golf depended on it. Jones battled his way to a pair of 72s over the weekend. That included playing the final fourteen holes of the championship in three under par, doing so on a bitterly cold, raw day in the company of a bumptious Walter Hagen and a gallery of 1,500 hearty patrons desperate for a Bobby charge and equally desperate for another spritz of corn whiskey to warm their insides. Those scores helped golf's emperor claw his way into thirteenth place. It was a respectable finish for a man who'd been retired for four years, expectations be damned.

By contrast, Runyan was right in the thick of the action for all four rounds. He shot a two-under-par 70 in the third round and began the final round steadily, until disaster struck at the fourth hole. His tee shot failed to carry the hazard left of the fairway by just inches, coming to rest in mud at the bottom of the ditch. He blasted it out to the fairway and then took aim at the green with a brassie from a tight lie. The shot came out low and failed to cover the hazard fronting the green. He took a penalty stroke, then pitched onto the green and two-putted for a double bogey seven. That all but ruined his chances, but he continued the tenacious fight, carding four birdies and ten pars over the final fourteen holes to shoot 71. His two-under-par total of 286 finished tied for third place with Ryder Cup teammate Billy Burke. Runyan's old boss Craig Wood finished runner-up, a stroke ahead. And the first Masters champion was Runyan's practice partner Horton Smith, who finished two shots ahead of Runyan.

Interestingly, Smith won the Masters playing with one of Runyan's drivers. Turns out, a week earlier Smith had visited Runyan's hotel room in Charleston and, while demonstrating a principle of the golf swing, had reached into Runyan's golf bag and pulled out a driver. Smith set it down and instantly liked the look of the club. It had a deeper face than his usual driver, but that meant he could tee the ball higher than normal. It seemed an odd match, considering that Runyan stood nearly six inches shorter than Smith, and yet they could share the same feelings about a golf club. But golf is an odd game, and its solutions often come from strange places—sometimes other players' golf bags.

"Take it," Runyan told his friend. Smith took the club and won the Masters.

There's no doubt that Runyan won some fan support that week. He had played alongside Bobby Jones in the eye of the storm for thirty-six holes, and he had come out in one piece on the other end. And while he failed to win, he was close enough that his laments truly carried some weight. A shot here, a shot there. If not for that damn double bogey on the fourth . . . what could have been?

Runyan also pulled some extra ink in the newspapers that week by virtue of his moonlighting as a sort of Masters correspondent for the United Press. He authored a daily column on his play and that of his fellow Masters contestants, although his sentences, which contained an awful lot of the usual jargon spewed out by the era's sportswriters, make you question if Runyan called on the ghostwriting services of a fedora-wearing, notebook-carrying member of the golf press to help him. No matter his methods, there were some insightful turns of phrase. He called his driver-borrowing, Masters-winning buddy Horton Smith a "genial chap." He compared the pressure of the final round to the feeling a pinch hitter gets in baseball: "Only those who have battled down the stretch of an important tournament can understand what a burden those final 18 holes can be. It's just three hours of ceaseless pinch-hitting." Of Bobby Jones's play before the final round he wrote, "He has been improving with the passing of each day, and maybe we pros are fortunate in having the tournament end tomorrow before Jones gets really warmed up."

A week later, Paul and Joan were in Virginia Beach, Virginia, for the Cavalier Open, and the form he had carried into the Masters returned. Prior to the start of play, Runyan noticed the rain-soaked greens were especially bumpy, so he gave himself a pep talk, deciding that he might have to simply accept an occasional three-putt. Don't panic, he told himself. Then Little Poison drowned the field like a giant wave shooting out of the Chesapeake Bay, firing rounds of 69-68-66-67 to win by eight shots over Harry Cooper. The Cavalier victory was Runyan's fourth win in five individual stroke play starts, and it capped off an unmatched winter season. Charles Houston, sports editor of the *Richmond Times-Dispatch*, wrote of the victor, "But this Runyan fellow is the story—a story of virtue unheard of rewarded richly. Runyan doesn't drink coffee for the fear of nerves, believes all golfers should have a lot of sleep and this and that. He lives by the book—and sticks close to par."

Make that under par.

AT THE U.S. Open that June at Merion Golf Club (then Merion Cricket Club) in Philadelphia, Runyan—"as cool as a slice of cucumber on ice," wrote Grantland Rice—was again among the betting favorites. Some pegged him as *the* favorite; prominent New York handicapper Jack Doyle gave Runyan 6-to-1 odds, behind only Gene Sarazen, who was a 5-to-1 favorite. Runyan arrived in Philadelphia a full week before the championship, and his confidence grew when he breezed around Merion with a three-under-par 67 on the Thursday before tournament week. When asked by sportswriters to speculate about a winning score, he told them the course was there for the taking, and the winning score could be quite low. For a man who rarely spoke out of turn, he might have been better off keeping his mouth shut. Runyan shot his 67 from a set of tees that were two hundred yards ahead of the tournament tees, and as the week went on Merion toughened up. With each successive practice round, Runyan found new obstacles in the layout. Chief among those hazards was the 445-yard eighteenth hole. The tee shot required a lengthy carry over a rock quarry just to reach the fairway. From a slightly forward tee position, Runyan could carry the quarry, where his ball would land on a downslope and scoot down the fairway, no problem. In the three practice rounds that followed his majestic 67, he failed to carry the quarry each time, due to the wind conditions or the placement of the tee markers. He knew this posed a problem, and so on Sunday before the tournament he left Merion to play an exhibition match with Bobby Cruickshank in Richmond. The *Philadelphia Inquirer* reported that the sudden departure was intended to give Runyan a change in scenery and take his mind off the maddening drive at the eighteenth.

The story of Runyan and Merion's eighteenth would take on a life of its own in golf lore. One legend suggested that Runyan, knowing full well he couldn't make the carry, took a wedge and pitched his ball onto the forward tee box—commonly referred to as the "ladies' tee"—then hit his second shot over the quarry. The strategy sounded like something Runyan might do, but he debunked the story years later.

"Never happened," he claimed. "Never even entered my head to do it. It's pure fabrication."

During his last practice round at Merion before the championship, Runyan stepped up to the eighteenth tee with a prevailing wind at his back and ripped a drive that cleared the quarry. Just to be sure it wasn't a fluke, he took out a second ball and cleared the quarry again.

Even as stories of Runyan's troubles with the closing hole circulated in the newspapers, he was still considered a tournament favorite among the golf writers. As for the boys in the locker room, it depended who you asked. One day after a practice round, Runyan was in the locker room playing bridge with Tommy Armour, Frank Walsh, and others. It had been a rough day on the course for Armour—who reportedly shot 87—and when Gene Sarazen came in and started complaining about Armour's slow play, the Silver Scot would have none of it.

"Ask Sarazen if he brought his eight-inch cups with him for this tournament," Armour wisecracked. You can almost hear the other players snickering, trying to hide their mirth behind highball glasses and club sandwiches.

A member of the press, who had somehow wormed his way into the locker room, asked Sarazen who he thought should be favored at Merion. Sarazen said he liked Denny Shute, and then he took a minute to list the reasons why. He also said Merion was harder than even Oakmont.

"What about Runyan?" someone asked.

"He will not win because he is the favorite," Sarazen said.

It was not the first time Sarazen had taken a poke at Runyan, and perhaps he intentionally spoke loud enough to be sure Runyan could hear him from his bridge table. He continued, "What has he ever done in an open tourney anyway? Finished 14th once, and that makes him the favorite. What's the matter? Have all you fellows gone cuckoo just because he connected in a few winter tournaments?"

Runyan kept on playing bridge. When asked for a response, he took the high road.

"Every man is entitled to express an opinion and be respected for it, if it is a sincere one," he said. "But you can quote me as saying that being a 'favorite' is not causing me one ounce of worry. Furthermore, I do not think I will buckle up at the end of the third round."

No matter Sarazen's reasons, he was right about Runyan that week. Little Poison struggled. The greens confounded him to the point that he decided to stroke his putts with cut spin so they would better hold their line. He shot rounds of 74-78-79-76, finishing fourteen strokes behind winner Olin Dutra. In the process, Runyan's worst fears had come true at the eighteenth hole. With the tee markers moved back, Runyan could barely carry the ball over the quarry. Instead of catching the downslope in the fairway, his ball was landing in knee-deep grass that required a pitch out, and he took fives and sixes on the hole all week.

If there was an antidote that would stifle Little Poison, it was long forced carries.

AT THE 1934 PGA Championship at Park Country Club in Buffalo, New York, Runyan was again a betting favorite. No matter his public comments about dealing with the pressure of expectations, his performance at Merion under the intense spotlight had failed to live up to the pretournament billing. If he had any self-doubt hidden underneath his steely exterior, he would have to conquer it to contend for the PGA title.

Nothing came easily at Buffalo. Well, nothing except his first-round match against Johnny Farrell, which Runyan won without breaking a sweat, 8 and 6. In the second round, he squeaked by Vic Ghezzi, 2 and 1. Then came Chicagoan Dick Metz. For a while it seemed that Metz would out-Runyan Little Poison himself, thanks to a series of spectacular recovery shots. Both players shot 71s in the morning round, and Runyan started the afternoon with an eighty-foot run-up shot on the first hole that he nudged to within two inches. Then he made a twenty-footer a hole later to take the lead. Metz eagled the day's twenty-seventh hole, but Runyan regained the momentum with a twenty-five-foot birdie putt on the next hole to gain a three-up lead. Metz refused to go quietly, pulling even on the thirty-fourth hole. Finally, on the thirty-fifth, Runyan stuffed his approach with a seven-iron to eight inches, guaranteeing a birdie and a one-up advantage on the final hole, which they halved, giving Runyan the victory. A day later Runyan took down Gene Kunes 4 and 2, setting up a date in the finals with his old boss Craig Wood.

Back in White Plains, Runyan's friends and the members of Metropolis Country Club followed his results closely in the newspapers. After he beat Kunes to advance to the finals, the Metropolis "Big Three" of Ed Waterman, Gerald Rosenberger, and Jesse Jelenko wrote to Runyan and promised they'd be in Buffalo the following day to help him "bring home the bacon."

On paper, the match clearly favored the master, not the apprentice. Wood, standing 6 feet tall and weighing 225 pounds, was a long hitter, much longer than Runyan. And he was hungry to capture a major championship, having been tantalizingly close at the prior year's Open Championship at St. Andrews (which he lost in a playoff) and at the Masters a few months earlier (where he finished runner-up to Horton Smith).

Runyan started the morning round fast with a birdie at the opening hole, but that was the last time he would taste the lead until the day's twenty-third hole. On the seventh hole, Runyan's tee shot sailed wide right into a patch of matted-down rough. As he addressed his second shot with a seven-iron, the golf ball rolled back against his club.

"Mr. Referee," Runyan shouted for the rules official. "Here's one on me. I accidentally moved my ball taking my stance."

The rules official never saw the ball move, but Runyan was adamant about the infraction and was assessed a penalty stroke, causing him to drop the hole to Wood. The players arrived on the eighteenth tee of the morning round all square. Runyan lunged into his tee shot and it hooked wildly offline, striking a state trooper standing adjacent to a clump of trees. From there, he tried a desperation shot with a fairway wood, and the ball landed in a creek near the green. After a penalty and a pitch, he made a half-hearted attempt at a long putt before conceding the hole to Wood, who finished the morning round one up. As expected, Wood was out-driving Runyan on every hole. But he had also out-putted Little Poison, and that had much to do with his advantage.

The action stayed nip and tuck in the afternoon round, and the gallery grew in size to some four thousand people. Sportswriter Jimmy Powers likened the combatants to a pair of dogs: Wood a husky St. Bernard and Runyan a snapping, cocky fox terrier nipping at Wood's heels.

Runyan finally regained the lead on the fifth hole of the afternoon round when Wood hooked a drive that struck a spectator. On the seventeenth, the large gallery horseshoed around the green to watch Wood play a lob shot to within eighteen inches. Runyan needed to hole his chip shot from forty-five feet to halve the hole—which he nearly did—but when it failed to drop, the match was again all square.

Much of the gallery sprinted toward the eighteenth fairway, lining it on both sides to catch a glimpse of the tee shots. The breeze was in the players' faces, and Wood socked a 260-yard drive down the fairway. Runyan, thirty yards behind off the tee, hit a fairway wood for his second that landed ten feet in front of the pin and raced through the back of the green. Then Wood made a critical error, hooking his approach under a weeping willow tree adjacent to some rosebushes near the men's locker room, twenty yards offline. Because his ball was beneath a scoreboard, he received a free drop. He surveyed the lie and his options for a full ten minutes before finally playing a marvelous pitch-and-run shot that finished ten feet from the hole.

Then it was Runyan's turn. He hit an uncharacteristically mediocre chip shot that finished a hair outside Wood's ball. The players were unsure who should play first, so PGA president George Jacobus was called in to measure each ball's distance from the hole. He determined that Runyan would play first.

"Tomb-like silence settled over the excited spectators as they draped themselves on the terrace in front of the clubhouse," read an Associated Press recap of the match. "Runyan carefully examined every blade of grass in the path to the hole."

Runyan stroked his putt. It hit the back of the hole and dropped in. The crowd cheered wildly, and the moment shifted back to Wood. He nervously bit off the end of the cigarette he'd been smoking, then studied his putt for more than a minute while the drama continued to build. Then he stepped in and holed it to send the match to extra holes.

All week long, Runyan had felt that everything at Park Country Club was conspiring against him. Perhaps that was a subconscious trick his mind was playing to narrow his focus, harden his will. But as the playoff got under way, the conspiring—real or imagined—felt too much to overcome. That's how he felt when he learned that sudden-death play would commence on a 535-yard par five. Wood drove his ball a full sixty yards past Runyan and flushed a six-iron to seven feet. Runyan had to take a brassie to reach the green in two shots. His ball struck the rear tire of a movie truck that was driving into position to film the action, and his ball settled into the greenside rough. Runyan felt the selection of playoff hole was ridiculous. "It was a 535-yard hole, and the peanut hitter is playing against one of the two or three biggest hitters in the game," he later said. "Where's there any equity in an extra hole playoff in that?"

Still, Runyan had a chance. He chipped to four feet, then caught a break when Wood missed his eagle putt. Runyan stepped in and holed his four-footer to continue the match. The players, exhausted, and the entertained gallery of thousands marched on.

In high-pressure situations like this, Runyan had taught himself a trick to help cope. He told himself over and over that whatever pressure he was feeling, the other guy—Wood, in this case—was feeling just as much, maybe more. It was a strategy he used throughout his career to help him focus on the situation, not his nerves.

On the thirty-eighth hole, Wood drove first and hit another hook that found the rough beneath yet another willow tree. Runyan hit a straight drive but still had 240 yards to the green. He grabbed his trusty brassie and lashed at the ball with everything he had. The ball landed atop a greenside bunker, then rolled back into the sand. Wood went for the green with a two-iron, his shot flying offline, right of the green, about sixty feet from the hole. He chipped, leaving himself a good twelve feet. Runyan stepped into the bunker and blasted out to eight feet. Wood's putt missed the hole by just inches, and he was in for a five.

Now Runyan faced an eight-footer to win the PGA Championship. He crouched over his ball and settled into his putting stance, with his elbows, covered by his long-sleeve shirt, bent in their customary manner. How fitting a scenario: the short-hitting Runyan, having dodged a landmine on the previous par five and then striping a near-perfect drive, had still faced 240 yards to get home. When his fairway wood found the sand, Runyan was back in his element. The boy from Arkansas, who had learned the game on sand greens, now needed to get up and down from a greenside bunker to capture a major championship. All those hours—the thousands upon thousands of chip shots, bunker shots, pitches, putts, and recovery scenarios—would now get tested on the grandest stage. The man known as Little Poison, having executed a better-than-average bunker shot, could end this thing with a putt.

Modern-day golf statistics reveal that a professional golfer putting from eight feet is a 50/50 proposition. On average, it takes one and a half strokes to hole out from that distance, meaning Runyan's putt was no sure thing—a coin toss, if you will.

Runyan buried the eight-footer. It carried just enough speed to topple over the front lip. In doing so, he buried whatever questions he had about his ability to perform under the most extreme pressure. He buried the demons—real or imagined—that he felt were working against him that week in Buffalo. He buried Gene Sarazen's six-week-old comments about his ability to handle the spotlight. He buried the sportswriters' nonsensical babble about his homespun technique. He buried all of it.

"Everything was against me in that tournament," he recounted decades later. "Everything. And still I won."

Paul Runyan was the PGA champion.

His friend and competitor Craig Wood, who had a front-row seat to Runyan's triumph, may well have been the person most impressed by Runyan's victory in Buffalo—or, as the most recent victim of Runyan's brand of golf voodoo, the most mystified.

"I don't know how he does it," Wood said. "I cannot completely understand how."

6

A Code of His Own

A week after the 1934 PGA Championship, Olin Dutra showed up at Metropolis Country Club to steal Paul Runyan away from the lesson tee for a friendly match between the two most recent major champions crowned on American soil. Runyan shot 69, Dutra 74, and Runyan closed him out 3 and 2. Both players looked underfed, Dutra still recovering from some mystery ailment that dated back to the U.S. Open at Merion (he was down to 185 pounds instead of his usual 200), and Runyan having dropped 5 pounds from the stress of competition at Buffalo, a grueling two-hundred-hole golf marathon over the course of a week. After golf, they shared a few laughs while discussing Tommy Armour's recent victory at the Canadian Open, a tournament he only entered because he had missed a train that was supposed to take him elsewhere. And they recounted Craig Wood's recent win at the New Jersey Open. Then they packed up and headed out for the next event, to be held in nearby Rochester, New York.

In early September, a full month after Runyan's win at Buffalo, he made news (barely—this was a small item in the Courier News *of Blytheville, Arkansas) when it was reported that his parents, Walter and Mamie, were the new occupants of a five-acre Arkansas farm. The purchaser? Their son Paul. Golf may have taken the Runyans' son away from the farm, and it may have literally taken the farm away from the family, when Walter's struggling operation was cast aside in favor of the expansion of the Hot Springs Golf and Country Club years earlier, but Paul hadn't forgotten the years of toil from his youth on the farm, when his parents scraped together a start for him and his brother. Now, in a small way, he could pay it back.*

But it was not that small of a way. After all, five acres was five acres. And it was *the Depression. More than one million American families lost their farms in the first half of the 1930s. Now the Runyans were getting one back.*

There was plenty of room, Paul told a reporter, for a cow, some chickens, and a truck garden.

THERE ONCE EXISTED the whiff of a notion that Paul Runyan was like a carnival sideshow, a popcorn-hitting lightweight who, once near the green, would start holing shots from just about anywhere, like a hot player at a craps table, catching an improbable run of good fortune with the dice. Picture Runyan, sinking long putts, getting up and down from everywhere, carving fairway woods from junky lies to chipping distance and holing out for improbable birdies like a human highlight reel. Any reasonable person watching such a display would have to assume that it would all end at some point. Come crashing down. The clock would strike midnight. Cinderella's luck would run out.

After the 1934 PGA Championship, there was still a general amazement that this dapper-dressing, short-hitting, 130-pound wizard could compete with pro golf's best players, but almost overnight he became viewed in the same class as those big-hitting name-brand pros like Sarazen, Hagen, and Armour, and even Craig Wood. That's what a major championship can do for a player's standing. Another way of saying it: after the PGA win, nobody was laughing anymore. That was the take offered by Jimmy Powers in the *New York Daily News* the day after Runyan's victory at Buffalo.

Other golf influencers soon followed Powers's lead—the Grantland Rices, the Tommy Armours, and, perhaps begrudgingly, the Ralph Trosts. It was Armour who articulated that Runyan's victory would make him a popular champion among golf galleries. "He is the type that attracts the average duffer, and I mean no offense," Armour told a reporter. "People will say to themselves, 'That Runyan kid is built along my lines. If he can get the scores and win the money from those big monkeys, maybe I can do a thing or two at my club.'"

Armour even suggested that there would be a rush to copy Runyan's grip, his clubs, and his technique. A stretch? Maybe. But then again, Runyan had a marketable platform, thanks to his deal with Spalding. Powers reported that Runyan's PGA victory earned him a $1,000 check from the company, presumably as a bonus. Runyan also received an offer to tour Australia and make a few extra bucks through a schedule of prebooked matches—an offer he refused, at first anyway, less than forty-eight hours after his victory over Wood.

Runyan suddenly found himself having to answer questions from the golf press on a whole new range of topics, like his ethnic background. "I will settle it once and for all," he told Jimmy Powers, like a political candidate looking to quash a brewing scandal. "I work for a Jewish club at Metropolis, but I am Scotch-Irish." Yet he had a knack for earning good press. Was that due to his own media savvy? Or a friendly group of sportswriters who couldn't help but like him? Both, perhaps. He gladly cooperated with stories about his work ethic and his busy schedule, telling Powers that a slate of lessons from 8:00 a.m. until dark awaited him back at Metropolis. "The training I received on my father's dairy farm helps me a lot. I'm probably the only pro in America who goes to bed at 10 PM every night, and I'm up at daylight."

At a time when millions of Americans were homeless, migrating across the country looking for opportunities, many of them overcome by fear and despair, feeling let down by government, by their leadership, by their supposed heroes, Paul Runyan provided hope for a new kind of sporting hero. Sure, he played an aristocratic sport, but he played it a different way. He was no blue blood. He played golf like the undersized fighter he was, willing to scratch and claw against bigger, supposedly better competitors. He could take a punch, and he knew how to throw one in return. On the golf course he backed down from nothing, and his victories, which always seemed shaped by his triumph over supposed shortcomings, seemed incomprehensible.

Other than Horton Smith, it's likely that no other golf professional knew Runyan as well as his old boss Craig Wood. With Wood having been the most recent victim of Runyan's sorcery, Ralph Trost tracked him down to better understand how the little man made it all happen. "Getting down in two from the far off places in the Runyan manner is so inconsistent with the common method of playing the game that even though one sees such accomplishments as his in one tournament after another it continues to smack of the occult rather than true skill," Trost wrote.

Wood, to Trost: "It is true that from several points of view Paul Runyan violates golf's unwritten laws. But it seems to me that after the thousandth violation the man must be admitted to have a code of his own."

Wood marveled to Trost at the shots Runyan attempted, as well as the precision needed to pull them off. For instance, he could barely fathom the pitch shots that Runyan played out of the rough in Buffalo, landing them short, bouncing them onto the green, and judging the line and distance perfectly.

"Luck?" Trost asked.

"If it happened just once, it would be," Wood conceded. "After playing against Paul Runyan one shakes that word 'luck' out of his vocabulary. The danged thing doesn't seem to fit. The experience gives a man a new slant. One learns to pay closer attention to the business at hand.

"He has the utmost faith in himself, complete control of his nerves, the stamina to keep on plugging, the mental nerve to withstand reverses."

THE SPOILS OF victory continued for Runyan that fall. On Saturday, September 29, two months after his victory over Craig Wood, the Metropolitan Section of the PGA hosted a testimonial dinner for Runyan at the Hotel Commodore in New York. The event was first class; the PGA rented the entire grand ballroom to wine and dine three thousand guests. The dinner included live entertainment and dancing. The three-hundred-person committee that sponsored the event included A. W. Tillinghast, Grantland Rice, Condé Nast, and Henry O. Havemeyer.

In October Runyan signed a contract to serve on the professional staff of the Miami Biltmore Country Club. For Colonel Henry Doherty, the president of the Florida Year-Round clubs, inviting prominent golfers into the club's stable of teaching professionals was part of a larger marketing plan to link sports celebrities with the Biltmore, thus enticing ordinary Joes and Janes to stay in the hotel while visiting Miami. Runyan was hardly the first pro golfer to represent the Biltmore; previously the hotel had courted Gene Sarazen and Walter Hagen, among others. The folks in Miami took good care of their players and spouses, offering them appearance money, perks such as bottles of scotch and tins of cigarettes, and entertainment—not that it was necessary. "If at any time the sponsors grew lax at providing entertainment, the players took over. Such as the evening that Walter Hagen came back from a fishing trip and dumped his entire catch, including an alligator, into the clubhouse," wrote Dan Jenkins in 1966.

The announcement of Runyan's deal with the Biltmore came on the same day, October 9, 1934, that he left New York for Louisville, Kentucky, to begin a stretch of golf that would keep him away from home for the rest of the calendar year. The Louisville Open would serve as a jumping-off point for Los Angeles, from where Runyan would travel—along with a group of American players, including Craig Wood, Harry Cooper, Denny Shute, Leo Diegel, and Ky Laffoon—to Australia to play in a series of tournaments down under, centering on the Melbourne Centennial Exposition. It seems Runyan simply changed his mind after first taking a pass on Australia in the immediate aftermath of the PGA. Maybe the money had some influence on his about-face. The tour was a shared arrangement, meaning the $30,000 of prize money would be split among the six players, $5,000 apiece. The newspapers referred to the group as the PGA Australian team or the Lakes Cup team, and Runyan was voted captain. The players' wives were invited to attend, and the PGA even purchased the steamship tickets, which cost $1,432 per couple.

Runyan's play in Louisville was mediocre. He pocketed $50 after finishing eleven strokes behind winner Horton Smith. Craig Wood finished second, two strokes behind Smith. Then it was off to Los Angeles, where they'd leave on the SS *Mariposa*, a three-year-old luxury ocean liner which could hold seven hundred passengers and crew members.

If the team's October 17, 1934, departure from Los Angeles lacked for anything, it was not drama, nor was it rain, which fell persistently. The golfers and their wives (only Ky Laffoon traveled sans spouse) arrived on board the *Mariposa* in two waves. The Runyans were in the first wave, during which a frantic search ensued after Leo Diegel lost his passport. Diegel dumped the contents of his suitcase all over the wharf, searching desperately for the missing document. Joan Runyan calmed the uproar when she located the passport in Diegel's hip pocket. Craig Wood and Ky Laffoon were in the second wave. Despite the *Mariposa*'s endless food offerings, the pair craved one last meal on land before sailing, so they went into Hollywood for dinner, causing the others in the traveling party to become sick with worry as the minutes ticked away. Wood and Laffoon (who also was reported to have lost his passport) arrived just in time to board the ship before the scheduled 10:00 p.m. departure, stepping aboard and blurting out to the stewards, "We're the other two."

Team captain Runyan purchased sea sickness medication for each player, which he handed out as the *Mariposa* got under way. The drama didn't end at the wharf. A Ryder Cuppian cloud hovered over the whole affair, and it centered on—guess who—Gene Sarazen, who was already in Australia when the PGA team set sail. Sarazen had initially been asked by the PGA to be part of the team but declined because he didn't want to split the purse. So what did he do? He went to Australia anyway, weeks ahead of the group of six, who, frustrated by Sarazen's tactics, kept an eye on his movements from the United States. They vowed to refuse to play anywhere in Australia that Sarazen and his running mate—Australian Joe Kirkwood, a regular player in America—got to first. Not wanting to upset the six American professionals and especially not wanting to upstage their own lavish preparations, Australia's Victorian Golf Union refused to grant Sarazen and Kirkwood permission to play an exhibition tour prior to the Melbourne Centennial Exposition event in November.

There was no shortage of exciting distractions at sea. For example, among the passengers with whom Runyan and the other golf stars rubbed shoulders was American actor Spencer Tracy, who was traveling with his older brother, Carroll.

The Americans had been at sea three weeks when they arrived in Sydney on Monday, November 5. However, there had been stops along the way—Honolulu, Suva, Pago Pago, and Auckland—where the players could leave the *Mariposa* with their golf clubs and practice.

In Sydney, the players and their wives were welcomed with a luncheon at the Lakes Club. Afterward the men played a practice round while the players' wives visited a nearby koala farm. The next day, the players took a bumpy flight to Brisbane for a match, then returned to Sydney and the Lakes Club. Meanwhile, the Victorian Golf Union loosened its position on the Sarazen matter and made arrangements for him and Kirkwood to play three weekend exhibition matches at other sites, away from the six-player main attraction.

The American team and their pleasant leader Runyan made a positive impression on the Australian golf fans and media. They were popular with galleries, quick to offer tips, and full of energy to play countless rounds and exhibitions. One member of the Australian press wrote, "Paul Runyan's golfing career is one of the romances of the depression." Another journalist wrote that any man who could find a way to make a comfortable living in such trying times deserved some respect.

"I'm just a plugger," Runyan explained to the Aussies. "My theory is that 90 percent of all luck is a question of good or bad judgment. I always try to create my good luck by good judgment. If my judgment is poor—well, I'm unlucky."

The depth of golf talent in Australia in the mid-1930s was not yet equal to that of the United States. The American players speculated that the average club champion from an American country club would qualify as one of Australia's better amateur players. Still, enthusiasm for the game was high, and the Americans were treated well. The Australian press got a kick out of Runyan's bag of clubs, which included six woods. And they raved about his course-record 67 at the Peninsula Country Club just outside Melbourne in early December.

The golfers left Sydney on December 15 aboard the SS *Monterey*. Their traveling party included one additional member, a speedy Australian racing dog that Craig Wood had purchased while abroad. The group would spend Christmas at sea before arriving at the port of Honolulu on December 27. From there, the SS *Lurline* took them to California, where they landed in San Francisco in the early morning hours of January 4—so early, in fact, that there was no porter around to help with their substantial amount of luggage. So Runyan, Laffoon, Diegel, and Jimmy Thompson, all wearing suits and ties and overcoats, loaded their trunks and bags and golf clubs onto a makeshift luggage cart themselves. There was little time to waste. They had to quickly work out their sea legs and start prepping for the Los Angeles Open, which was set to begin in a few days at the Los Angeles Country Club.

Golf was not foremost on Craig Wood's mind; he was anxious to learn where there was dog racing.

WHEN PAUL RUNYAN stepped off the boat from Australia in early 1935, he did so as arguably the most consistent professional golfer in the world over the previous eighteen months. Would that superb run of shotmaking suddenly go cold? Hardly. He would capture five titles over a two-year period (1935 and 1936), and he would finish 1935 with the lowest scoring average in professional golf (72.3), earning him the Radix Cup award. Runyan's margin was razor thin; he finished one-tenth of a stroke ahead of second-place Henry Picard and two-tenths ahead of Horton Smith.

The highlight of Runyan's five victories was his second win at the North and South Open at Pinehurst, in March 1935. But this victory was different than his 1930 triumph, when he had come out of nowhere, a virtual unknown, to put his stamp on a top-flight golf tournament.

Runyan found Pinehurst to be a course on the cusp of transition when he arrived in 1935, thanks to brooding architect Donald Ross, who, reportedly upset at being passed over by Bobby Jones to design Augusta National (Jones had tabbed Alister MacKenzie instead), was ready to turn his crew loose on numerous course upgrades that would transform Pinehurst and bring it back into the national spotlight. Some of the work had already begun. In 1933 Ross's crew laid five miles of irrigation pipe down the fairways to water the new winter rye grass. The following year, Ross got his hands on a strain of Bermuda capable of survival as a putting surface, and he built three experimental greens to test it. In the summer of 1935, months after the North and South had finished, Ross would complete the changeover from sand greens to grass on the entire No. 2 course. Along with reworking the bunkering and building two new holes in the middle of the golf course (the fourth and fifth in the revised routing), the course changes (specifically, the conversion to grass greens) would be enough to convince the PGA of America to award Pinehurst the 1936 PGA Championship.

But when the pros rolled into town in March 1935, the greens were still sand, and that would be a significant advantage for the young pro who'd learned to putt on sand greens in Hot Springs, Arkansas.

Runyan grabbed the tournament lead like a bloodhound, shooting an opening-round six-under-par 65 on a rainy day when just two other players, Felix Serafin and Ray Mangrum, broke 70. The wet conditions meant that Runyan had to hit fairway woods into some of the longer par fours, but the challenging weather failed to deter him in the bogey-free masterpiece. How impressive was that 65? After the round, Runyan dubbed it "the greatest single round of shotmaking I have ever played in my life." He followed it with rounds of 71-72-68 to win the tournament by eight shots. His was the lowest cumulative score in the thirty-three-year-history of the North and South Open.

It's worth noting that his winner's check of $1,000 was $500 less than his check at the same event in 1930—owing to the severity of the ongoing Great Depression.

Runyan's other victories in 1935 came at the Westchester Open in August (where he won by four strokes) and the Grand Slam Open in Louisville, Kentucky, in October (where he won by two). He would repeat at Westchester in 1936 and capture the Metropolitan PGA title.

A week before Runyan's 1935 Westchester victory, he played an exhibition match at Salisbury Country Club alongside Frank Strafaci, the recently crowned U.S. Public Links champion (and future grandfather of 2020 U.S. Amateur champion Tyler Strafaci). Their opponents that day were Tommy Goodwin, a handsome 6-foot-3-inch, card-playing, baritone-singing, shark-fishing amateur golfer who was in the midst of a run of four New York State Amateur victories, and legendary slugger Babe Ruth, who had just retired from baseball. Goodwin, known for his trademark V-neck T-shirts (and in later years, mesh tops, resembling football practice jerseys), and the Babe towered over Runyan and Strafaci, and they made a match of it. However, that was mostly Goodwin's doing. The Babe was a competent golfer but a little bit outclassed by his playing companions on this day (he shot 87), and Runyan and Strafaci closed out Goodwin and Ruth 2 and 1.

Runyan remembered the Babe from his spring training stops in Hot Springs back in the 1920s. Any young man of that era would never forget Babe Ruth. As a young apprentice, Runyan had rubbed shoulders in Hot Springs with superstar athletes such as Walter Johnson, Jack Dempsey, and Gene Tunney. Was there any chance the Babe remembered Runyan, who would have been a pint-sized caddie or an apprentice trying to grow a mustache back then? Who knows.

RUNYAN WAS BACK in Miami in December 1936 for the Biltmore Open. He failed to factor into the tournament, which was won by Ralph Guldahl, but he hung around the Biltmore after the event concluded, as part of his deal to serve on the club's professional staff. You never know who you might meet at a prominent golf club in a touristy spot like Miami, and the following week Runyan made the acquaintance of a group of friendly political heavyweights, including Stephen Early, press secretary to President Roosevelt. Others in the group were Mississippi senator B. P. "Pat" Harrison; former Ohio governor James Cox; George Allen, commissioner of the District of Columbia; newspaper publisher Dan Mahoney; radio executive Harry Butcher; and economist Merle Thorpe. These men got to know Runyan and liked him. They also had a plan to hatch, and they needed their new golf pro to pull it off.

The Early group, which regularly played golf in Washington with John J. Pelley, president of the American Association of Railroads, was frustrated by continually losing money to Pelley, a supposed eight handicap who regularly shot in the low 80s. They asked Runyan if Pelley would know Runyan by sight, and when he said no, they got him to agree to help them get even.

A chance meeting was orchestrated in the Biltmore locker room; the group clearly worked hard to establish a believable backstory. Runyan was introduced to Pelley as "Mr. Paul," a youngish-looking businessman vacationing from Muncie, Indiana, who liked to play golf and carried an eight handicap. The group shared a few beers and lunch (it's doubtful that Runyan had anything to drink, unless he really went for an Academy Award), then arranged an afternoon match with the usual side bets. They invited their new friend "Mr. Paul" to join them.

"Sure. Why not?" he said.

Pelley pulled Mr. Paul aside before the match and suggested, "Well, since we're both eight handicaps, how about a few side wagers?"

"All right," said the faux businessman from Muncie. "Although I'm not sure how well I'll play on a strange course."

Pelley figured his ship had come in.

A small crowd gathered around the first tee as the group began its round. Runyan put his tee in the ground and played first. Mr. Paul's motion was a bit awkward but nothing all that unusual for an 80s shooter. He hit a wild hook into the left rough, the sort of out-of-control shot you might expect from a nervous vacationer playing in front of new friends, and as the ball settled into an unfortunate spot, Pelley turned to a friend and winked.

"Kid, if you teed your ball a little lower, you wouldn't be so wild," Pelley suggested.

Mr. Paul battled his way to a 40 on the front nine, good enough for a one-up lead over Pelley. The match was close, and nothing about Mr. Paul's 40 came easy. He missed most of the fairways but scraped together some impressive recovery shots, including a pair of deliberate hooks from trouble that landed gently on the green. After seeing the second such miraculous escape, Pelley muttered something about Mr. Paul's handicap. Whatever suspicions Pelley may have had about his opponent, he clearly failed to recognize him as one of professional golf's top players.

"Those were lucky shots," assured Mr. Paul's caddie, who was in on the gag. "He'll blow up anytime now. Just you wait."

At the turn, Runyan said to Pelley, "I've been playing over my head, and I feel badly about it. To make things square, you take a stroke here and we'll play double or nothing."

"No, that wouldn't be fair to you," Pelley said. "You've been playing nicely, and you've won." Pelley said there was still a back nine to play, and he had his mind set on a comeback.

On the next hole, Runyan cranked a drive that ran out 250 yards down the middle of the fairway and then flushed a three-iron right toward the pin, from where he two-putted for a four. Pelley became even more suspicious but played on. This routine went on for the rest of the round, and you know how it ended—with Pelley owing, big. Mr. Paul birdied the twelfth, thirteenth, and fourteenth holes. He would be returning to Muncie with enough cash to buy Main Street. Pelley's friends had to love it.

In the locker room after the round, the group sat around a table full of food and drinks. A waiter approached the table to page Runyan. "Mr. Paul Runyan, Mr. Paul Runyan. Mr. Paul Runyan, you are wanted on the telephone."

Runyan turned to the railroad executive. "Excuse me, Mr. Pelley," he said. "They want me on the phone."

Runyan left the table in a hurry. Pelley, upon learning that he had been hustled, was surely furious. And his Washington companions sharing the table? The sound of their laughter carried throughout the grounds of the Miami Biltmore. Just to show there were no hard feelings, they returned all the cash they had won from Pelley.

Could this con have been carried out by another professional golfer of Runyan's pedigree? Maybe, but it's doubtful. It's hard to imagine tall and handsome Horton Smith going undetected by a mark. He was too graceful. Same for cocksure Gene Sarazen. Or even Walter Hagen, who would have insisted on upping the stakes every hole, assuming he even made it to the first tee on time. Never mind Bobby Jones. He was far too famous. But Runyan, with his skinny frame, ever-present sway, and lash at the ball? He was just what central casting sent down when you asked for an eight handicapper. Perfect for the part.

THE FOLLOWING SPRING Runyan was in Fox Chapel, Pennsylvania, for the 1937 PGA Championship, played at the Pittsburgh Field Club. On the eve of match play he received a Western Union telegram from his Biltmore pals Early and Butcher.

"Best wishes for continued success in the big tournament," they wrote. "Pelley would advise, 'My boy, don't tee your ball too high.' May the Muncie boy make good."

PART 3

On the Delaware

7

A Talent Nonpareil

"He was a great athlete, and he had a great eye. Sam knew a lot about the golf swing. Hogan was the practicer, and I think Hogan said that if he could have caddied for Snead he would have won all these tournaments. Sam said, 'How could I not know what the hell I'm doing? I've hit a million golf balls.' And that's true, he practiced a lot.

"He really knew the game well. I think he liked, to some extent, to play up the fact that he was a hillbilly who didn't know what he was doing. In reality, he would chafe at that. If people said that he was a natural who didn't know anything about the swing, he'd say, 'I know a hell of a lot about the swing.' And he did. He was a smart athlete and a very smart golfer.

"Bob Toski had some great stories about Sam. Toski was playing with Sam. Now, Toski's a little guy, and Sam was a very long hitter. Toski was trying to keep up with him, and his feet were off the ground. He was jumping, he was swinging so hard. And Sam said, 'Bobby, you've got to keep your feet on the ground.' And Toski said, 'I can't. I'm trying to keep up with you.'

"Sam said, 'Well, put some fucking rocks in your pocket.'

"Smart guy. A lot smarter than people think."

—Al Barkow, in a telephone conversation with the author

SAM SNEAD'S ARRIVAL on the big-time professional golf scene ranks high up on the list of the all-time great launches in the history of the sport—maybe the greatest ever. Snead was aided by two clubs, a driver and a putter, that he acquired on the eve of the 1937 Los Angeles Open.

Seems he was on the range after qualifying for the LA Open that January when fellow professional Henry Picard—who later suggested to a struggling Ben Hogan a subtle weakening of his grip that helped lessen Hogan's sometimes wild hook—offered him the chance to take a few cuts with his George Izett driver, which was heavier than Snead's driver and had a much stiffer shaft.

Snead liked it immediately. "God, this is good," he said, holding the club as he gazed down at its head.

Picard told him to hang onto it. Snead later called the driver "the single greatest discovery I ever made in golf." He kept the club in his golf bag for the next two decades. When the clubhead began developing small cracks, Snead patched the cracks with wood filler.

Not long after putting Picard's driver in his bag, Snead was on the putting green with Leo Walper, who proposed a putting contest. Snead didn't have his own putter, so he borrowed one from Walper's bag and made three in a row. That ended the contest but not Snead's affection for the Calamity Jane–inspired wand. Walper offered it to him for $3.50, and Snead happily took the deal. Then he went out and shot rounds of 71-71-72-69 and finished sixth in the tournament, winning $400. It was a brilliant end to a brilliant week that began when Snead turned up on the first tee for a practice round alongside Dutch Harrison and Bob Hamilton, who were in the process of hustling a few dollars out of a couple of club golfers who were easy marks. Neither pro recognized Snead (or had even heard of him), and when he asked to join the group they agreed. Snead started with a pair of birdies that got their attention and continued winning holes throughout the round. Whenever Harrison or Hamilton would hit an approach shot close, Snead would hit it closer. The hustlers were being hustled, even if the young man doing the hustling had no clue he was doing it.

When the round ended, Snead asked, "What time tomorrow?"

"Son, you work your side of the road and we'll work ours," Harrison said.

After his high finish in Los Angeles, there would be no mistaking Sam Snead.

A week later, Snead won the $5,000 Oakland Open at Claremont Country Club with scores of 69-65-69-67, finishing two shots ahead of Ralph Guldahl. The payout was $1,200. "You're going to end up having your picture in the *New York Times*," someone said to him.

"How?" Snead wondered. He'd never even been to New York.

Did Snead not know how press photos circulated in newspapers across the country? Or was he playing dumb, toying with people, cultivating the Virginia hillbilly legend? It was the latter, he later explained to Al Barkow, telling him, "I wasn't quite that naïve." The story and others like it helped Snead's legend grow. A week after Oakland, Snead avoided the distractions of Hollywood celebrities and won the weather-shortened Bing Crosby Pro-Am at Rancho Santa Fe Country Club, taking home $500.

Around the time Snead emerged as a force in professional golf, PGA of America president George Jacobus tabbed promoter Fred Corcoran to manage the week-to-week activities of the professional golf circuit. Jacobus and Corcoran realized that Snead, with his prodigious drives and syrupy swing and athletic physique, presented a unique opportunity to promote professional golf, and Corcoran proposed to work on Snead's behalf to set up exhibitions and other money-making side hustles. Corcoran struck a handshake deal with Snead to serve as his manager, an arrangement that made other pro golfers upset. Jealous, at least. It was a conflict of interest, they cried. But what could they do? In just a handful of events, Snead had proved that he could quickly become *the* most popular draw in professional golf. The Snead deal was noteworthy for Corcoran because it effectively made him the first sports agent—although his name often gets lost in history, thanks mostly to the titanic impact of Cleveland-based lawyer Mark McCormack, who founded International Management Group (IMG) in the 1960s and inked deals to represent Arnold Palmer, Jack Nicklaus (for a time), and Gary Player.

Legendary sportswriter Grantland Rice had been on hand to watch Snead shoot 68 at the Crosby Pro-Am and came away a believer. That February, Rice penned a column announcing Snead as golf's next big thing, a budding star. Rice quoted sports editor Duke Ridgley, who described Snead as a "big, lanky and loose-limbed" Virginia boy who was "shy as a mouse." Rice's column was picked up by newspapers across the country, and pretty soon Snead teetered on becoming a star. John J. Romano, in the *Miami Herald*, described Snead as "one of those self-made golfers one reads a lot about in fiction but seldom appears on a golf course matching his long drives and steady putting against the cream of the professional crop."

Snead's hot play on the West Coast was a harbinger of his 1937 season. In early August, he captured the St. Paul Open, despite some shaky putting over the final few holes. In December he won the Nassau Open and the Miami Open. He was untouchable in Miami, shooting 68-67-66-66 and winning by five shots. Wilson Sporting Goods, one of Snead's sponsors, used the opportunity to place an ad in the *Miami Herald*, directly opposite a recap of the Miami Open, touting the company's clubs and its HOL-HI K-28 golf ball, which utilized what the manufacturer called "fly-wheel action" to increase a player's control.

When Snead came in with his final-round 66 in Miami, he drew some oohs and aahs from spectators, media members, and golf professionals lingering around the scoreboard. "Greatest player since Jones or Hagen," someone remarked. Another person asked, "Wonder how they will ever beat him?" And still, much of his potential seemed to remain untapped, that is, many spectators were convinced that Snead was failing to get the lowest possible scores out of his rounds. Many lamented missed short putts and unnecessary penalty shots. It didn't matter. Snead won anyway.

For the season, Snead won five times, finished second three times (including once as runner-up to Ralph Guldahl at the U.S. Open), and finished in third place five times. He earned more than $10,000, which made him pro golf's second-highest money winner that year.

And where was Paul Runyan while Snead was dazzling the golf world in 1937? He was right there, hiding in plain sight, logging steady finishes in many of the same tournaments. While Snead was capturing the spotlight, Paul and Joan were still getting settled in a house they had purchased the previous spring, a Georgian colonial at 62 Malvern Road in Westchester County, New York. When Snead won in Oakland, Runyan finished in tenth place, ten strokes back. Harry Cooper and Snead set the pace over the winter season, but Runyan was close behind, carrying a 71.35 stroke average (compared to 69.9 for Cooper and 71 for Snead). When Snead won in Nassau that December, Runyan tied for fourth, four strokes back.

Much of Runyan's energy in 1937 was spent getting used to new equipment. It took some work, but once he had fine-tuned his set of clubs, that effort led to some of the best golf of his professional career. Around 1936, he recalled, Spalding started taking the advice of other players, instead of relying solely on the wisdom of Bobby Jones. "And that was when the clubs worsened," Runyan said.

Spalding had released a set of clubs that Runyan felt placed the center of gravity too close to the top of the club. A weak player like Runyan would struggle to get the ball airborne.

Runyan contacted Victor East at Spalding to voice his concern. Runyan was no Bobby Jones, but he was in the prime of his career and an important asset to Spalding. The company paid him a reported $1,500 annually, plus golf clubs. He figured they ought to listen to his views on equipment.

"Victor, I can't use these this year," he told East. "You've got to make me a set of clubs that's going to help me get them up."

"Tell me what you want," East said. "And I'll have them hand forged."

Runyan asked East for long irons (one-iron through five-iron) with jigger-style heads. He instructed the club maker to round off the soles of the clubs, then gradually thin out the head toward the topline. For his short irons, Runyan asked for conventional-shaped heads that were hand-ground to look more compact. "Shorter this way, shallower that way, and a little thicker down here," he explained to East.

"He gave them to me, and they were the best set of clubs I ever had," Runyan said. "I shot lights out in 1937 and '38 with that set of clubs."

One sign that Runyan was starting to get comfortable with the new clubs came at the 1937 PGA Championship in May, held at Pittsburgh Field Club in Fox Chapel, Pennsylvania. Runyan jumped out to the opening-round lead during stroke play qualifying, shooting a 68 that could have been even lower had he holed a few more putts. "The green is nothin' but cup when he starts to putt," Runyan's caddie bragged to one member of the golf press.

Byron Nelson equaled Runyan's score later that day to tie the lead. Snead got off to a rocky start after he grabbed his ball on the fifth green and allegedly removed a chunk of mud from its dimples. The incident sent the rules committee into a lengthy conference, but the fan support for Snead never wavered. Clearly, he was the gallery's favorite player. Ultimately, Denny Shute prevailed in Fox Chapel, defeating Jug McSpaden to capture his second consecutive PGA Championship.

For the 1937 season, Runyan made a little more than $5,000 in prize money—good enough for eleventh place in the hierarchy of golf earners.

The press in Pittsburgh tried to cast Runyan as an aggrieved party for having been left off the list of Ryder Cup qualifiers that had been released just before the PGA Championship, but that view didn't prevail. Was Runyan motivated by the supposed snub? Maybe. But he knew well enough that playing opportunities would follow good results. And PGA officials put him on a short list of players—one that included Nelson and Snead—who, if their play warranted, could be late additions to the Ryder Cup team after that June's U.S. Open.

For Runyan, that Ryder Cup was not meant to be. The final spot on the team would go to Byron Nelson, and the United States would be victorious in England.

AS THE 1938 golf season dawned, few people in the golf community questioned Sam Snead's place as the dominant force in professional golf. He would win his share of tournaments; they just knew it. The only question remaining was how many victories stars like Harry Cooper and Gene Sarazen could wrestle away from him.

Golf's more pressing issues at the start of the year centered on the state of the game. There was talk of formally organizing pro golf's tournament schedule, which today is commonly known as the PGA Tour. Paul Runyan, for one, was in favor of an organized professional circuit. He envisioned a tour—or multiple tours—that would offer playing opportunities to the game's best competitors. Those less adept at tournament competition would have better luck finding openings as golf instructors at the country's best clubs. The idea of formalizing the tour had been floated roughly a decade earlier but had never gained enough traction to become a reality. Now, it seemed, the timing might be right.

The other news that garnered some attention was a rule change that prohibited players from carrying more than fourteen clubs during a round of golf. The rule had been given a trial run at the Miami Biltmore Open in late 1937, and most players, it seemed, were in favor of it. Johnny Revolta, who won the tournament (not the same tournament in Miami that Snead won), was rumored to have carried just eleven clubs during the final round, and other players joined him in carrying fewer than fourteen. At Snead's win in Nassau, before the rule change took effect, he had carried *more* than fourteen clubs. Interestingly, many professionals figured Snead would benefit the most from the rule change. That's because he and other long hitters had little use for fairway woods. Most par fours were played with a driver and some sort of short iron or wedge, and the long holes simply meant that he had to use a long iron to reach. Only rarely did Snead need to hit a fairway wood to approach a green.

The Los Angeles Open in early January 1938 was the first significant event to implement the fourteen-club rule. Snead shot rounds of 73-75-71-69 to finish in the money but well behind (by fifteen shots) winner Jimmy Thomson. Runyan finished two shots back of Snead. The following week, Snead successfully defended his title at the Bing Crosby Invitational. Runyan finished eleventh, eight strokes behind.

The next week, at the Pasadena Open, Runyan started hot with a three-under-par 68 to share the first-round lead. However, his fast start was overshadowed by Snead, who withdrew under strange circumstances on the twelfth green. From the start, Snead did not seem himself that opening round. He shot a front-nine 41, then missed a short putt for par at the eleventh hole. When he found his ball stymied behind a large tree on the next hole, Snead decided he'd had enough. He picked up his ball and began walking toward the clubhouse.

"I'm heading back to the hills of West Virginia," he was heard to say.

Whether Snead knew it immediately or not, he had made a big mistake.

"Now this business of picking up, or quitting, in golf is regarded as a close equivalent of going down without being hit and is supposedly not very cricket," wrote Charles Curtis in the *Los Angeles Times*. Snead's untimely departure sent a buzz through the spectators and other players in the field. Some folks on the grounds of the Brookside course had harsh words to say about the young phenom. Others speculated that

Snead, who liked to play fast, had been upset at playing companion Jimmy Thomson's deliberate pace on the putting greens.

An hour later, an apologetic Snead returned to Brookside to face the music. He explained that he really had no intention of going back to West Virginia. Instead, he would stay on the West Coast and continue playing the events where he was committed.

"I just quit because I was playing lousy," he drawled. "I'm sorry about it now. Guess I was a bit hasty."

Snead's apology, whether prompted by Fred Corcoran or self-motivated, was a smart idea. Sports fans of the 1930s had little patience for a quitter, and an apology could help to heal any hurt feelings. In fact, that very day of Snead's brief walkout, underdog prizefighter Jim Braddock, after having been knocked around for the better part of eight rounds, finished with a spectacular fury in the ninth and tenth rounds to upset British heavyweight champion Tommy Farr in front of seventeen thousand fans at New York's Madison Square Garden. The surprising win over Farr would be Braddock's eighty-eighth and final professional fight; a week later he would announce his retirement from boxing and intention to go into business with manager Joe Gould. If Snead hoped to continue to win over fans, walking off the golf course—especially when viewed alongside a long-shot hero like Braddock—would do little to help cast him as a sympathetic figure.

RUNYAN FAILED TO hold on to his lead in Pasadena and finished in a tie for tenth with Ben Hogan, who was still trying to tame that hook. Runyan's play would remain steady but unspectacular the rest of the winter and spring. He logged a series of high finishes but rarely threatened to win.

The withdrawal debacle at Pasadena seemed to take some wind out of Snead's sails, at least for a few months. By late March he was in Greensboro, North Carolina, with fresh legs. Galleries six thousand strong turned up to watch him battle for the title at the Greater Greensboro Golf Championship. *Charlotte Observer* sports editor Jake Wade called Snead "one of the great golfers of his generation. Perhaps he is the greatest." The local fans agreed, and their enthusiasm was reflected in the large throngs that followed Snead during each round.

But mistakes continued to dog Snead. Just a week before the Greensboro contest, when he was at Pinehurst for the North and South Open, he had again picked up midround, this time on the thirteenth hole. His actions upset many of his fellow players, but most fans came to his defense. So did Jake Wade, who tried to make the case in his column that picking up midround was Snead's business and nobody else's.

"Snead has made himself enormously popular here," Wade wrote. "They scoff at the scorn in which his critics have held him for conduct in other tournaments when, out of the running, he picked up his ball and blithely sailed away."

Snead surely felt the pressure building around him. He needed to deliver, and that's just what he did in Greensboro. But even his spectacular play at Sedgefield Country Club failed to escape controversy. Runyan was a party to the episode.

On the eighth hole of the third round, Snead and Ralph Guldahl both hit their drives toward a creek, presumed to be marked as a water hazard. Both players' caddies set their golf bags on the bank of the creek that was believed to be part of the hazard. Snead's caddie had placed the bag close to his boss's ball—close enough that he seemed to be guarding it. This prompted Runyan, the third member of the group, to question the caddies' motives. He asked if the rules forbade placing your golf bag in a marked hazard, immediately in front of a golf ball. Could that be deemed to have improved your path to the hole? The players continued on, and after the round rumors started to circulate on the Sedgefield grounds that Snead and Guldahl might be disqualified or face, at minimum, a two-stroke penalty. That's when Homer Wheeler, who chaired the local rules committee, announced that there would be no penalty. Wheeler's declaration seems to have been made simply to calm the crowd, because he continued asking other professionals for opinions on the matter. As complaints arose from other players, the rules committee in Greensboro wired to the United States Golf Association for a decisive opinion.

Meanwhile, the final round got under way. Snead led by four strokes—or just two, depending on how the pending ruling shook out. Tournament officials found him eating lunch before his starting time and explained that there was still the possibility of a penalty.

Under such duress, Snead went out on the front nine and played some of his best golf of the week, turning in just thirty-one strokes. He came home in thirty-seven, good enough for a final-round 68 and a 271 total, which gave him first place by five shots over Johnny Revolta. Runyan and Guldahl tied for third, ten strokes back.

Then word came from the USGA: no penalty. The gallery let out a football stadium–sized roar once it was clear that Snead had won, then began crowding around him and begging for autographs. A police escort finally nudged through the throng and gave him some breathing room. Tournament organizers presented him the winner's check for $1,200.

Sam Snead was out of the doghouse and back on top.

8

"Lawdy, the Man Ain't Human"

It's all still there, mostly, if you know where to look. Steve Taggart can point it out to you. As the longtime director of golf at the Shawnee Inn and Golf Resort, the broad-shouldered Taggart is uniquely qualified to guide you around the Shawnee Country Club, which had first been conceived by famed architect A. W. Tillinghast. Some of the holes that were part of the course's routing at the 1938 PGA Championship are still there, fully intact. Others are hidden, partially buried. Taggart will point out deep swales that used to be bunkers, raised plateaus that were once teeing areas, former green pads that have grown out (including the one where the 1938 PGA climaxed on Saturday, July 16, 1938). And he can describe how Tillinghast routed holes across the large ridge (or "spine," in golf design-speak) that goes through the property. At one point in the early 2000s, plans were being finalized to restore the course to Tillinghast's routing (one of them, anyway). Trees had been marked for removal. Contracts were ready to be signed. This restoration was set to happen. Somehow, it didn't. Taggart wonders what life at Shawnee would have been like had the plan gone through. Maybe someday it will; the original A. W. Tillinghast golf course—what a must-see golf destination that would be. Taggart's been around long enough to know that business can be complicated and sometimes things don't work out for damn good reasons.

Jon Kirkwood, whose family has owned the resort since 1977, will chuckle when it occurs to him that his family's ownership stint has outlasted that of any of its predecessors. His tour of Shawnee includes great stories about growing up on the property as a young man. He'll show you the spot where they grow fresh vegetables to serve in hotel dining. And he'll turn nostalgic as he takes you out to his favorite spot on the far edge of Shawnee Island that overlooks the Delaware River, away from the hotel. Everything about Kirkwood and his family's stewardship of this Shawnee oasis is sincere. Many in the Kirkwood clan own houses a stone's throw from the resort. They live it and breathe it every day.

Then there's the hotel, once called the Buckwood Inn. It's not hard to imagine what it looked like in 1938 or earlier because it's still in operation, in many ways frozen in time, right down to the countless sepia-toned historic photographs that adorn the walls. On the bottom floor there's even a Runyan Room, named in honor of you-know-who. Supposedly, Dwight Eisenhower had a soft spot for Shawnee. So did Fred Waring's friends in the music and entertainment business, folks like Jackie Gleason, Bob Hope, and Lucille Ball. In 1954 Arnold Palmer was competing at Shawnee when he met his future wife, Winnie, in the hotel.

Amid a heat wave in the summer of 1938, more than one hundred of the world's best golfers turned up at Shawnee to find out who was golf's best at match play. Runyan was one of them, having trained a week in advance just for the heat. Sam Snead was there, determined to etch his name onto one of golf's biggest trophies. Other contenders included Denny Shute, Ralph Guldahl, Ed Dudley, Shawnee's own pro Jimmy Thomson, and prickly Gene Sarazen, who was tangled yet again in a rift with one of golf's governing bodies. Each one probably felt deserving, but titles are won on merit, not self-belief. Sam Snead would be the first to tell you that sometimes things don't work out for damn good reasons.

THEY CALLED IT the golf capital of America. If that statement was a stretch, it was only so by a whisker.

Situated along the banks of the Delaware River, surrounded on all sides by the Pocono Mountains, the Shawnee Country Club and the adjoining Buckwood Inn at Shawnee-on-the-Delaware, Pennsylvania, provided an idyllic setting to stage a major championship in 1938. The club got its much-deserved chance that summer, thanks in large part to the industrialist and inventor Charles Campbell Worthington, known as C.C.

It was Worthington's father, Henry Rossiter Worthington, who had invented the direct-acting steam pump and subsequently founded the Worthington Pump and Machinery Company. When the elder Worthington died, C.C. took over the company, which continued to perform well enough to allow him, by then a millionaire, to indulge in an opulent lifestyle. Golf was chief among his passions, and the bug hit him hard. (Like his father, C.C. had a knack for inventing things and later developed a horse-drawn gang mower for cutting grass at golf courses—the Worthington gang mower. As technology evolved, he eventually modified the design so it could be pulled by tractor.)

C. C. Worthington and his family started vacationing in the Delaware Water Gap area in the 1890s, and when he retired in 1900 at age forty-six, he had more time to devote to his friends, the Shawnee community, and golf. In 1903 he acquired some eight thousand acres on both sides of the Delaware River. Worthington sought to share with his closest friends the many charms of the Shawnee lifestyle that meant so much to him, and in 1908 he set out to construct a first-class hotel with capacity for 250 guests. He insisted on building a fireproof hotel, constructed out of cement and hollow tiles. The food served on the premises would include vegetables grown in on-site gardens and nearby farms, the creamery would provide fresh milk and butter, and the drinking water would be gravity fed directly into each room via two miles of pipe that originated at Sunfish Pond, a forty-four-acre spring-fed glacial lake that Worthington owned on the east side of the Delaware River.

Worthington also wanted his guests to have top-notch recreation facilities. In 1904 he built Worthington Hall—today known as the Shawnee Playhouse—to bring entertainment and culture to Shawnee residents and visitors. Then he tabbed his longtime friend and fellow golf enthusiast Albert Warren (A. W.) Tillinghast, who had frequently vacationed with Worthington and his family in Shawnee (and who would eventually purchase his own cottage there), to design a golf course. For Tillinghast, it would be the opening salvo of a nearly unmatched design career.

Born into a family of means, Tillinghast—the well-dressed, smooth-talking, waxed mustache–wearing, self-proclaimed creator of the double dogleg—liked to gamble and drink and fancied himself a common man, a proponent of public golf. He designed his courses with a hands-on philosophy, gathering inspiration in the field, living in the dirt, laboring over every detail alongside his hired hands. And he could be persuasive. When Baltusrol Golf Club hired him in 1918 to redo its golf course, he talked its officials into starting over and building two courses on the same piece of property. Of course by 1918 he had established a track record of beyond-satisfactory work, which aided him as he pitched the Baltusrol members.

In the late fall of 1909, Tillinghast, then in his early thirties, took his first peek at the land where he would design the Shawnee Country Club. "I immediately saw that the conditions were most unusual," he later wrote. "It seemed as though nature had ordained that this particular section of the beautiful Delaware Valley should be prepared for the royal and ancient game of golf." With his attention to detail, he was surely inspired, if only in some small way, by the numerous Native American relics that were unearthed during construction of the course at Shawnee—reminders of the days when the Shawnee and Lenape people called Shawnee Island home.

Likely at Worthington's suggestion, Tillinghast set out to construct a golf course built for championship competition, yet playable enough that resort guests could still enjoy a relaxed round. Tillinghast's first routing was a par seventy totaling 6,011 yards. Six holes were routed on land snaking around the Buckwood Inn, while the other twelve holes sat on an island—Shawnee Island—surrounded by the Delaware River and its smaller tributary on the north, known as the Binniekill. In the course's earliest days, players and spectators would have to board a ferry to cross the Binniekill, but eventually that gave way to a wooden footbridge players could walk across.

The Spanish colonial–inspired Buckwood Inn opened for business on May 27, 1911. Advertisements for the hotel touted that all guests who arrived by train would be met by automobiles to transport them to the resort. Shawnee was two hours by train from New York and three hours from Philadelphia. As automobiles became more popular, Worthington constructed a fireproof garage at the inn with enough room for fifty cars. He even added a complete line of spare parts, in case any of those cars needed repairs.

Tillinghast must have reserved a special place in his heart for his first design, because he continued to modify the course at Shawnee over the ensuing three decades. As his design business flourished throughout the country, Shawnee became a sort of testing ground for his work, where he could retreat and tinker. His pal Worthington generously gave him the leeway to do so. A significant rerouting took place around 1914, placing fifteen holes on Shawnee Island and just three holes—the first, seventeenth, and eighteenth—on the Buckwood Inn side of the Delaware River. The sixteenth hole, which had been Tillinghast's original thirteenth, played across the smaller berth of the Delaware River and was thus nicknamed the Binniekill Hole. Tillinghast described it simply in his own notes as a hole that's "all carry across the Binniekill." It was a sort of island-green par three that in 1912 became party to a unique feat in golf lore when a competitor in a qualifying round for the Shawnee Invitational for Ladies hit her tee shot into the Binniekill, whose current carried the ball more than a mile downstream. Her husband took up the oars of a small rowboat and, as they plied the waters of the Delaware, tried to locate the ball. Once it was found, the woman proceeded to take 165 more strokes to complete the hole, playing most of the way back through the woods that surrounded the Binniekill.

Tillinghast's 1914 revision increased the course's length to 6,500 yards, and by the 1938 PGA Championship the course would measure 6,655 yards and play as a par seventy-two. To make sure the conditions were pristine, the club invested $20,000 in the property in anticipation of the championship. Many of the professional golfers who'd be visiting Shawnee for the 1938 PGA Championship were already familiar with the layout, which steers us back to its place as the golf capital of America. Worthington and Tillinghast together conceived the Shawnee Open, a professional golf tournament, held annually beginning in 1912. At that first playing of the tournament, a conversation began about forming a golf association; four years later the organization known as the PGA was formed with fifty or so members, and by 1938 it had grown to nearly two thousand members. In 1913 the Shawnee Open reached elite status with the presence of European stars Harry Vardon and Ted Ray. That tournament was won by two-time defending U.S. Open champion John J. McDermott, who, in the trophy room of the Buckwood Inn, sullied the moment with a patriotic yet cringeworthy speech proclaiming the end of European dominance in championship golf. Over the years, the Shawnee Open produced many noteworthy champions: Walter Hagen in 1916, Jim Barnes in 1919, Harry Cooper in 1929, Ed Dudley in 1930 and 1936, and Lawson Little in 1937. The game's top players knew the layout because they played it each year. Not even Jimmy Thomson, the long-hitting Shawnee pro, would have much in the way of a course-knowledge advantage. The winner of the PGA Championship would simply have to play the best golf.

Tillinghast had a hand in bringing the PGA Championship to Shawnee, thanks to two years he spent touring the country in the mid-1930s on behalf of the PGA of America, offering golf clubs free course consultations during that period when his design work had slowed due to the Great Depression. Awarding the championship to Shawnee was the PGA's way of thanking Tillinghast for his contributions to the organization and to American golf. By the time the Great Depression took hold of the country, he had already designed Aronimink, Baltusrol, Philadelphia Cricket Club, and Winged Foot, among many other historic courses.

Aside from the golf course, players in the PGA field at Shawnee would have to contend with the weather. A significant heat wave settled over the entire Eastern Seaboard early that July, and players would have to tolerate high temperatures throughout the championship. The annual average July temperature in nearby Allentown was 76 degrees; during tournament play those figures were soaring toward triple digits, made worse with intense humidity. On July 8, two days before the start of play, the weather station at Allentown-Bethlehem reported a temperature of 91 degrees at the close of business. The *Morning Call* newspaper in Allentown reported that on Sunday, July 10, the Reverend August Buettner, assistant rector of Sacred Heart parish, was overcome by heat while celebrating an early morning mass and was taken to a nearby hospital. It was his second heat-related attack that week. To find some relief from the heat, large crowds had overwhelmed Allentown's swimming pools—including an estimated 5,500 people that Sunday afternoon.

It's unknown if Paul Runyan had friends in the weather bureau or inside sources on the grounds of Shawnee or was simply a keen observer of atmospheric science, but none of this was news to him. In the weeks leading up to the PGA Championship, he had concluded that handling the weather conditions would play a significant factor in the outcome, so he left his home on Malvern Road to head north about thirty miles so that he could spend a week training at Bill Brown's Health Farm, a 180-acre training resort located on the Hudson River in Garrison, New York, near West Point. Brown, a former boxing commissioner who'd also been an athlete, had opened the facility in 1909 after it became evident to him that professionals engaged in business needed a place to get away from everyday life and focus on their physical health. Sometimes called Bill Brown's Physical Training Farm or Brownsdale, for short, it was "friendly and informal with old fashion comfort and modern methods" that offered "the ideal place for a physical tuning up and a mental rest," read one brochure. Upon arrival, every guest met with a physician to determine an individualized training regimen. "We do not take anyone who requires a nurse, for Brownsdale is in no sense a sanitorium," asserted the author of that same brochure.

Runyan stayed at Brownsdale a week to train for playing golf in the hot weather. As he put it, "working like hell" in a hot climate taught him the importance of perspiring, what to do, and what not to do to stay fit. The facilities at the Brown Health Farm offered everything Runyan needed to prepare for hot and humid conditions. There were expansive locker rooms, rubbing tables for a massage, hiking trails, steam rooms, a swimming pool, tennis courts, and more. He could reset his diet, catch up on sleep, and get his body and mind ready for competition.

It's safe to assume that teetotaling, nonsmoking, early-to-bed Paul Runyan was more fastidious in his personal habits than most men or even most other professional athletes who plopped down $125 for a weeklong stay at the Brown Health Farm. Abstaining from booze and cigarettes was routine business for Runyan. But there were other, less obvious, health choices he employed, all intentional, that he explained to golf journalist Guy Yocom decades later.

"In hot weather, you don't drink a Coca-Cola. You don't drink ice-cold water. If you're going to drink anything, drink something that's tepid, hot tea or certainly just tap water," he told Yocom.

Runyan learned that a change from one extreme temperature to another can close your pores and limit perspiration. He also learned never to eat ham in the morning before a round of golf, particularly in hot weather. Ham took too long to digest, and, as he explained, "it just lays in your stomach in a lump."

So what *did* Runyan eat before and during rounds of golf? Cottage cheese. Honey. Toast. Maybe some hot tea. He would rather go hungry than put something in his stomach that was hard to digest. When it came to his clothing, he was careful to wear apparel that was thick enough to absorb his perspiration. He admired workers in steel mills who wore heavy wool jackets and wool shirts. To keep cool, they'd drench their clothes in lukewarm water.

When Paul Runyan left Brownsdale for Shawnee-on-the-Delaware—presumably by way of White Plains, where he reconnected with Joan and stayed just long enough to pack a bag full of enough golf attire to last the week in Shawnee—he did so brimming with confidence, even cockiness. He had prepared to face tough conditions, and now it was time to perform. Of all the potential land mines waiting to derail him at Shawnee, he was determined that the heat and humidity would not be among them.

ON THE EVE of the championship, bandleader (and future owner of the resort) Fred Waring and his famous radio orchestra officially kicked off the PGA Championship with a live concert in the ballroom of the Buckwood Inn. Themed "Swingtime in the Poconos," a thirty-minute portion of Waring's radio show could be heard coast to coast between midnight and 12:30 a.m. It was reported that the pretournament jamboree was the first in the history of the PGA Championship. Sports commentator Ted Husing served as radio announcer during Waring's performance, introducing professional golf's leading men to the radio audience listening around the country. Despite Paul and Joan Runyan's mutual love of dancing, it's hard to imagine Runyan staying awake until midnight simply to saunter onto the dance floor and take a bow for a radio broadcast. Could he have turned in early, set an alarm for 11:45, then tumbled out of bed in his $8-per-night room at the Buckwood Inn, donned a tuxedo, and headed down the main staircase and into the ballroom to give the crowd a momentary thrill? Perhaps. Maybe he and Joan danced the rumba and really caused a stir. Or maybe he slept through the whole thing. No matter what hour his head hit the pillow that night, Runyan had to be considered among the contenders for the championship, even if he failed to crack the short list of betting favorites. Earlier that day, the undersized pro demonstrated solid form while shooting 71 during a practice round at Shawnee.

Those favorites who had the attention of the golf press were Billy Burke, who shot 69 in his practice round that Friday; Ed Dudley, twice a winner of the Shawnee Open; U.S. Open champion Ralph Guldahl, who carried pro golf's best scoring average through the first six months of the year; long-hitting Shawnee professional Jimmy Thomson; and wiry two-time defending PGA champion Denny Shute. And of course there was the young buck from the backwoods mountains of Virginia: long-hitting Sam Snead, the crown prince of pro golf in 1938. He was on everyone's radar.

Snead arrived at Shawnee in good form. In addition to his early season victories at the Crosby and in Greensboro, in May he partnered with Vic Ghezzi to win the Inverness Four-Ball Invitational in Toledo, Ohio. A poor showing at the U.S. Open in June (which included a final-round 80) might have been enough to throw some folks off his scent, but he rebounded later that month with a victory at the Goodall Round Robin. On the Thursday before the PGA Championship began, Snead teamed with Billy Campbell to win the West Virginia pro-amateur best ball tournament; a day later Snead captured the West Virginia PGA with scores of 66-67.

Play began on Sunday, July 10, the same day that millionaire aviator and movie producer Howard Hughes and a crew of three left Floyd Bennett Airport in New York bound for Paris and, Hughes hoped, a trek around the world. In Munich, Hitler opened an art exhibition by declaring that Nazi Germany wanted nothing to do with modern artists, whom he considered to be cultural Neanderthals. And in Shawnee-on-the-Delaware, Pennsylvania, 120 of the world's most accomplished professional golfers teed off in threesomes—spaced just six minutes apart—starting at 9:00 a.m. Eastern Standard Time.

Snead shot a three-under-par 69 in the first round of stroke play qualifying. Runyan shot 70. Everyone was chasing Runyan's buddy Harry Cooper, who missed just two greens in regulation and opened with 67. Twenty-nine-year-old Frank Moore was a stroke behind at 68, and Henry Picard and Terl Johnson joined Snead at 69. Gene Sarazen, in the field but feuding with PGA officials over his role on the upcoming U.S. Ryder Cup team, shot 72.

Thirty-one players broke par at Shawnee on day two, including Frank Moore, who fired his second straight 68 to capture medalist honors at eight under par for thirty-six holes. Snead shot 70 to finish qualifying just three strokes back of Moore. Runyan bettered par for the second straight day and finished qualifying at 141.

The following day, with the field whittled nearly in half, sixty-four players would begin first-round matches, played mano a mano, to determine who was professional golf's best match-play player.

Runyan awoke that Tuesday, his thirtieth birthday, to a surprise. Well-known New York bookmaker Jack Doyle, the "sage of Broadway," had made Runyan even money in his first-round match against Levi Lynch. Runyan was perplexed that he wasn't favored, and he would remain that way for the rest of the week. In fact, the rest of his life.

"Broadway" Jack Doyle, a semibald, bespectacled, blue suit–wearing, sports-wagering savant, had been a fixture in New York athletics for decades. He had opened a billiards parlor in 1906 at Broadway and Forty-Second Street, half a block from Times Square, which he held on to until late 1937, when poor health forced him to sell the establishment. But he refused to abandon his post as America's bookmaker. A few weeks after news broke that he was unloading his pool hall in December 1937, the famous odds layer made public his views on the upcoming 1938 sports scene. Doyle made the New York Yankees the shortest-priced favorite in the history of Major League Baseball, tabbed Fighting Fox as the Kentucky Derby front-runner, and warned that, in college football, "always take Pittsburgh and never bet against Notre Dame in any one game." If Doyle had a weakness, it was golf, where he was something of a Johnny-come-lately. He was quick to admit this shortcoming. However, with his mystique came credibility. And, sometimes when it mattered most, he could be right, like he was when he listed Ralph Guldahl and Dick Metz among his five favorites to win that year's U.S. Open (along with Sam Snead), a full six months before the tournament. Guldahl and Metz went out and finished first and second, proving Doyle right.

At the start of match play at Shawnee, Doyle made Guldahl, Denny Shute, Sam Snead, and medalist Frank Moore 8-to-1 favorites. When Doyle made Runyan and Levi Lynch a pick 'em before their first-round match, Runyan was miffed. If he needed a match to light the fire in his belly that week, he got it from Jack Doyle.

"I'm a previous champion, and this fellow hasn't done anything," he said once about Lynch, still bewildered.

Doyle was on site that week in Shawnee, wearing a dapper-looking pair of broadcloth pants that were "thin from sitting around on hard benches outside and inside the clubhouse at Shawnee looking for bets on the PGA Championship," wrote one sportswriter. That's exactly what Doyle did. All over the Buckwood Inn, he placed signs that read, "Jack Doyle Mutuel Betting" to help scare up some business.

Runyan easily beat Lynch in his eighteen-hole first-round match, 5 and 4. That afternoon he drew Tony Manero, who had won handily in the opening round. Doyle made Runyan a 3-to-1 underdog.

Manero, with his thin mustache and Hollywood smile, bore an uncanny resemblance to the actor Cesar Romero. But that mustache wasn't all he had going; he was a major champion, having won the 1936 U.S. Open. Coincidentally, Manero had gained inspiration that week in 1936 from none other than bookmaker supreme Jack Doyle. At the start of the week at Baltusrol, Doyle had given Manero 200-to-1 odds to win, 100-to-1 odds to finish second, and 50-to-1 odds to finish third. Manero decided to place a $20 bet on himself across the board. The next day his odds dropped only slightly: 100-to-1 odds to win, 50-to-1 to finish second, 25-to-1 to place third. Still insulted, Manero again bet $20 on himself across the board. Manero was playing well, and when his odds remained fixed the following day, he bet another $20 on himself. When it was all finished and he had won the U.S. Open, Manero walked away with not only his winner's check of $1,000 but a return on his wagers of something like $18,000, which was a massive payday in 1936.

Manero gave Runyan a tough match, but Runyan prevailed, 3 and

2. Did Jack Doyle's name come up that afternoon as the twosome cruised around Shawnee Country Club? You have to wonder. And if Doyle *was* a topic of conversation, it's hard to imagine anything nice was said by either player.

On the other side of the bracket, budding young stars Sam Snead and Byron Nelson appeared to be on a collision course. Snead opened with an easy 4-and-3 victory over Frank Champ and followed it up by disposing of Terl Johnson by the same margin. In his third-round match he would defeat Felix Serafin, again 4 and 3. Nelson took out Clarence Yockey and Al Krueger in the opening rounds, but what truly got the golf world's attention was the Texan's morning round of eight-under-par 64, en route to a twelve-up advantage at one point and an eventual 11 and 10 thrashing of Harry Bassler in the first of the thirty-six-hole matches.

Nelson's torrid play was enough for Associated Press sportswriter Paul Mickelson to declare him the tournament favorite. That might have been a jinx. Nelson responded by losing his next match to Jimmy Hines, 2 and 1, throwing cold water on the brewing semifinal showdown with Snead.

"It just wasn't my turn to win," Nelson told a sportswriter the following day from his home. "Guess I got hot too early."

If you were a Sam Snead fan—a faction that seemed to be growing by the day since his sudden take-off in 1937—suddenly the path to victory looked a lot clearer.

RUNYAN KEPT GETTING the cold shoulder from Jack Doyle. On his second day as a thirty-something, he played Ray Mangrum, the older brother of the more famous Lloyd Mangrum, who would win the 1946 U.S. Open (and who might have won the 1950 Open at Merion, if not for Ben Hogan and that famous one-iron to the seventy-second hole that photographer Hy Peskin captured on his Speed Graphic camera—you know the photo, the one that all serious golfers have framed on their wall, with spectators lining both sides of the fairway, watching anxiously to see if the Hawk could get into a playoff). Doyle made Ray Mangrum the favorite, and the Texan would push Runyan to his limit.

Runyan shot 69 in the morning round to go two up, which is the same advantage he held as he stood on the seventeenth tee that afternoon—dormie—only to watch Mangrum birdie the par-five seventeenth and par the 234-yard par-three eighteenth. Runyan went par, bogey, and suddenly the match was headed for extra holes. But just when it seemed that Runyan might have lost control of the match and his game, he won the first extra hole to close out Mangrum.

How had he conjured such a stunning reversal when it seemed all was lost? Conditioning might have played a factor. It was a hot, sun-drenched day at Shawnee. An Associated Press photograph that ran in the *Philadelphia Inquirer* showed Gene Sarazen carrying an oversized umbrella, holding it aloft to shield himself and his caddie from the sun. Heavyweight boxing contender "Two Ton" Tony Galento, training in Philadelphia, became so fed up by the oppressive heat, which made it nearly impossible to do road work, he left the City of Brotherly Love for Summit, New Jersey, to prep for his upcoming fight with light heavyweight champion John Henry Lewis.

On a day that sultry, Runyan believed his fitness played a role in victory.

"I was smarter than they were, all of them," he told Al Barkow. "There wasn't a one of them who knew how to take care of himself in 100-degree sweltering heat. It was 100, 102 with a humidity of ninety, and it just wilted them. In match play I knew how to take care of myself."

What did that mean, exactly, beyond avoiding ham for breakfast and Coca-Cola at the turn? For one thing, it meant that Joan Runyan's role in her husband's preparation took on added importance that week. Runyan had noticed that the Delaware River water was especially cold, so he filled the tub in his hotel room and took a long soak each morning before he left to play. Rounds that week were going fast, and most matches finished in less than three hours, he recalled, which allowed plenty of time to retreat to his room at the Buckwood Inn for another soak to lower his respiration before the afternoon round.

"I'd have my wife draw the water, and before I had my lunch I'd take another cool bath," he said. "I'd stay in it until I actually was chilled, then I'd go back and have my lunch and a warm-up. Oh, I was getting stronger as the week went on, and they were all wilting."

ON THURSDAY, JULY 14, about the time Howard Hughes landed in front of twenty-five thousand spectators at Floyd Bennett Airport in New York (2:34 p.m. Eastern), having navigated his Lockheed Super Electra around the world in a record time of three days, nineteen hours, fourteen minutes, and ten seconds, Slammin' Sam Snead was putting the final touches on his 8-and-7 dismantling of quarterfinalist Jim Foulis at Shawnee Country Club. Snead's morning 70 put him four up over Foulis, and he slammed home a fifteen-foot birdie putt on the day's twenty-ninth hole to end the match.

Runyan drew a tougher assignment in the quarterfinals: his old pal and money game partner Horton Smith. Smith grabbed the early advantage, but Runyan's twenty-foot putt on the sixteenth hole of the morning round gave the little man his first lead. Runyan birdied the first hole of the afternoon after hitting his approach to two feet, and he kept the birdies flowing on the opening nine with a fifteen-footer at the fifth and a seven-footer at the eighth. He eventually closed out Smith 4 and 3.

The field was now down to its final four: Runyan, Henry Picard, Sam Snead, and giant-killer Jimmy Hines, who had impressively beaten Denny Shute and red-hot Byron Nelson in succession.

The Snead-Hines match was described by sportswriter Bob Brumby as "a thriller down to the final blow." Snead had been breezing through the bracket all week, playing strong golf and looking nearly untouchable, but Hines pressed him in a manner previously unseen by spectators that week at Shawnee-on-the-Delaware. Hines enjoyed a one-up advantage after the morning round. That was quickly erased on the opening hole of the afternoon, when Snead holed a thirty-foot putt to even the match. On the 342-yard par-four fifteenth hole, a subtle dogleg right that featured a wide-open tee shot, which allowed the players to let loose a big drive, Hines stuck his approach to nearly gimme distance. Snead, meanwhile, faced a twenty-foot putt for birdie, but without hesitation he stepped up, stroked the putt, and dropped it to halve the hole with birdie. On the par-five seventeenth, playing back toward the Buckwood Inn after crossing the Binniekill, Snead launched a three-iron to within ten feet, then holed the eagle putt to trump Hines's birdie and take a one-up advantage to the difficult closing hole. Both players had birdie putts on the final green, but when Hines's attempt slid by, the match was Snead's.

In order for Runyan to join Snead in the finals, he would have to outwit Henry Picard, the "Chocolate Soldier" from Hershey Country Club in Hershey, Pennsylvania. Picard steered right into his unofficial role as pro golf's chocolatier, gladly handing out a supply of chocolate bars at every tournament he played. Reportedly, Milton Hershey would reciprocate by matching Picard's tournament earnings and thereby supplementing the golfer's income. Not only would Runyan have to overcome a partisan Pennsylvania gallery, but Picard was in the midst of a run of strong play, having already won twice that season, at Pasadena and the Masters.

Runyan also believed he possessed an insight into Picard's demeanor, saying once, "Henry Picard gave the air that nothing could ruffle him, but that was the exterior. Inside he could get ruffled easily."

Fortunately for Runyan, he caught Picard on a day when his putter was as cold as a Pennsylvania winter, and not even the humidity steaming off the Delaware River could heat it up. Reporter Bob Brumby counted at least seven makeable putts that Picard missed, which might have flipped the match. Runyan, meanwhile, won the day's opening hole to seize the lead and kept up his own steady putting, one-putting nine times on the day. He never gave Picard an opening and cruised to a 4-and-3 victory.

It was now official: Paul Runyan would play Sam Snead for the 1938 PGA Championship.

"DAVID TEES OFF against Goliath in the final round of the PGA Championship over the lightning-fast, sun-baked Shawnee Country Club course here tomorrow," wrote Bob Brumby on the eve of the Runyan-Snead match.

Brumby had nailed it. This was a David versus Goliath matchup, but it was more nuanced than the often-abridged version of that biblical quarrel. Grantland Rice described the PGA finale as "the old battle between a hard puncher and a boxer," which illuminated a further truth about the match: Snead was the hard puncher and Runyan the boxer. But for all the differences in how Runyan and Snead played golf—and to be sure, there were many—as individuals they had much in common. Start with the fact that both were products of spa resort courses considered among America's best: Runyan from Hot Springs Country Club in Arkansas and Snead from the Homestead Resort in Virginia. Now here they were, playing for a major championship on one of the country's premier resort courses. As kids, they both had liked to box. Both began in golf as caddies, and both worked in golf shops as apprentices to older professionals; each one even did a stint making and repairing clubs.

Those similarities mostly ended when they walked onto a golf course. Snead was tall, weighed 175 pounds, possessed long arms and an unhurried rhythm, and seemed to glide when he walked. Runyan was shortish and slightly built, weighing just 130 pounds with a sleeve of golf balls stuffed in his pocket. He swung with a choppy rhythm and always seemed to walk like he was running five minutes late for an important meeting.

Snead was a long hitter, a graceful swinger, yet he sometimes struggled with distance control and selecting the right club for the shot at hand. He was talented enough to hit almost any shot with any club in the bag, but sometimes he'd try to smooth a four-iron when the shot called for a six, and he'd airmail the green into trouble. Runyan could little afford to make such an error in judgment, so he viewed the game through a different lens. It was imperative that he hit the ball straight and hunted angles that gave him the least-obstructed path toward the flagstick.

If you enjoyed watching contrasting styles of play, this was your match.

On the morning of the finale, a Shawnee locker room attendant went looking around the clubhouse for Jack Doyle while carrying $1,000 that someone had given him to bet on Snead at 2-to-1 odds; those were the odds that Associated Press sportswriter Bill Boni had reported. The attendant found Doyle and tried to place the bet, but there was a catch. Those were not Doyle's odds. According to Runyan, Doyle had made Snead a 10-to-1 favorite.

Hold the phone: 10-to-1? Had Runyan embellished the Jack Doyle story over the years, through his various retellings? Or, perhaps, had the whole narrative been a ruse from the beginning, a motivational tactic Runyan employed at Shawnee to get in the right mind-set to play? Great athletes through the years have sometimes invented perceived slights to gain an edge. What to make of this? Runyan was the underdog, yes, but 10-to-1?

If you start digging, you'll find Jack Doyle's name mentioned frequently in the sports sections of East Coast newspapers throughout the 1930s. In most of those newspapers he's giving odds on major sports such as baseball, college and pro football, boxing, and racing. Other stories touch on happenings at his pool hall, almost as if the sports scribes had an unspoken agreement to keep Doyle's pool hall in the news in exchange for juicy gossip and betting odds for their newspapers. Golf was not Doyle's bailiwick, but he *had* laid odds on the PGA Championship at the start of match play; that fact was reported by syndicated sports columnist Henry McLemore, a Grantland Rice chum who, in his varied career, had covered the Lindbergh kidnapping and the ongoing gambling wars in New York. And it was longtime *Washington Star* golf writer Walter McCallum, a well-liked reporter who later became a war correspondent providing firsthand accounts of D-Day and the Battle of the Bulge, who reported that Doyle was on the grounds of Shawnee during tournament week, conducting business in the lobby of the Buckwood Inn. It was McCallum who wrote the story about the locker room attendant carrying a $1,000 bet and that Doyle's odds, whatever they *actually* were, were not 2-to-1. While nothing that either man reported indicated 10-to-1 odds in the finals, nothing refuted it either.

Ultimately, Runyan's version of the Jack Doyle saga that week at Shawnee may be history's principal version. Without someone unearthing Doyle's own ledgers, there seems to be no evidence to refute it.

Maybe Runyan had made it part of his morning routine, after a cold soak in his tub and a few spoonfuls of cottage cheese, to race down the stairs of the Buckwood Inn like a kid on Christmas morning and find Doyle seated on a wooden bench on the hotel's veranda. Runyan would look him straight in the eye through the bookmaker's thick eyeglass lenses and ask him for the day's odds. You can picture Runyan, after hearing each morning that Broadway Jack thought the safer money was on someone else, rising from the bench, winking, and in his own gentlemanly way wishing Doyle a lovely day before sprinting down the thirteen steps of the main entrance to the Buckwood Inn and heading straight for the practice tee to begin his warm-up, on his way to proving the world wrong.

SHORTLY BEFORE THEIR 10:30 a.m. starting time that Saturday, July 16, Sam Snead and Paul Runyan arrived at the first tee of Shawnee Country Club to pose for press photographs. The Wanamaker Trophy was there on the tee, sitting on a small, round, four-legged wooden table against which each player leaned his golf bag. Runyan, wearing dark blue pleated slacks, a light-colored golf shirt with button-down pockets on the left and right breast, and "Paul" stitched onto the right collar, removed his light blue porkpie hat and offered his right hand to Snead. He cradled the hat between two fingers in his left hand and palmed something else, a small tin, perhaps. Maybe it was breath mints or salt tablets.

Wearing a long-sleeve button-down shirt and tie, Snead, nearly four years younger than his opponent and with a pronounced widow's peak, removed his tam-o'-shanter cap and extended his own right hand to meet Runyan's handshake. Both players smiled, although Runyan's smile was wider and warmer, if only for that moment it took the photographer to capture the embrace.

Spectators, many of them wearing their Sunday best a day early—men in shirts and ties and light-colored pants and women in summer dresses—surrounded the first tee. There would be an estimated crowd of three thousand that day at Shawnee, believed to be the week's largest turnout. If that number seems small, remember that Shawnee was a resort course, located two hours by train from the region's largest metropolitan areas and secluded by design. There were a limited number of hotel rooms available near the resort; most of the Buckwood Inn had been taken up by players and sports reporters. The local population, also limited in number, still turned up for the thirty-six-hole final, anxious to see if David had any chance in hell to topple Goliath—at 10-to-1 odds. Runyan wasn't the only underdog competing that day. In California, the racehorse Seabiscuit and backup jockey George Woolf took aim at the $50,000 Hollywood Gold Cup. In front of fifty-five thousand fans, Seabiscuit would be victorious.

A black-and-white Movietone News newsreel, which likely played nonstop in movie houses coast to coast over the coming days, featured footage from the day's play at Shawnee. Narrator Ed Thorgersen's voice-over performance helped tell the story.

"The camera highlights in the world of sports," he began as an image of Runyan waggling his driver on the first tee came on the screen. "Dapper Paul Runyan of White Plains, New York, tees off in the thirty-six-hole final of the PGA Championship at Shawnee-on-the-Delaware."

Runyan, wearing his porkpie hat, transitions from two smooth waggles into his backswing, winding up onto his right side—making a pronounced lateral shift, almost a sway—his left heel lifting a few inches off the ground as he nears the top of his swing, then lunges into the shot, chasing after it with his right hand, following the flight of the ball down the fairway. Joan Runyan, not visible on the newsreel, is there on the tee, watching her husband begin his round, noting the time so she can count the hours until drawing water for his bath.

Then, with the Pocono Mountains in the background, there is Snead, seen from head-on, wearing on his left hand a golf glove that cuts off just below each knuckle, like a chauffeur. He makes one purposeful waggle before beginning a backswing characterized by a deep turn of his hips and an even deeper upper-body turn, his hands extending to the heavens and his clubhead dipping only slightly past parallel, and then unleashes a powerful stroke with his driver that sends the ball whistling down the fairway like a freight train. We hear Thorgersen say, "Slammin' Sammy Snead of West Virginia," before the audible "thwack" of Snead's driver compressing the golf ball overtakes Thorgersen's voice. Even to the untrained eye, the difference in clubhead speed between the two players is noticeable.

Runyan missed a short birdie putt at the first, and they halved the hole with pars. Same at the second after Snead missed a makeable putt. Then on the third, a 458-yard par five with out of bounds on the left, heavy Shawnee rough on the right, and a narrow opening to a well-protected green—a Snead hole, on paper at least, if you believed that driving distance was an advantage—Little Poison struck the first blow. Snead, over the green in two, seemed to hold the advantage, as Runyan's ball was in a bunker, some thirty yards short and right of the green. But Runyan blasted out to eighteen inches, winning the hole with the day's first birdie.

Both players birdied the 400-yard par-four fourth hole, Runyan by holing a twenty-five-foot putt and Snead making a five-footer to halve.

Runyan asserted himself at the fifth hole, a short, 110-yard, uphill par three with a steep slope fronting the green. To set the scene: Runyan's ball, after two strokes, rested three and a half feet from the cup, while Snead, having hit a smooth eight-iron that landed right beside the pin, lined up a birdie putt from the opposite side of the hole.

"Arriving at the green of the short fifth hole, Snead lines up a six-foot putt," narrated Ed Thorgersen on the Movietone News highlight reel. "His ball misses the cup, and Runyan is stymied. To halve the hole, he must sink this putt. But how? After much thought, Runyan decides to use a niblick. The crowd is tense. So is Runyan, for that matter, but watch."

Snead's putt had barely missed, sliding by the left side of the cup and finishing seven or eight inches past the hole. But Runyan was stymied: Snead's ball was directly in his path to the hole. The scenario is no longer possible in modern golf, not since the stymie was abolished in 1952. Even in 1938 there were cries to dump the rule (and an experiment to test removing any obstructing ball within six inches of the cup). Just that morning, columnist Henry McLemore, taking issue with the stymie, had written, "I wish Donald Duck were a golf writer. I wish this because Donald is the only animated thing capable of registering sufficient indignation over the golf stymie rule." McLemore pointed to two separate putts within gimme distance, both stymied, that had cost Jimmy Hines in his match against Snead the day before. McLemore argued that the stymie went in direct opposition to the first principle of golf: to get your ball as close to the hole as possible. Many players he interviewed said they would rather putt first from distance, thus increasing the likelihood of stymieing an opponent.

Now Runyan: after four minutes of deliberation, he grabbed his niblick, sized up the shot from a few feet behind his ball, and hitched his pants with his left hand. He took his stance, bending over from the waist, gently hovering his club behind the ball. Snead crouched down a few feet away, watching his opponent with the grip of his club gently resting against his chin. Runyan took one final look at the hole and the spot where he wanted to land his ball, then pulled his club away a few inches, chopping down at the back of the ball, which elevated quickly and carried a few feet, barely ankle height, landing in an area between Snead's ball and the cup that was no larger than a grown man's hand. It took one short hop and dove into the hole for a three. The hole was halved.

The crowd cheered. Runyan could feel the energy pumping throughout his body. As impressive as the Houdini act with the niblick had been, his body language in the three seconds that followed said more about his state of mind. After his ball disappeared into the cup, he took one step forward with his left foot, bent down, and in one smooth motion grabbed Snead's ball and flicked it toward him, then grabbed his own ball out of the cup, stood up with his head held high, and began walking off the green. It was pure chutzpah—Runyan the showman. His quick hands were reminiscent of an expert billiards player clearing the table before racking it. He handed the club to his caddie, who held the flagstick, and grabbed his driver out of his golf bag for the tee shot at the sixth. And the whole time his eyes remained forward, fixed on the green's exit point. He had the momentum. He looked confident, maybe even cocky. It seemed like nothing could stop him.

Metropolis Country Club members, Runyan's family, and friends around the country followed the action on their radios. In New York, New Jersey, Arkansas, California, Pennsylvania, Ohio, and elsewhere they kept their hands on the dial and hung on Ted Husing's every word, hoping their collective will could carry Little Poison to victory.

Runyan finished the first nine of the morning round two up, and his confidence surged. "I can win," he told himself. He added to his advantage with back-to-back birdies at the eleventh and twelfth. When

Snead made bogey at fifteen, Runyan's advantage grew to five up. Growing frustrated, Snead smacked his ball into a greenside bunker and tossed the putter in after it.

The match had the makings of a woodshed beating. It was made all the more remarkable because Snead was consistently driving well past Runyan. This, of course, surprised no one. On the fourth, Runyan drove it 230 yards, Snead 270. At the sixth, Runyan hit it 240, Snead 295. At the seventh, it was Runyan 235, Snead 270. It went on this way the entire day, with Snead well past Runyan by 30, 40, sometimes 70 yards. But Snead failed to capitalize on his advantage.

After witnessing a string of Runyan recoveries, Snead was so bothered that he felt he couldn't have made a putt in a bathtub.

"This isn't golf, it's magic," he said to Runyan.

On the 135-yard par-three sixteenth—the Binniekill Hole—Runyan hit a seven-iron that finished thirty-two feet right of the pin. Snead hit an eight-iron that finished thirty feet away, on the opposite side of the hole as Runyan. An International News photographer snapped a photo of the pair as they walked to the green. In that image you see Paul Runyan crossing the Delaware River with enough swagger to make George Washington blush. He's a comfortable half step ahead of Snead, who by that point had tucked his necktie in between the second and third buttons of his shirt. You can imagine the clanking of their metal spikes on the one-hundred-yard-long footbridge, the gentle swaying that the caddies and sportswriters and hundreds of spectators following behind must have felt. Runyan removed his porkpie hat to let his forehead catch some sun. Maybe he felt a hint of cool breeze wash over his face from the river below. The look on Snead's face is that of a helpless man, probably wondering how, in just a matter of a few hours, he had gotten five holes down to professional golf's shortest hitter.

Each player two-putted the sixteenth, birdied the seventeenth, and parred the eighteenth. After a bogey-free 67, Runyan took a five-up lead to lunch.

"Boy, I can't match this kind of going," Snead said.

"The old Runyan luck is still holding out," Runyan replied.

Any hope Snead or his legion of fans held out for a comeback that afternoon was quickly quashed after Runyan birdied the par-four second hole, despite being thirty-five yards behind Snead off the tee. His lead grew to six up.

Then on the par-five third, Runyan holed another fifteen-foot putt for birdie. After a marvelous bunker shot to five feet, Snead missed his birdie putt. Seven up. The boxer had the hard puncher on the ropes.

"Runyan must have spent the intermission in a Turkish bath and stored his clubs in a fireless cooker," wrote Henry McLemore. Quite the opposite—the real recipe was a soak in the cold water from the Delaware River Valley and a few bites of toast and honey washed down with a tall glass of room-temperature something-or-other.

Only on the day's twenty-fourth hole, the lengthy (464 yards) par-four sixth, did Runyan falter. Needing a four-wood to reach the green, Runyan's second shot sailed long. After whaling on a drive three hundred yards, Snead hit a five-iron to forty feet. Runyan hit a masterful pitch shot to four feet but missed the putt, and Snead two-putted to win the hole. The bogey was Runyan's first since his fourth-round match against Horton Smith, a remarkable string of sixty-five holes under major championship conditions.

Snead seemed likely to chip away at Runyan's lead on the next hole. He was on the par five eyeing a thirty-footer for birdie, while Runyan had strayed into the rough over the green. With his caddie tending the pin and spectators three rows deep circled around the green, Runyan grabbed his wedge. He opened his stance significantly for a high, lofted pitch. He drove the flange of his wedge into the ground underneath the ball, which came out softly, settling twenty-three feet away. Snead two-putted, forcing Runyan to make his putt just to eke out a halve. Like he had so many times that week, he holed the midrange putt, thwarting Snead's momentum.

One hole later, Runyan, "merciless as an executioner," hit a 220-yard drive (65 yards behind Snead) and a two-iron from more than 200 yards to four feet, from where he holed out for another birdie. Runyan was back to seven up.

Runyan's final birdie came on the par-five tenth. Snead, having driven into the rough, topped his second shot and struggled to make par. Runyan hit a wedge for his third to thirteen feet, where he holed another putt for birdie. On the day the twosome played seven par fives. Despite his tremendous length advantage, Snead failed to win a single one.

In making another biblical reference to the match, golf columnist Ralph Trost, while harshly overlooking the fact that Snead shot even par for the match, could barely contain himself as he described Sam's despondency: "Through all this Sam, who had been a relentless golfer for six days, evidently rested on the seventh and appeared the stooge, the guy who went around to make it look like a contest."

Runyan reached the tee of the day's twenty-ninth hole, the 369-yard par-four eleventh, with an eight-up lead. The crowd could sense what was likely to happen. Unless Snead won the hole, the match would be over. Eleven was a dogleg left that played over a ridge that ran through the middle of Shawnee Island. Jack Patroni, Shawnee's resident pro in 1938, wrote in the tournament program that it was his favorite hole. The hole no longer exists today, not since another Shawnee rerouting decades after the 1938 PGA made space for more golf holes on Shawnee Island. But if you know where to look on the west side of the island, you can still make out the remnants of the old green pad, adjacent to a fairway bunker on a present-day hole.

Runyan drove it 240 yards off the tee, Snead more than 280. As the players marched down the fairway and the crowd gathered around the hole to find a good vantage point, a spectator, running toward the green, stepped on Snead's ball, nearly embedding it, according to one report. PGA president George Jacobus, the match referee, allowed Snead to take a drop without penalty.

"They think I'm going to win this match doing something like that," Snead joked, forcing a smile.

Runyan's second shot found the green, eighteen feet away from the hole. Snead grabbed a seven-iron. "Well, I'll see if I can get this one up there and win a hole for a change, anyway," he said to nobody in particular. He hit a fine shot that finished seven feet away.

Runyan rolled his first putt close to the hole. When Snead missed his birdie, Runyan only had to hole out from a few feet for par to end the match. He settled into his bent-over putting stance. Snead watched from a few paces away, his left hand on his hip. Spectators gathered around the green, some of them even a few steps onto the putting surface.

When Runyan made the putt to close out the match, he immediately looked toward Snead, extending his right hand for a moment of sportsmanship. Dozens of spectators rushed onto the green, and a few of the most excited ones, all men in their late teens or early twenties, darted toward the hole to see who could be the one to grab Runyan's golf ball. They ran so fast that Runyan stood no chance of saving it.

Paul Runyan was once again a major champion, having beaten the game's best player by a margin so convincing that nobody could call him lucky or his play fluky. He had played twenty-nine holes that day at Shawnee in eight under par, and his 8-and-7 margin of victory was the most lopsided in the history of the PGA Championship. In 196 holes of tournament play that week at Shawnee Country Club, Runyan had shot twenty-four under par.

When asked to summarize his own destruction in the immediate moments after the match, Snead, whose sweet southern voice typically spooned out his words like molasses, was stunned, his voice reduced to a soft murmur.

All he could manage to say was, "Lawdy, the man ain't human."

9

No Days Off

"On the 29th, White Plains licked White Sulphur."

Those words were used to describe the climax of the Runyan/Snead match in Time *magazine a week after the* PGA *Championship. The article, titled "Little Poison," was all of five hundred words and introduced Runyan to the average American, describing the champion as a "hobgoblin even more terrifying" than the nerves a player faced in match play. The "wispy, 135-lb. colleague affectionately known as 'Little Poison'" used "deadly potions of accuracy and control" to whip six of professional golf's best players, including Snead, "the biggest titan of them all."*

And what of Gene Sarazen, Denny Shute, Ralph Guldahl, and other betting favorites? "All agreed that they were just as well pleased that they had not lasted until the final round."

Hyperbole? Sure, maybe a little. But this was becoming Runyan's reputation. He was so proficient at his style of golf—short-hitting, accurate iron play, deadly chipping and putting—that he could break his opponents' spirit. Many of the world's best golfers preferred avoiding him altogether over risking the embarrassment of suffering a head-to-head loss like Snead's.

Runyan latched onto this and used it to his advantage. "I've taken some pleasure out of being the little guy who has beaten the big fellows," he said once—more than once, actually. "At match play, don't think that isn't an advantage, because a big guy would rather lose to a big guy."

THE WALK BACK. It's unique to match play. In stroke play, you finish your round on the eighteenth hole, or sometimes the ninth, which typically places you smack dab at the clubhouse, or near it anyway. Not always so in match play. Frequently matches end in far-off spots on the golf course. In the case of Runyan's decisive victory in the finals of the 1938 PGA Championship, the eleventh green at Shawnee Country Club—while hardly the far end of the property—left him a significant distance from the Buckwood Inn. As the crow flies, it's roughly 915 yards from the eleventh green to the footbridge that crosses the Binniekill. That bridge adds another 100 yards, and then it's a smooth 425-yard walk to the golf shop, located in the lower level of the Buckwood Inn.

That's a total distance of 4,320 feet, give or take. More than three-quarters of a mile. It was a hike. And for Sam Snead, still feeling the fresh sting of Runyan's bite marks, that walk had to have been pure agony. It must have made those late-night adolescent walks home from the drugstore where he worked, through the dense Virginia woods full of bears and snakes and other dangerous wildlife, seem like child's play. If he had been offered the chance to be dragged to the clubhouse solemnly through the Delaware River in a body bag, away from the feverish throng of spectators, he might have taken it.

As for Paul Runyan, did he even notice the walk at all? At one point, the fedora-wearing standard-bearer who'd been following the match let Runyan carry his sign, which identified the final margin of victory: RUNYAN 8 UP. Runyan cradled his putter underneath his left armpit and raised the sign over his head. Dozens of spectators, nearly all of them male, gathered around him and walked alongside, each smiling as wide as Runyan was. There were a couple of teenage boys wearing short-sleeve shirts, their sleeves rolled up like James Dean's. Grown men in neckties were part of the throng. So was a man with a small camera, who stepped in front of a press photographer to snap his own keepsake photo. Did these people realize that the shellacking they had just witnessed had been a once-in-a-generation golf upset? And what of the folks who had wagered money on Snead? Where were they? Speaking of wagering, where was Jack Doyle? Or the other bookmakers who'd been roaming around Shawnee all week? And how about those faithful few who had taken a flier on Runyan at such long odds? Had they hotfooted it back over the Binniekill to collect? Did any one of them, suddenly flush with cash, start a tab in the bar of the Buckwood Inn?

Reporter Walter McCallum caught up with an exasperated Jack

Doyle a week later, after the dust had settled at Shawnee. Turns out, Doyle had left town before the final match between Runyan and Snead. Just to show there were no hard feelings, he sent Runyan a telegram on the morning of the finals. He wrote, "If my rooting helps you are already in good luck, Jack Doyle."

McCallum described the week at Shawnee as a "fiasco" for Doyle, asserting that there was little to be gained for bookmakers in the gentlemanly but fickle world of professional golf.

"Golf is peanuts," Doyle told McCallum. "I don't think I'll try it anymore. It's peanut money. It's hardly worth fooling with."

WHEN HE GOT back to the clubhouse, Runyan found Joan sitting on a bench. She wore a light-colored dress, high heels, and a bow in her hair. He leaned over the edge of the bench and planted a kiss on her lips. Then, with the standard visible behind them, Runyan grabbed his wife in a bear hug and lifted her a few inches off the ground, posing for a nearby photographer. With an embarrassed look on her face, you can imagine her saying, "All right, Paul, that's enough. Put me down!"

Bob Brumby wrote, "Runyan's pretty wife, Joan, must have thought she had married an angel, so perfect was her ever-loving husband today."

That angel could be a ruthless gentleman warrior. "The new champion is one of the nicest little guys you ever would wish to meet," wrote Charles Bartlett in the *Chicago Tribune*. "He is soft voiced, sharp minded, and his manners have made him known throughout the game as a little Lord Chesterfield. At the same time, he is such a deliberate, calculating party on a golf lot that his competitive name is Little Poison."

PGA president George Jacobus put on a sport coat to present the Wanamaker Trophy to Runyan. For the victory, he made $1,100. Snead took home $600 in second-place money. Having removed his necktie and loosened the top button of his shirt, Snead reached around Runyan's left shoulder and removed the lid of the trophy for a peek inside. Was he looking for the prize money?

Jacobus thanked the Philadelphia Section of the PGA. He congratulated Shawnee president Arthur Brown and the club's professionals, complimenting them for the week's near-perfect playing conditions. Then Jacobus presented Runyan the trophy and the winner's check.

"Shall I hand you this check, Paul, or shall I give it to Mrs. Runyan?" he asked.

"You might as well allow me to hold it for a minute, George," Runyan quipped, by now familiar with this routine. "Mrs. Runyan will get it eventually."

Then Jacobus gave Snead his runner-up prize. "You shouldn't feel downhearted, Sam," he said. "This is only your second year in the championship competition. Your time will come later, without doubt."

Snead shook his head. "That's just what you told me last year when I was runner-up at Detroit."

At every turn, Snead was gracious toward Runyan and with the press. He shook hands, faked a smile for pictures, and answered questions as best he could—even if he was still staggering in disbelief at what had just happened.

Snead was hardly alone.

"I still don't believe it," Runyan confessed to a reporter, one of the first to ask him a question. After some thought, he offered a more substantive analysis.

Runyan: "I was very much surprised that Sam should be so much off his game after the fine golf he'd been playing all week. Perhaps it was because he'd gone into the match feeling that he could wear me down by out-hitting me off the tees. But as it turned out that wasn't much of an advantage, because I could get home just as well as he could on every hole but the 567-yard seventh, and he couldn't reach that in two, either."

Decades later, in an interview with Al Barkow, Runyan proffered an empathetic but direct take on the match—and Snead. "I think he was the best sport under the circumstances," Runyan said. "It must have been one of most galling experiences of his life. Got to have been. Because he drove it bullet straight."

For Runyan, who was always a short hitter, playing alongside a stronger player was just business as usual. "His length didn't bother me, because I was the shortest hitter in the annals of golf to be as successful as I was."

Barkow spent time with Snead later in life and sensed that any embarrassment Snead felt over the defeat had been short-lived. "He just took it," Barkow said. "Sam got beat, you know. He didn't play well, and Paul played very well, but Sam didn't take it like a U.S. Open loss. He just got beat by the little guy."

IF YOU HAPPENED to stroll by the practice tee at Metropolis Country Club in suburban White Plains, New York, on Sunday, July 17, and noticed a familiar figure on the end of the range, you might have been tempted to rub your eyes, certain you were seeing a ghost. There, giving golf lessons, was the club's teaching professional, Paul Runyan, the guy you had just read about in the morning newspaper while you sat at your kitchen table in your bathrobe and sipped your morning coffee.

Less than a full day removed from his greatest professional triumph, $1,100 richer and incalculably more famous, at least in golf circles, Runyan went back to work at Metropolis like he would have on any other Sunday morning. If there ever was an opportunity to have a captive audience of students, this was it. Did he bring the Wanamaker Trophy with him that day, to put on display in the golf shop for all to see? It's easy to imagine.

Maybe Runyan went right back to work to try to feel normal after what must have been a whirlwind twenty-four hours. The *Arkansas Gazette* reported that Runyan had been flooded with telegrams from his old friends in Arkansas, congratulating him on his triumph. No doubt his parents, Walter and Mamie, had taken a few bows back in Arkansas on behalf of their son.

The congratulatory notes came in from all over. The first to arrive, just minutes after the final putt had dropped, was from golf writer O. B. Keeler, who'd made a career out of covering the great Bobby Jones. Others who wrote included Bobby Cruickshank; Horton Smith and his wife, Barbara; Mannie Dias and Edmund Waterman from White Plains; his old Little Rock pal Harry Tenenbaum and family; the Carey salt-tycoon family from Hutchinson, Kansas; the club secretary of Forest Hill in New Jersey; the entire membership of Palma Ceia Golf Club in Florida; and many other friends from around the country.

Golf writer Herb Graffis, while simultaneously pitching Runyan to play the following week's Chicago Open, called him a "mitey monarch of the links" and described his victory as "Napoleonic."

Milton B. Reach, a vice president of Spalding, wrote to congratulate Runyan and referenced David's slingshot-aided takedown of Goliath. "When the bonus check for this event comes to me for signature I can assure you it will be signed with an Amen of praise," he wrote.

Snead headed west. He would compete the following week in the Chicago Open, played at Olympia Fields. There he would find redemption. He shot a course-record 64 on the No. 1 course and closed with rounds of 73-70 on the No. 4 course to take the title by a shot over Ralph Guldahl.

The *Chicago Tribune* ran a photo of Snead the following Monday. He's shown standing in between low amateur Wilford Wehrle and Dick Metz, who finished third. Snead's wearing a nearly identical outfit to the one he wore the week before in the finals at Shawnee: long-sleeve shirt, tie tucked in between his second and third buttons, tam-o'-shanter cap. He removed his cap when the picture was snapped. He raised his right hand to salute the Chicago crowd and directed his eyes skyward, as if to thank a higher power for granting him a quick end to his golfing nightmare. But the credit really went to Snead himself, for not sulking and for immediately getting back to the business of winning golf tournaments. As he was learning—and as Paul Runyan already knew—in professional golf there were no days off.

1. Paul Runyan, pictured at Concordia Country Club in Little Rock, Arkansas, got his start in golf as a caddie and apprentice to Jimmy Norton, the professional at Hot Springs Golf and Country Club. Courtesy of Jeff Runyan.

2. Walter and Mamie Runyan, Paul's parents, worked a series of odd jobs when their boys were young. Eventually, Walter established himself as a dairy farmer in Hot Springs. Garland County Historical Society.

3. In its earliest days Hot Springs Golf and Country Club had a sand-green golf course. Garland County Historical Society.

4. Paul Runyan met Joan Harris while sprinting through the golf shop at Concordia Country Club and knocking her over. Shortly thereafter, they were married. Courtesy of Jeff Runyan.

5. Runyan's victory at the 1930 North and South Open at Pinehurst surprised everybody, including himself. Courtesy of Jeff Runyan.

6. Self-taught Sam Snead was mostly unknown until he burst onto the professional golf scene in 1937. New York Times Co./Archive Photos via Getty Images.

7. Moments after winning the 1933 Agua Caliente Open in Mexico, Paul and Joan Runyan were presented with a wheelbarrow full of silver dollars that totaled $1,500. Courtesy of Jeff Runyan.

8. Amateur sensation Johnny Goodman (*left*) and prickly pro Gene Sarazen (*second from left, wearing bow tie*) turned up at the trophy ceremony when Runyan won the 1933 Florida All-Year-Round Open at the Miami Biltmore. Bettmann via Getty Images.

9. The 1933 U.S. Ryder Cup team. *From left to right*: Horton Smith, Gene Sarazen, Craig Wood, Paul Runyan, Walter Hagen, Olin Dutra, Denny Shute, Leo Diegel, Billy Burke, and Ed Dudley. Walter Hagen Jr., who traveled with the team, is kneeling in front. Historic Golf Photos, the Ron Watts Collection.

10. On land or sea, the Runyans were a well-liked couple in professional golf circles and known for their love of dancing. Courtesy of Jeff Runyan.

11. When golf legend Bobby Jones hosted the first Masters Tournament, in 1934, he was paired with Paul Runyan for the first two rounds. Bettmann via Getty Images.

12. Paul Runyan, shown staring down an iron shot, partnered with Horton Smith to win the 1933 International Four-Ball in Miami. The following year, they lost to Al Espinosa and Denny Shute on the final hole of the championship match, despite a furious rally. Courtesy of Jeff Runyan.

13. While traveling to Australia in 1934 on the *Mariposa*, Runyan made the acquaintance of actor Spencer Tracy (*second from right*) and his brother Carroll (*far left*). Courtesy of Jeff Runyan.

14. Caddies at Quaker Ridge Golf Club rewarded Paul Runyan with a ride atop their shoulders after his course-record 67 in the second round of the 1936 Metropolitan Open. Bettmann via Getty Images.

15. Paul Runyan, shown arriving by train in Pasadena, California, in 1937, saw much of the world in the 1930s, and his suitcase and golf bag showed the wear and tear to prove it. Courtesy of Jeff Runyan.

16. Joan Runyan was always elegantly dressed when she watched her husband compete at golf tournaments, and she made sure he looked just as neat. Courtesy of Jeff Runyan.

17. Harry Tenenbaum (*right*) played countless rounds with Paul Runyan at Concordia Country Club in Little Rock before Runyan achieved stardom in professional golf. They're pictured here in 1938 with Ralph Schwartz (*left*). Courtesy of Jeff Runyan.

18. Shawnee Country Club was A. W. Tillinghast's first course design, and in 1938 it hosted the PGA Championship with the adjoining Buckwood Inn. Shawnee Inn and Golf Resort.

19. Not even an ankle-deep water hazard at Shawnee Country Club could keep Sam Snead from steamrolling into the finals of the 1938 PGA Championship. AP Photo.

20. With a large crowd gathered around the fourth green at Shawnee Country Club and Sam Snead in close for birdie, Runyan holed this twenty-five-foot putt to halve the hole. Bettmann via Getty Images.

21. Sam Snead (*right*) was gracious in defeat, shaking Paul Runyan's hand and smiling for photographers. Bettmann via Getty Images.

22. After defeating Sam Snead, a joyful Paul Runyan, carrying the sign, walked back to the Buckwood Inn surrounded by elated spectators, opportunistic photographers, and stunned sportswriters. Bettmann via Getty Images.

23. During his time in the navy during World War II, Runyan befriended prominent amateur golfer Johnny Fischer (*right*). Courtesy of John Fischer.

24. Paul Runyan, pictured at the 1947 Pasadena Open, stepped away from full-time professional golf for five years after the war, playing a reduced tournament schedule. Courtesy of Jeff Runyan.

25. The Runyan family. *From left to right*: Joan, Paul Jr., Jeffrey, and Paul. Courtesy of Jeff Runyan.

26. Dapper golf shop assistant Jack Taylor (*second from left*) became one of Paul Runyan's most trusted friends during the second half of his career. Courtesy of Jeff Runyan.

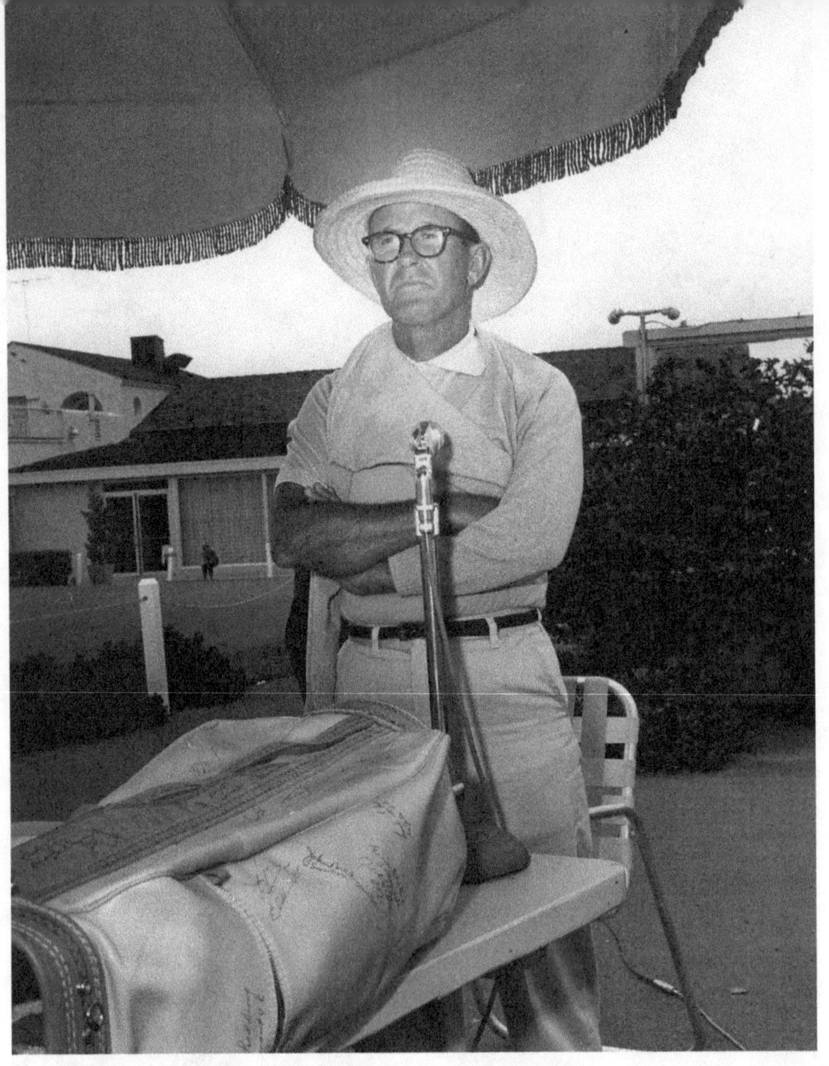

27. At La Jolla Country Club, Runyan handled every imaginable club pro duty, including starting groups off the first tee. Courtesy of Jeff Runyan.

28. Runyan doubled down on his competitive aspirations in the 1960s, twice winning the PGA Seniors' Championship and the World Seniors' Championship. Courtesy of Jeff Runyan.

29. Following Joan's death, Runyan married Berniece Harbers in July 1983. Courtesy of Jeff Runyan.

30. Jeff Runyan (*left*) caddied for his dad (*right*) during the final years of his playing career as a senior golfer. Courtesy of Jeff Runyan.

PART 4

Go West

10

"Whatever Became of Paul Runyan?"

When war broke out, golf found itself in a tight spot. So did the men and women who played the game. A casual stroll around a golf course could do wonders to calm a person's nerves. For a few hours you could forget about real-world tensions and focus on your backswing or your putting stroke or fret about the speed of the greens. But couldn't a leisure pursuit such as golf, especially in a time of uncertainty, seem unpatriotic, tone deaf? That worry was on the minds of many golfers before government and golf officials stepped in and said no—it's okay—play on, if you can. Golf, they claimed, was good for your mental and physical health and thus good for the war effort.

The game's next big hurdle was supplying its constituency. A national rubber crisis put golf balls in short supply. They became so scarce, a rumor circulated through the professional ranks that tournament players were going to be allowed a full ten minutes to search for a lost ball instead of five. Of course, this was only a rumor. The PGA *entered into an agreement with a company that specialized in golf ball salvage and offered to dredge up water hazards from coast to coast. Then they would sell their treasures—some of which had been submerged in water for a decade or more—to golf clubs around the country, who would in turn sell them to golfers, who would put them into play. The Red Cross organized golf club drives to piece together starter sets for the troops. Golf would not go down in America without a fight.*

And for professionals like Paul Runyan and Sam Snead and countless others, not to forget entertainers such as Bing Crosby and Bob Hope, golf would serve a higher purpose—to entertain and inspire. The competitive circuit would take its lumps but find a way to survive. And the game in general would do its country a much-needed service.

PAUL RUNYAN WAS not ready to close the book on 1938. In early October, he and Jug McSpaden headed for South America. They left Newark for Miami via Eastern Airlines, then the following day boarded a Pan Am flight for Argentina. Together they would play tournaments in Argentina, Brazil, and Puerto Rico.

Buenos Aires was especially kind to Runyan. On the same day that Seabiscuit and War Admiral made final preparations for their much-anticipated match race at Baltimore's Pimlico Race Course, Runyan captured the Argentine Open by shooting a seventy-two-hole score of 282, good enough for a one-stroke victory over two local professionals. He was paid 1,500 Argentine pesos for the win, equivalent to $385 in the late 1930s.

That Sunday, October 30, 1938, author and filmmaker Orson Welles caused a national panic when his "War of the Worlds" radio broadcast caused some listeners to believe that a Martian invasion was under way on American soil. A day later Welles told reporters that neither he nor anyone else involved with the broadcast believed the episode would cause such an uproar. Frayed nerves caused by a near decade-long global economic depression were no help.

Runyan rounded off his South American tour by advancing to the semifinals of the South American Masters Tournament. The exhibition matches proved not as successful for Runyan and McSpaden, at least in Runyan's eyes. "Won two, lost two, and tied the rest," he explained to a newspaper reporter.

While Runyan may have landed the heaviest punch of the 1938 golf season with his 8-and-7 runaway over Sam Snead at the PGA Championship, it was Snead who had the most impressive season of anyone in professional golf. He earned what was then the all-time record in single-season prize money, $19,534, and was awarded the Vardon Trophy. Runyan brought home $7,550 and finished fifth on the money list and second for the Vardon award.

Back on native soil, Runyan stopped in Memphis, Tennessee, in late January 1939 on his way to spend a few days visiting his parents in Hot Springs, Arkansas, before making his way down to San Antonio for the Texas Open. While in Memphis, he granted an interview to reporter David Bloom, and the *Commercial Appeal* ran a photo of Runyan, leaning against his golf bag, wearing a topcoat and hat, with a book cradled under his left arm. Nothing Bloom reported was especially insightful to someone who followed pro golf (or Runyan) closely. It was mostly a get-to-know-ya story for his Memphis readership, with Runyan discussing his views on match play versus medal play, life on the competitive winter circuit, and his recent South American trip. However, he made one reference to his play at the PGA Championship at Shawnee that should not be overlooked; it seems that the passage of time had caused him to reflect on his play in Pennsylvania the previous July, a task that had simply seemed too big in the moments after his stunning upset over Snead.

"When I beat Snead in the PGA," he told Bloom, "that was the best golf I ever played in all my life. I was simply right."

Knowing that his best golf was good enough to thoroughly annihilate one of the most talented golfers of all time must have made Runyan feel satisfied. As he looked forward on his career, it's possible—having set the standard for his personal best—that he asked himself some questions, such as: Can I ever play like that again? And how can I do it more often at golf's biggest events?

Unfortunately, Runyan's window for seeking out those answers and trying to apply them in tournament play, at least in the short term, would be closing faster than he or anyone could ever have imagined, thanks to larger forces in the world that would disrupt pro golf and sports in general.

RUNYAN CONTINUED TO be a factor in professional golf as the 1930s came to a close. From 1939 through 1941, he notched six top-twenty finishes in major championships, including four top-tens. (He continued opting out of the Open Championship, as had been his practice since he missed the cut in 1933.) Those finishes were highlighted by a couple of quarterfinal appearances at the PGA Championship, a fifth-place finish at the 1941 U.S. Open, and a tie for twelfth at the 1940 Masters. Runyan's record during the first nine renditions of the Masters was remarkable, particularly on a golf course that he felt—and most agreed—favored a long hitter. In those nine Masters he recorded five top-tens and never finished lower than thirty-fifth place.

Runyan ended a three-year winless drought in May 1941 with his victory over Gene Sarazen at the Goodall Round Robin. He played that week with a new putter, described in one newspaper as "a putter with a square piece of wood for a handle." Another publication called the putter a "monstrosity" and likened its handle to "a sawed off fence picket." It was a new model, a Bristol Built from Horton Manufacturing in Bristol, Connecticut, that utilized a paddle grip. Runyan had apparently served as a consultant on the project. In fact, Runyan's collaboration with Bristol went through the bag. For the 1939–40 golf season, he had helped develop a set of Paul Runyan woods, Runyan Pyramid irons, and three styles of "Little Poison" putters for the company.

As for the paddle-grip putter, sometimes Runyan took his grip with his hands close together, and other times he separated his hands on the grip by as much as six inches. (Ultimately, Runyan's experiment with the paddle-grip putter would be short-lived, but he continued to explore the effect of separating his hands on the grip.)

Golf media hailed the Goodall win as a victory for the average duffer, whose short-hitting conquering hero, with a swing just as unorthodox as theirs, had once again vanquished the game's biggest names. The following day Runyan was back on the golf course, trying to lock up a qualifying spot in the upcoming U.S. Open, which would be played at Colonial Country Club in Fort Worth, Texas. (He would qualify and finish fifth.)

On Sunday, December 7, 1941, Runyan was on a golf course in Miami, playing alongside Harry Cooper in preparation for the upcoming Miami Open at Miami Springs, when a caddie passed along word of the surprise Japanese attack that had taken place that morning at the U.S. naval base at Pearl Harbor, Hawaii. The group was stunned by the news.

Cooper expressed his shock over the attack, then tried to lighten the moment with humor. "Every one of them should be forced to play this course for a month just for punishment."

Just like that, the United States was directly involved in World War II. In some corners of the sports world, the reaction to the news was swift. Baseball slugger Hank Greenberg, the 1940 American League

Most Valuable Player, pledged to reenter the army within a few days of the attack at Pearl. Hard-throwing pitcher Bob Feller quickly applied for enlistment into the navy.

What would happen to golf? The short answer was a little bit of everything. Some players would join the service and disappear for the duration of the war. Others would play sparingly, whenever they could arrange a long-enough furlough. Byron Nelson, who was kept out of the service due to a blood disorder, maintained a busy slate of exhibition matches and tournaments. Some tournaments would continue on, with organizers patching fields together as best they could, often at the last minute. Others were canceled entirely. The Open Championship, which would have been impossible to stage in the European theater of the war, was halted in 1940 and wouldn't resume until 1946. At Turnberry, Scotland, the hotel adjacent to the golf courses was used as a hospital, while the courses were flattened for use as a Royal Air Force (RAF) landing strip.

The Masters was played in 1942, and Paul Runyan, playing with a sore shoulder, grabbed the early lead with a five-under-par 67 in the opening round, on his way to finishing third behind Byron Nelson and Ben Hogan.

A few days after the tournament, Augusta National chairman Clifford Roberts wrote Runyan a letter complimenting him on his fine play at the Masters and acknowledging his strong record since the tournament's inception. He noted that Runyan's cumulative score since the first Masters in 1934 was unmatched, nudging out the likes of Ed Dudley and Craig Wood.

"I want to congratulate you on your fine record in this tournament and also want to express the hope that we can some day put your name as a winner on one of our plaques," Roberts wrote.

When he received the letter, Runyan pulled out a golf pencil and tabulated his scores (286 in 1934, 289 in 1935, and so on), just to double-check Roberts's arithmetic.

The following spring, there was no Masters. A herd of cattle, reported as one hundred head, grazed the property, and a fence had been erected to keep them out of the clubhouse. Only a caretaker was on site to keep an eye on things. The Forest Hills hotel, where Gene Sarazen and other veteran players had regularly held court, was taken over by the army and used as a hospital. Augusta National founder Bobby Jones, by then forty years old, had volunteered for military service and was away. He went ashore at Normandy a day after the D-Day invasion, and his unit was assigned to the infantry, where Jones spent time interrogating German prisoners of war before his 1944 discharge as a lieutenant colonel. The Masters would remain on hiatus until 1946.

When gasoline rationing took effect, Runyan got rid of his six-wheel Buick, which had more than one hundred thousand miles on it. The car had been a trusted friend and had needed only minor repairs. But he saw no need to keep it.

Sam Snead's manager Fred Corcoran, still overseeing weekly tournaments on the professional circuit, proposed a ten-man team match between the leading pros in the service and those who were civilians. The match could benefit the Red Cross and would function much like the Ryder Cup, Corcoran figured. Of those leading pros in the service, Dutch Harrison was serving as an air sergeant in North Carolina; that's also where Lieutenant Horton Smith had been assigned. Ben Hogan was stationed with the air corps in Texas, Lawson Little was stationed at a base in Kansas, and Jimmy Thomson was in San Diego with the coast guard. Eventually Snead would land in San Diego, too.

Corcoran was forced to examine golf's big picture when it came to the game's place during wartime. John Kelly, the assistant director of civilian defense in charge of physical fitness—and himself a golfer—sought to introduce the game to the hundreds of millions of Americans who would not be joining the armed forces, if for no other reason than physical fitness. Kelly hired Corcoran as his golf deputy, which was a new, specially created position. Dreaming up ten-on-ten exhibition matches was part of his job description. So was encouraging regular Joes and Janes to play the game for exercise or as a diversion. The real trick was finding a way to use the former (tour pros) to influence the latter (average Americans) and somehow help the war effort. That's where Corcoran's knack for promotions proved its worth.

Corcoran and Kelly conjured up the Hale America series of tournaments, with proceeds benefiting the Navy Relief Society and the USO. In 1942 Runyan played in the Hale America National Open, a sort of substitute for the U.S. Open, at Ridgemoor Country Club in Chicago. Ben Hogan won the title by three shots with an un-Open-like seventeen-under-par total of 271. Runyan finished well back with a 288 total. After his first-round 72, an openly disgusted Runyan lamented that any accomplished player who knew the golf course and couldn't break 70 should be shot. A short while later, a car backfired in the parking lot at Ridgemoor, prompting trick-shot artist Jack Redmond to crack, "There goes Runyan. He's destroyed himself."

Runyan's wartime destination would be the U.S. Navy. The Associated Press reported in December 1942 that Runyan had enlisted as a seaman first class and would be assigned to physical training under Lieutenant Commander Gene Tunney, the former heavyweight champion, who had accepted a commission to set up a physical fitness program for student pilots. Runyan and Tunney shared some history. One winter back in the 1930s they had partnered up at the Seminole Pro-Am. On the first hole, Tunney hit a 310-yard drive and stuck his approach a foot and a half from the hole. Runyan was in awe and started to think that he and Tunney would be an unbeatable duo. Then he watched Tunney jab that short putt eighteen feet past the hole. Tunney may have been a technical genius in the boxing ring, but it was a different story on the golf course.

The Runyans were no strangers to the navy. Paul's brother Elmo had been in the navy for nearly two decades and had been standing on the flight deck of the USS *Wasp*, a 741-foot-long aircraft carrier, when the Japanese torpedoed the ship while it was transporting reinforcements to Guadalcanal on September 15, 1942. Elmo had just gotten out of an aircraft he had been flying in for some four hours. The force of the explosions sent men and equipment flying around the deck of the carrier. Aircraft that were suspended overhead came crashing down on the hangar deck. Countless men suffered painful burns and life-threatening injuries, but still they fought to save the *Wasp*. Lieutenant Runyan went to his battle station on the hangar deck as assistant damage control officer and helped fight the fire. Eventually, orders were given to abandon ship, and Runyan was among the last forty men to enter the water and await rescue; that, too, was a dangerous proposition. Sharks were circling the area near the *Wasp* until servicemen on the destroyer that arrived to aid the rescue started picking them off with rifles.

More than 194 people were killed or went missing during the attack. The *Wasp* sank that night, about seven hours after the attack began. In January 2019 its wreckage was discovered by the research vessel *Petrel* at the bottom of the Coral Sea off the coast of Australia.

Back home in the United States following the sinking, Lieutenant Runyan, his wife (Margaret), and their son (Thorne)—who would one day become a navy man himself—retreated to Hot Springs for a few weeks on leave. About that time, news broke that Elmo's more famous younger brother would be joining the navy.

It's hard to know what effect military service had on Paul Runyan the golfer. He found plenty of time to practice and competed sporadically—not often—but it's a difficult task to quantify how the disruption of the war affected the quality of his golf. Certainly it interrupted his playing schedule, to which he had bound himself for more than a decade. When he did turn up to compete in a professional tournament during the war, it usually made news. Most pretournament newspaper columns included a list of the big-name players who would be competing and those who were absent, plus an acknowledgment of how much money in war bonds the players would be competing for that week.

One newspaper ran a photograph of Runyan jumping on the back of another navy man, who was lying face down on a table, with a handful of chief petty officers gathered around observing. Supposedly Runyan was demonstrating artificial respiration, even if it looked more like a reenactment of professional wrestling. Based on the photograph, it seemed that Runyan still maintained a spirited attitude.

In early 1943 Runyan was assigned to the naval training station in Norfolk, Virginia, where he would spend the majority of his time during the war. He pleaded for sea duty, but he remained in Norfolk in the Fifth Naval District's recreation program. The navy restricted his outside tournament play to liberty time, which effectively ended his prospects of playing seventy-two-hole tournaments. Most of his competitive golf would thus be limited to weekends and military exhibitions. His days were spent teaching physical education and giving golf lessons to troops. Joan Runyan, while her husband was busy demonstrating artificial respiration and proper chipping technique to sailors, worked at a Norfolk book shop.

If you were an athlete, Norfolk seemed like the best possible duty station to hang your hat. Some called it the "sports capital of the South." From the world of baseball, Bob Feller, Phil Rizzuto, and Pee Wee Reese had all been assigned to Norfolk. Quarterback Ace Parker and fullback Joe Maniaci also called Norfolk home. And in golf, Runyan was joined by Chandler Harper, top amateur Johnny Fischer, and Sam Snead.

The story of Snead's induction into the navy is worth revisiting. In the summer of 1942 he was in Washington DC, waiting in line to be sworn in, when he said to one of the seamen in charge, "Hey, what's the chances of me skipping this one and doing it next week? They're having the PGA Championship over in New Jersey, just below Atlantic City."

He must have asked the right guy.

"One of the scrambled eggs said, 'Why don't you go ahead and get inducted, and they'll probably let you go,'" Snead said in a retelling of the incident.

Then the man asked him what the tournament would be worth, in dollars.

"It'd be $2,000 if I win plus $2,000 from Wilson Sporting Goods, who I represent," Snead said.

The seaman told Snead to call the draft board and explain that he'd taken his physical and ask if he could be inducted the following Monday so he could play in the tournament. Snead did as he was told, the navy agreed to the plan, and Snead went out and won the PGA Championship at Seaview Country Club with a 2-and-1 victory over Jim Turnesa. It was Slammin' Sammy's first major championship. Snead later recalled the victory as "the one I enjoyed the most."

IN NORFOLK, RUNYAN became especially close with Johnny Fischer, one of the country's top amateur golfers. Fischer, the 1932 NCAA individual champion and three-time Big 10 Conference champion at the University of Michigan, had won the 1936 U.S. Amateur Championship and was a regular competitor in the Walker Cup Matches. When Fischer became a father in 1943, he asked Runyan to be godfather to his son, who was also named John.

Together Runyan, Fischer, Harper, and Snead became the core of the Norfolk navy golf team, which played exhibition matches to help raise money for various war-related causes, including the Red Cross and the Navy Relief Fund.

"Even in the middle of the war, they set up matches to entertain troops and give them something to do," said John Fischer, Runyan's godson, who grew up to become a lawyer and a golf historian. "They had a lot of athletic events. They had baseball teams, football teams, all composed of service members. I have a letter my father wrote to one of the people in the law firm where he worked, and that letter listed the Norfolk baseball team. They had what looked like an all-star lineup."

Despite being an amateur in the company of professionals, thirty-year-old Fischer fit in well around Snead, Runyan, and Harper. He was quiet, but his golf game spoke volumes, and the pros respected his ability. Years after the war, Fischer, who made it a habit to travel regularly to some of golf's biggest events, whether he was competing or not, would often visit Augusta for the Masters and seek out Snead. Several times he traveled to the Greenbrier to play with Snead. And he kept in regular contact with Runyan.

"My father played in a lot of tournaments," said John Fischer. "He played the Western Open all the time, several U.S. Opens, the Cleveland Open. Because it was during the Depression he could only afford to play in a couple big tournaments each year. And all the other players were there, too. The Sneads and Runyans were playing in those events. We had a great tournament here in Cincinnati called the U.S. Pro-Am, where they paired touring pros and top amateur players from around the country in a thirty-six-hole, two-day pro-am that had a purse that was similar to what tournament purses were. Tommy Bolt was my dad's partner. He stayed at my parents' house when he came to play. Tommy Bolt was a club thrower, and my dad would never throw a club or anything. The worst he would say was, 'Oh nuts.' But they got along famously. He couldn't stop laughing when he was around Tommy Bolt."

Due to the regimented nature of life on a military installation, sometimes the Norfolk golfers had to sneak in their rounds at daybreak to allow adequate time for their required duties. Fischer, who began his navy stint as a physical education instructor, received a commission and became a navy lawyer, prosecuting soldiers who had gone AWOL or demonstrated unbecoming conduct. "I can't believe that," his son John said, "because it didn't seem like his personality."

The navy commission further complicated Fischer's practice schedule. "It wasn't like there was extra time," his son said.

Whenever he needed help with his putting, he went to Runyan. Fischer had always been known as an excellent putter, but he had never seen a better putter than Runyan. Fischer used a wristy pop stroke. Runyan preferred a pendulum motion governed by the big muscles. Even after watching him and observing his technique up close, Fischer was never quite sure what magical ingredients made Runyan's recipe work. It just worked.

Fischer was hardly the only man in Norfolk to seek out Runyan for golf advice. When he wasn't teaching conventional physical education (or doing other navy stuff, like taking his turn as a traffic cop, pulling over speeding Norfolk motorists), Runyan could usually be found on the practice tee, giving golf lessons. The driving range at Norfolk faced due north, which meant that Runyan looked to the west—and into the sunshine—all afternoon long.

"By the time night comes, if I can see at all I don't believe it," he joked to a reporter while on leave. "I think it's a mirage."

The reporter asked him if there was anything he could do to avoid getting crow's feet. Sunglasses perhaps? A visor?

"Nothing can help me much," Runyan said with a squint. "Nothing but a navy full of left-handers. They can look west while I look east. How marvelous that'd be."

On May 23, 1944, the Norfolk golf team traveled to Bainbridge, Maryland, to play the Bainbridge naval team, which was led by Texan Jimmy Demaret, winner of the 1940 Masters. Runyan shot 69 in his match, but it wasn't enough to overcome Demaret's 66, and the Bainbridge team won the contest. (A year later, Runyan and Chandler Harper would play Ed "Porky" Oliver and Jack Isaacs, who were representing the army, at James River Country Club in front of a crowd of three hundred people. Runyan was the low man, shooting 73. After the exhibition, players and spectators alike bought war bonds, which were available at special booths set up around the course.)

Exhibitions like these sometimes made the newspapers, albeit in small snippets. It was difficult to gauge the quality of a player's game simply by reading an exhibition score from golf played on an unknown course against a tiny field of players. For Runyan, by then a chief petty officer, the Bainbridge event in 1944 served as a tune-up before the Red Cross Open that would be played in June at Wykagyl Country Club in New Rochelle, New York.

Byron Nelson began the week as the betting favorite, and he delivered a four-stroke victory over Vic Ghezzi. Making one of his rare competitive appearances since joining the navy, Runyan finished well back (twenty strokes behind Nelson, ten behind Sarazen, eight behind Craig Wood, and four strokes behind Tony Manero), collecting $164 for his efforts.

By late 1944, having been away from full-time competitive golf for more than two years, Runyan had started to fall off the radar. That December, during the playing of the San Francisco Open, someone in the clubhouse at Harding Park asked, "Whatever became of Paul Runyan?"

"Last I heard of him he was in the navy," said Fred Corcoran, who was waiting in the clubhouse that day. "A chief specialist. I think he was running a golf course for the navy in Virginia."

Corcoran got it mostly right. But when pressed about the state of Runyan's golf game, he kept talking, and folks in the clubhouse kept listening, including one reporter from the *San Francisco Examiner*.

"Funny thing about Paul," Corcoran continued. "He stopped winning because he lost his distance. I know—that's like saying Lefty Gomez went into a hitting slump. Paul never had any distance, so how could he lose it? But he did. He actually did."

Corcoran believed Runyan had lost the timing in his swing, and thus Runyan had lost his distance, as well as his way. Ralph Trost had noticed that Runyan seemed slightly off the mark at the Red Cross Open at Wykagyl, hitting the ball on the heel of the club and lacking distance. It wasn't much, Trost wrote, but enough to matter, especially for an already short hitter.

Was there any truth to this? It's hard to say, because Runyan had mostly been away from competition while he was in the navy. He lacked the playing résumé to put Corcoran's claims on trial. Could this have been sour grapes from Corcoran—Snead's right-hand man—over the outcome of the 1938 PGA at Shawnee? That's unlikely. Corcoran doesn't seem like the type who would have harbored any sort of resentment, certainly not six years after the fact. Even in the aftermath of the PGA, Corcoran had written a lengthy recap of Runyan's match with Snead for a PGA publication, and his writing was as fair and complimentary in its assessment of Runyan's play as could be expected from any veteran golf journalist.

That leaves two possible explanations. Perhaps, due to Runyan's absence from mainstream competitive golf during the war, Corcoran had lost touch with Runyan and was speculating based on rumor or hearsay—in effect, talking out of school. Or maybe he had watched enough of Runyan's intermittent play at Red Cross exhibitions and occasional tour stops where Runyan turned up to recognize that something *was* amiss, that Runyan wasn't the same guy. Maybe the short hitter had gotten even shorter and the magic had washed up.

SAM SNEAD, HAVING spent the latter part of his twenty-five-month hitch in the navy on the West Coast, received a special medical discharge in the fall of 1944. He was suffering from a balky back, and after leaving San Diego he headed home to White Sulphur Springs for a brief rest. Then he planned to play a few Red Cross exhibitions before reevaluating his back after medical treatment.

In July 1945 Runyan, still stationed at Norfolk, won the Virginia Open by three strokes over Paul Schindo, who had been the professional at Westchester Country Club in New York before the war. Runyan's navy pal Chandler Harper finished third. Runyan beat the field and a rain-soaked golf course with straight driving, which seldom put him in any real trouble. For a player whose game had reportedly abandoned him, he didn't play like it.

Two months later, on September 10, eight days after Japan's formal surrender, which ended World War II, Runyan was discharged from the navy. That same day, Joan gave birth to a son, Paul Jr. The new parents would head west, for Pasadena, California.

Why California and not White Plains? Or Arkansas? Or even Florida? That answer came, at least partially, on October 4, just a few weeks after his discharge. United Press International reported that Runyan was quitting pro golf to enter the world of private business. In a statement, Runyan said that he had been in professional golf "long enough."

Quitting? For what? He had just won a state open. Now he was leaving? None of it made sense.

The war had ended. Hitler was dead. So was FDR. The bombs had been dropped. The troops were coming home. The Depression was starting to become a distant memory. Americans were anxious to turn the page and begin a new era in the country's history. And Paul Runyan, the popcorn-hitting son of a dairy farmer with the unmatched putting touch who in the last fifteen years had bagged enough golfing scalps to fill a trophy room, was saying sayonara.

Poof—gone, like one of his drives—into the California sunset. Just like that.

Why was he quitting? And what was his plan?

11

La Jolla

"He was never one of those guys who said, 'Go ask your mom.' He made a decision, and it was never based in anger.

"I had a lot of freedom in La Jolla in those days. You could walk down to the beach and hang out. I'd go up and work for him in the afternoon after school, then we'd come home together. Our family always ate dinner together. We watched television together, had discussions. I understood who my dad was. I didn't badger him to be more of a father, didn't ask, 'When can we go to the beach?' He would do the things he could when he could. We went camping once or twice. There was a man named Bert Finch that had a big property up in Poway, with a stream and horses. We'd camp down by a creek. Dad had this fancy new Rambler station wagon, and he bought a bunch of gear. He was actually pretty good at the woodsman thing, because of his life on the farm with his father.

"I remember a couple times being rude to Gertye, my grandmother, and later on when my testosterone was flowing, I sassed my mother a couple of times. When I told my mother to shut up, I was about thirteen. It only happened a couple of times, because I really respected my mother and dad intensely. There was one time when Mom had gone to him and told him what I had done. At that time he was teaching my brother and me how to box. He came into my room, and he had these big fourteen-ounce gloves. I looked at him and kind of had a feeling that I was in trouble. 'What are you going to do with those?'

"He said, 'I wouldn't let another man talk to my wife that way, and I'm not going to let you.' We put the gloves on. I didn't even know he had boxing gloves. I stood up in front of him in my boxing stance, and he moved around a little bit and then, 'Smack.' I went back. 'Had enough?' He went 'Smack'

again, and I went down on my butt. I jumped up and went at him, and he went, 'Smack, Smack.'

"He looked at me with tears in his eyes and said, 'Don't ever make me do this again.'

"He was a hell of a father in his own way, he really was."

—Jeff Runyan, in a conversation with the author

PAUL RUNYAN HAD been chasing golf since 1921—a quarter of a century. It had been the primary focus of his entire adult life and most of his adolescence. Ever since he had looked his father in the eye and told him he wanted to be a golf professional, not a dairy farmer, Runyan had maintained a single-minded focus on the game. To suddenly give that up and pursue other interests was no small decision.

Had he burned out, grown tired of the chase? Did he feel that he had accomplished all he could as a player? Had the war affected his outlook on life? Then there was his lifestyle to consider. As a pro golfer, he had seen much of the world. Was he determined to get off the road and settle down, focus on raising a family? After all, he and Joan were new parents. And what was Joan's role in the decision? Had she pulled him away? Had fatherhood?

These are all relevant questions. And none of them addressed the possibility that his game may have abandoned him while he was in the service, as Fred Corcoran and Ralph Trost had speculated. A still more burning question: If not golf, then what? What had Runyan meant when he said he was entering private business?

The answer was jewelry.

It seems a member at Metropolis Country Club in White Plains, whose New York company manufactured jewelry, needed a wholesale sales representative in Southern California. The man told Runyan he'd be perfect for the job. At the time Runyan was without a club job. Tournament golf alone was much too big a risk. He and Joan had committed to starting a family, and he needed a reliable income. His friend from Metropolis recognized the opportunity.

"He thought I'd make a hell of a salesman and assured me I'd make a lot more money than as a golf pro," Runyan said.

The new gig started out well enough. And it's true, Runyan had the personality for a sales job. Anyone who could make a career out of pleasing wealthy country club members knew a thing or two about dealing with people. Runyan was a well-spoken, good-looking guy. He cleaned up well in a suit and tie. He could be punctual, likable, persistent, yet not too aggressive. Yes, the more you thought about it, the more convincing the idea of Runyan the sales rep sounded. But why not sell golf equipment or sporting goods, a product line he knew better? Surely someone at Spalding could have arranged a job opportunity.

His new home city of Pasadena, California, had picked up steam during the war. Once a city that had relied on tourism to carry the economy, it was now a center of industrial research and manufacturing. It was home to the California Institute of Technology, the Jet Propulsion Lab, the Rose Bowl—not to mention natural beauty and ample sunshine. And now, Paul and Joan Runyan and son. If you were going to settle down and trying something new, joining the newcomers who had flocked to Pasadena during the postwar boom made a lot of sense.

As a wholesale jewelry sales rep, Runyan earned a reported annual salary of $30,000, which was more than twice what he'd been making in the golf business. In the spring of 1946, a photograph made the rounds in the newspapers; it showed Runyan, dressed in a suit and tie, displaying his wares to a jewelry store owner on a sales call in Los Angeles.

He wasn't the only pro golfer to explore a new career path following the war. Jug McSpaden tried his hand at selling men's suits and sportswear in Palm Beach. Vic Ghezzi joined up with the Supreme Food Company to help sell mayonnaise. Byron Nelson helped market golf umbrellas (a side hustle that predated the war).

Despite the reports, Runyan had not quit golf cold turkey. In fact, he played more tournament golf as a jewelry sales rep than he had during the war, although it still paled in comparison to the volume of competition he had been used to before entering the navy. Intentional or not, he was becoming a bit like his old pal Bobby Jones, the full-time lawyer, part-time golfer (and full-time American hero). However, Jones had competed as an amateur, while Runyan maintained his professional status.

Runyan's tournament results were fair. At the 1946 U.S. Open at Canterbury Golf Club in Ohio, he finished in twenty-first place. That fall he came within a whisker of beating Ben Hogan—who'd come out of the war playing scorching hot golf—at the Dallas Open at Brook Hollow. Runyan shot a final-round 71 to Hogan's 73 and finished in second place, tied with Herman Keiser, two shots behind Hogan.

A year later, the 1947 U.S. Open was played at St. Louis Country Club, and Runyan tied for sixth with Hogan and others, seven shots out of the playoff between Lew Worsham and Sam Snead. At the start of the week, Hogan had been a guest columnist for the *St. Louis Star-Times* and wrote that Runyan was one of his dark-horse picks to win, due to the demanding green complexes at St. Louis Country Club.

Runyan reportedly played that week in St. Louis wearing large, tortoiseshell-frame eyeglasses. Had his vision been a problem? Could that have been to blame for his "slump?"

At age thirty-nine, Runyan won the 1947 Southern California PGA Championship at Long Beach Recreation Park, beating defending champion Fay Coleman in the finals by a familiar margin, 8 and 7. Runyan's hot play that day included a morning 64, eight under par. The field that week at Long Beach included 1946 U.S. Open champion Lloyd Mangrum.

With a little extra money in his pocket, Runyan joined Annandale Golf Club in Pasadena, which had been founded in 1906 by an influential group of Pasadena locals, including George S. Patton Sr., father of the famed four-star general nicknamed "Old Blood and Guts." Annandale offered Runyan a top-notch venue where he could play, practice, and prepare his game for competition, be it a major championship or a Southern California Section PGA event.

Paul and Joan bought a Victorian house surrounded by fruit trees on a large piece of property in Pasadena. Joan's mother, Gertye, moved in to help out with the housework and raising their young child. Gertye was a farm girl at heart, accustomed to waking up in the dark to start baking, cleaning, and caring for the baby (and later the couple's second child).

After a few years, the jewelry business started to lose its luster, though the money was still good. As Runyan had been promised, his salary was more than twice what he'd been making as a golf pro. But the money provided only so much fulfillment.

"Any time you get up in the morning and have to go to work hating what you're doing, well, you've got to get out, if you can," Runyan said. "And I got to hating it more and more. Hated fighting the traffic. Hated dealing with jewelers. They were such bad sports!"

In particular, Runyan became frustrated by missed appointments. He would call and arrange to meet with a jeweler, but when he showed up for the meeting, the owner was nowhere to be seen. As a golf pro, Runyan would never have failed to show up to give a lesson.

"Instead of coming out and facing you and telling you they weren't buying that day, they'd send out some excuse, that they were out or had gone to New York or some place," he said. "And all the time you knew they were behind a door."

Publicly, Runyan gave no indication—at least not yet—that he was second-guessing his new occupation. After finishing twenty-five strokes behind Hogan at the 1948 Glendale Open, Runyan told a reporter, "I'm glad I'm in the jewelry business instead of golf. Imagine competing with Hogan for a living. Think I'll hurry home and polish up my sales talk."

What he really wanted to say was that he'd hurry home and polish up his résumé. Surely there was a club that needed a golf pro.

THE RUNYANS WELCOMED a second child into the world on January 31, 1948, when Joan gave birth to a seven-pound, six-ounce boy at St. Luke Hospital in Pasadena. They named him Jeffrey. That happy moment was offset a little more than a year later when news arrived on March 19, 1949, that Paul's father, Walter, retired farmer and dairyman, had died in Arkansas at age sixty-six. According to the death certificate from the Arkansas State Board of Health, the elder Runyan had died from pneumonia of the right middle lobe, which had been plaguing him for a week.

Mamie Runyan was in no rush to leave Arkansas. In 1962 her son Elmo, recently retired as a navy commander, would return to Hot Springs to help look after her. Within a few years, he would get involved in business, and in 1967 he was appointed manager of the

Hot Springs Convention Auditorium. He was a member of a local Baptist church, served as president of the Shrine Club, and became a thirty-second degree Mason—not to mention holding memberships in more lodges than you could count on one hand. One family member described him as a "classic, cigar-chomping career military guy." After his death, the Odd Fellows lodge on Whittington Avenue in Hot Springs would be named in his honor.

In California it was clear that his younger brother was itching to get back into golf. In June 1949, a couple of months after he captured the Santa Ana Pro-Am, Runyan offered a series of free evening golf clinics at the Wilshire Driving Range on Wilshire Boulevard. The clinics were written up in the *Los Angeles Times*, which seems to have been no accident. Runyan was unabashedly still a golfer, and he was perfectly happy if everyone in Southern California knew about it.

Then Runyan heard from his own club, Annandale, about a job. Longtime pro Harry Brooks was planning to cut back his duties, and the club wondered if Runyan had any interest in coming on in early 1950.

On Monday, October 24, 1949, Brooks suffered a heart attack in his car on the way to work and died. The opening for a club pro at Annandale was immediate. A few days later the *Pasadena Independent* published a story indicating that Runyan would likely take the job. However, the announcement only became official in November, after the board of directors approved the hire.

After a five-year dalliance in the jewelry business, Paul Runyan was once again a golf club professional.

RUNYAN HAD ALWAYS played and taught golf with an eye toward the angles, searching for the most fail-safe way to do things. As a player, he simply knew no other way. If there was a golf course he could overpower, he had yet to play it. He lacked the physical tools that would have allowed him to play loose and carefree. His brand of golf required that he knew how far his ball carried, how far it would roll, and on exactly what line it would fly. He also had a keen awareness of mathematics. Perhaps it was because he'd grown up in a gambling town or had caddied for wealthy businessmen who liked to gamble, but he always knew the odds, whether it was his odds of two-putting from a certain distance or a bookmaker's odds that he'd win a match. At Annandale, in the presence of instructors from Cal Tech and scientists from the Jet Propulsion Lab, Runyan's fascination with numbers and scientific detail reached a whole new level. As one former student said, "The golf nut engineers and scientists who worked at those places had a big influence on him. He got to thinking about engineering and angles and all that."

The result was that Runyan added a new, scientific dimension to his golf instruction. He incorporated terms such as effective loft, angle of approach, and suspension point (which he believed was the axis of the golf swing, described in his own writing as the spot at the nape of the neck where the top of the spine protrudes slightly). He delved into statistics; by his figuring, he realized that on shots within four feet of the edge of the green he could hole out in an average of 1.97 strokes, meaning he was more likely to chip in than simply get down in two. He also became fascinated with the swing concepts of English golf instructor Ernest Jones, whose "swing the clubhead" philosophy focused on a golfer's ability to maneuver the clubhead through space (and not on body movement). Jones, whose teaching had influenced Runyan's friend Horton Smith, published a book on the golf swing in 1952, and it seems likely that Runyan found a copy and read it.

Runyan blended these schools of thought with his strongly held beliefs about short-game technique and delivered the message to his students with uncompromising, unapologetic specificity. As he once wrote, "At times I may seem overly specific in my instruction. So be it."

His thinking was also progressive when it came to golf analytics. One year he passed by Byron Nelson coming off the golf course at Augusta National. Nelson, usually mild tempered, was red faced and furious, looking like he might have a stroke. Runyan asked him what was wrong.

"If you had putted for me this afternoon, you'd have broken 60," Nelson said.

"Wait a minute, Byron. What did you take?" Runyan asked.

"Sixty-six," Nelson said, still fuming.

"Why are you so upset?" Runyan asked.

"Well, I've already said if you had putted for me you'd have broken 60."

"How many greens did you hit?"

Nelson explained that he had hit every green in regulation and had hit all the par fives in two shots.

"How many short putts did you have?" Runyan asked.

"I had two six-footers, two or three ten-footers, and the rest were somewhat longer," Nelson said.

Runyan grinned. And he recalled something his friend Horton Smith had written.

Runyan said, "Well, isn't it quite reasonable to think thirty-four putts isn't so bad on these tricky greens, when you've hit all the greens and had no really short putts? You had two five- or six-footers and a couple just a little longer. Remember what Horton wrote. It isn't how many putts you've taken but where you took them from that establishes whether you did or did not have a good putting performance. And since you had no chip shots, there's no way you could have as few putts as me, even if you were as good a putter as I am, which you are not. There's no way you can get the ball as close to the hole after two shots as I can after three."

Runyan was explaining what would one day become known in golf analytics as "strokes gained," a metric used to measure performance based on the expected number of strokes needed to hole out from a specific distance.

Runyan's own game seemed to get buoyed by his return to the club pro scene. In 1951 he advanced through U.S. Open qualifying at San Gabriel Country Club, shooting rounds of 71-66 to tie Jerry Barber for medalist honors. The Open would be played that June on the South Course at Oakland Hills Country Club outside Detroit, Michigan, a brutal par seventy that measured nearly seven thousand yards and was nicknamed "The Monster." The day before Runyan left by train for Michigan, he played a round at Annandale and decided to try out a putter from the sales rack in the golf shop. A new batch of putters had just arrived, and he always liked to give new equipment a test drive so that he would know what to recommend to members. All he did that day at Annandale was fire a 61. He stuck the new putter into his golf bag and slammed his regular putter into the sales rack in the golf shop. Off he went to the U.S. Open.

Runyan got to Oakland Hills and began his practice rounds, and after a few days he realized that he'd made a terrible mistake. "I didn't have time to understand its variables," he said of the new putter. Still, his game was good. In fact, he was playing some of the best golf that he'd ever played at a U.S. Open. Sam Snead held the first-round lead, but Runyan was just two strokes back after a 73. Playing alongside big-hitting Al Besselink, Runyan had played thirty of his seventy-three shots that day with woods. Only once did he hit an iron from the fairway. In between shots, Runyan chewed on small lumps of sugar, supplied by Joan from the gallery. Someone joked, "On the long holes Paul uses three woods and one putt." Besselink spoke to the press after the round, sounding like he had just witnessed a magic act. His comments were eerily familiar to those made by the professionals from the 1930s who'd watched Runyan perform the same routine.

As the tournament wore on, Runyan realized his new putter would eventually become a liability. He called up the golf shop at Annandale and asked to have his old putter sent to Oakland Hills immediately. (It showed up in the middle of the third round, but he couldn't change midround.) Somehow, slinging fairway woods into greens, he cobbled together good scores and kept pace with the leaders. Oakland Hills was playing tough, but Runyan was up to the challenge. After fifty-four holes, the forty-two-year-old club pro from California was just one stroke back of leaders Jimmy Demaret and Bobby Locke.

Good-luck telegrams came in from everywhere, including Pasadena. "Best of luck cousin," wrote Hienie and Berniece Harbers.

"Seems like old times—good luck. We are all pulling for you," wrote the Jelenkos, his friends from White Plains.

The entire membership at Annandale wrote to wish him good luck. "No nicer guy could win the national open," they said.

Could he actually pull this off? Could Little Poison strike again, at a long, difficult U.S. Open of all places? On a course nicknamed "The Monster"?

The answer was no, no matter how big the headlines would have been. He stumbled badly out of the gate in the final round, shooting

39 on the outward nine. He came home in 36 for a 75 and finished tied for sixth, seven shots behind Ben Hogan, who blazed through the field with a closing 67. Still, Runyan's performance had turned some heads. The *Los Angeles Times* devoted a correspondent to Runyan's special week in Michigan, with that write-up almost treating it like a victory. The newspaper called his performance "a tremendous showing for the little man who has been absent from the tournament trail for a decade."

It seemed Runyan was the only one unhappy about his result at Oakland Hills. That's probably because he knew how close he was to nabbing an improbable victory, and he had only himself to blame for taking the wrong putter to Oakland Hills.

"I never played golf in an Open better in my life for 72 holes," he said, bemoaning his performance in the tournament. "And I finished sixth. Because of this damn putter."

RUNYAN WAS HAPPY at Annandale. He told someone that it was "the best job I've ever had." However, he had a family to consider, and Annandale—more specifically, its proximity to Los Angeles—was not the best situation for his loved ones. His son Paul Jr., age nine in 1954, had developed nasty allergies, and the family doctor advised relocating. The Runyans spent their summers near the beach, and there young Paul's allergies improved, but when they returned to their house on Markham Place in Pasadena, located less than two miles from Annandale and eight miles from downtown Los Angeles, the allergies raged on. The doctor blamed the smog from nearby Los Angeles, and Paul and Joan wholeheartedly believed it.

"Smog Drives Annandale Golf Pro from Job" was the headline that blazed across the top of page 25 of the *Pasadena Independent* on October 22, 1954. The article indicated that Runyan would stick around Annandale through the end of the year before leaving for his new job at La Jolla Country Club, near San Diego.

The sound of crackling bonfires and the sight of early arriving parade-goers huddled in blankets dominated the streets of Pasadena in the early morning hours of January 1, 1955. Thousands would jam the city to catch a glimpse of the Tournament of Roses Parade that day, an early appetizer for the afternoon kickoff between Ohio State and the University of Southern California at the Rose Bowl (which would get spoiled by persistent rain). One hundred miles to the south, Paul Runyan, having left Pasadena in the rearview mirror, began his first day on the job at La Jolla Country Club. His arrival signified the start of a new era for the club and for Runyan the instructor. Countless lives would be impacted by his presence at the club, and every one of them could thank the LA smog for stirring up Paul Jr.'s allergies.

La Jolla Country Club was and is a beautiful setting for golf. Perched on a hillside above the affluent town of La Jolla—between the edge of the Pacific Ocean and the Mount Soledad foothills—the William Bell–designed golf course, a kikuyu grass paradise that spanned all of 6,583 yards, offered views of the Pacific Ocean from every tee and every green. Bell's work was well known throughout the western United States and included San Diego's Balboa Park, Bel Air Country Club, Stanford Golf Course in Palo Alto, and the Ojai Country Club (with George C. Thomas) in Ojai, California.

Established in 1927, the club had staggered through the Depression and the war years when money was tight but seemed to be hitting its stride by the early 1950s. Among the club's members was Thomas Lanphier Jr., a World War II fighter pilot who had been given partial credit for shooting down Admiral Isoroku Yamamoto, commander of Japan's Imperial Navy. Lanphier had moved to San Diego in the 1950s to take a post with a large defense contractor and would become La Jolla's club president in 1958.

Not even termite trouble and dry rot, which threatened to condemn the clubhouse in 1955, could derail the club's momentum. The membership raised enough money to completely restore the clubhouse, which included expanded locker rooms and dining facilities. And now the club had hired a sought-after instructor with a national profile. Everyone there thought they had hit the jackpot.

Runyan's impact was felt immediately. He was a whirl of perpetual motion. Always conscious of his own physical fitness, he'd sometimes run wind sprints to pass the time between lessons. That sort of activity will raise eyebrows at a country club, especially on the uneven, sloping terrain that connected the golf shop to the practice tee at La Jolla.

He helped develop new competitions at the club, such as the Outhouse Open, which stipulated that players had to tee off atop a mattress and putt around a toilet seat. He routinely posted his scorecard somewhere in the clubhouse after a round, daring members to try and beat him with their own net score. In 1957 the club chose to redesign the second hole to settle an ongoing land dispute with the city of La Jolla; Runyan was tapped to design the hole. He fashioned a 157-yard par three with a long, narrow green set into a depression, surrounded on all sides by tall banks that created a funnel effect. The new hole was constructed for $7,000. Clearly Runyan had quickly become the face of La Jolla Country Club.

Runyan got to know a young, up-and-coming professional named Gene Littler, who'd grown up around the club and was just getting his career started. In 1950, at the age of nineteen, Littler shot 63 at La Jolla, setting the course record (which stood until Phil Mickelson shot 60 in late July 2004). When he wasn't competing, Littler was usually at the club practicing. "There I watched in awe as Paul dashed back and forth from his pro shop to the lesson tee," he wrote. "His enthusiasm seemed boundless. It infected the members at the club."

Chuck Courtney, whose family had moved from Minnesota out to the West Coast during the war while his dentist father served as an officer in the navy, was a promising junior golfer at the club when Runyan arrived. Courtney was the perfect age to latch onto a mentor. The new pro's impact was profound and immediate, Courtney recalled.

"Fortunately, we just lived a couple of blocks from the club, so I was there all the time. Runyan was very inspirational. Immediately he got the whole golf scene at La Jolla Country Club organized. He was just the most enthusiastic person about the game, the rules, the competition. And about having people enjoy the game. That's the essence of the guy.

"All of us hung on every word he had to say. He taught a lot, and I'd go out to the practice tee and hang close enough by him to pretend like I was practicing, but I was basically listening to what he had to say. He had a huge influence on me."

Runyan's sons, Paul and Jeff, hung out with Courtney and other junior golfers who were about the same age. Their dad encouraged them to play golf—and they did—but the country club lifestyle they were exposed to extended far beyond the golf course.

"We grew up in Camelot at La Jolla," said Jeff Runyan. "It was pre- a lot of things in the early to mid-1950s. It was just magical. La Jolla was a little artistic, intelligent enclave with some of the best artists and thinkers in the world."

In part to help meet new people, Joan Runyan would often open up her home for parties. The crowd would be a diverse mix of thinkers, professionals, and political ideologies of every stripe. The discussions were fascinating, said Jeff Runyan.

"In those days there were a lot of socialists, almost communists, in La Jolla in the postwar years. And she would bring together staunch conservatives and Democrats, and in those days they didn't seem all that far apart. I would get dressed up and hang out and listen. I was a pretty good guitar player then, and sometimes I would play a few tunes for the parties. La Jolla Country Club always had a couple good piano players in the membership, and people would sing and play the piano."

The membership at La Jolla in those days was a mixture of retired navy admirals, local businessmen and their families, doctors, lawyers, and professionals—even a few "rough and ready guys, too," Courtney explained. Runyan was masterful at handling all of them.

One day a group of Southern California Golf Association officials showed up as guests at the club. There were eight of them, all there to play golf, and two starting times had been reserved, completely aboveboard. A small group of members who regularly used those starting times came into the golf shop, upset, and asked to speak to Runyan. It's a scene that's been played and replayed at every country club in the nation at one time or another.

"Who are these people?" one of the regulars asked, somewhat rudely. "What's going on? Those are *our* starting times."

Runyan was annoyed but kept his cool.

"Gents, would you step outside for a moment please?" he asked.

He walked them out onto the putting green and made sure he had their attention.

"Gentlemen, these folks are guests at our club. Don't you think we should treat them as such?"

It was a simple plea, and not one of the members had a worthy rebuttal. That was that. The new pro at La Jolla Country Club walked back into his golf shop and went about his business. The huffing members cooled down and waited another ten minutes, basking in the California sunshine and cool sea breeze before starting their round behind officials from the SCGA.

"Runyan had cut his teeth as a young man on the East Coast, dealing with these kinds of people at fancy clubs," Chuck Courtney said. "He carried himself with such dignity and poise. It's hard to fault the guy. For somebody with an eighth-grade education, he was quite something."

Over the course of his time in La Jolla, many nights Runyan would be awakened by a telephone call from the San Diego Sheriff's Department because a caddie had been picked up for drunken and disorderly conduct. Without fail, Runyan would bail them out and keep it hush-hush. As the person primarily responsible for their training, he had a soft spot for caddies and went out of his way to help, regardless of skin color or financial status.

The golf shop at La Jolla was as much Joan Runyan's turf as it was Paul's, probably more. Courtney described her as the "head haberdasher" in charge of stocking the shelves with the latest in golf fashions. Her husband, a well-dressed, stylish teaching pro, was the perfect model for the polos, sweaters, and slacks she carried in the golf shop. He wore whatever she suggested.

"Whatever they made from the golf shop was a big part of their income," Courtney said. "And Runyan being Runyan, the members were very loyal to him. People bought stuff just because it was him, and he owned the shop. That's one of Paul's legacies. Treat people well, take care of their families, learn their children's names and their grandchildren's names, and teach them how to play golf. And they'll support you."

Joan's deputy was Jack Taylor, a tall, well-dressed, ex-military golf shop assistant who was as loyal to the Runyans as anyone in their inner circle. Many days Taylor would show up for work wearing a

Brooks Brothers shirt and sport coat. Because of his fashion sense, he helped Joan Runyan buy the shop merchandise. Taylor drank a dozen cups of coffee and smoked more than a pack of cigarettes daily. As Jeff Runyan described, "He lived really well and spent all his money on us, good food, and really nice clothes." Over time Taylor became like a surrogate father to the Runyan boys. He was a frequent dinner guest and never missed a birthday or holiday. If the Runyans left town for a golf tournament, they trusted Taylor to look after the golf shop and club operations. Taylor also became Paul Runyan's most trusted set of eyes whenever his own golf swing went awry. Runyan would confide to friends that Taylor had one of the best swings he'd ever seen.

As Chuck Courtney matured as a player, he started caddying at La Jolla, hoping he could learn by watching other players while earning a few bucks on the side. Over the years, by his estimation, he caddied for Runyan more than one hundred times. He learned how Runyan would almost always take the flagstick out while chipping, expecting to hole every shot. ("The flag just gets in the way of my ball going in the hole," he'd say.) He marveled at the fairway woods the little pro would hit on his approach shots, trying to roll the ball onto the green. And he recalled countless days when Runyan would hole out from off the green several times a round. There was a deep bunker on the right side of the par-four twelfth hole, so deep that you'd have to stand on your tiptoes just to see out of it, and Courtney caddied for Runyan on consecutive Saturdays when the pro holed out from that bunker to a short-sided pin on the right side of the green.

"To even keep it on the green would have been a great shot," he said. "But he was a magician with a wedge."

About the time Runyan arrived at La Jolla Country Club, another magician emerged onto the scene, and their collaboration became one of the more noteworthy student-teacher relationships in that era of golf. His name was Phil Rodgers, a pudgy, cocky golf prodigy whose high school golf team had playing privileges at the club. Rodgers, who had learned the game as a boy at a San Diego pitch-and-putt called Presidio Hills, started caddying at the club and came to know Runyan, who, recognizing the boy's immense talent, quickly took him under his wing.

Rodgers was a couple of years older than Chuck Courtney, and as a golfer he was on another level. Runyan described Rodgers as a "finished player" when they first met, but he was referring primarily to the boy's full swing. Runyan taught Rodgers almost everything he knew about the short game, and almost immediately Rodgers improved. Runyan provided Rodgers with structure and a reliable system for playing short shots, two things the youngster desperately needed.

"He was a master at course management and gave me an excellent education in how to use the golf course and my skills to the best advantage," Rodgers wrote. "I accepted Paul's advice, not merely because he had been a very successful player on the tour, or because I knew from my own experience that he was right, but also because the game became more interesting."

Rodgers, whose family had little extra money, won the 1955 International Jaycee Championship at seventeen, earning scholarship money for college. He would attend the University of Houston and play under Coach Dave Williams. In 1958 Rodgers would win the NCAA individual title. His winning margin in the finals over Purdue sophomore John Konsek: 8 and 7.

Runyan stressed to Rodgers that a heightened attention to detail was needed to play golf at the highest level.

"He took me from being one of the top ten juniors in the country to right at the top," Rodgers said. "He had ideas about everything. He was a very, very meticulous man."

Rodgers and Courtney both pointed to Runyan's handwriting as an example of how detailed the man could be. "It was beautiful," Rodgers said of the handwriting. "And absolutely perfect, free of grammatical error."

Courtney said his mentor's penmanship reminded him of the examples of perfect cursive that teachers tacked to the wall above chalkboards.

Runyan recommended that Rodgers become a lifelong learner. "If you're going to play at a high level, you need to learn everything you can about it," he told him.

That involved more than technique. He encouraged Rodgers to understand golf club design, club making, architecture and course setup, course management, and anything else related to golf. Rodgers would learn these things eventually, but in his youth he was mostly concerned about beating whoever was in front of him.

One day in the late 1950s, the man in front of him was Runyan. It's unclear who first issued the challenge, but a duel was arranged at the club between Runyan and Rodgers, teacher versus student. They'd play a five-hole match on the ninth through thirteenth holes and would use only one club. Runyan chose a four-wood. Rodgers picked a wedge that he had doctored with a four-iron shaft. Early in the match, Runyan found a greenside bunker and had trouble getting out with his four-wood. By the time they came to the final hole, the crowd following the twosome had grown to an estimated one hundred persons. Rodgers had the lead, and Runyan asked to press so he could get even.

"No," Rodgers told his mentor.

Runyan was livid. Rodgers remained defiant. They played the hole, and Rodgers clinched the match by holing a twenty-foot putt. The student had beaten the teacher. Runyan was so upset that Rodgers had denied his press, he gave him the silent treatment for what Rodgers remembered was a full year. However, by the time Rodgers had turned professional and was in contention to win the 1962 Los Angeles Open as a rookie, they were friendly again, and Runyan called him on the morning of the final round to offer some encouragement. It worked. Rodgers fired a 62 to win by nine shots. A few days later, Runyan told a reporter that his protégé had a bright future.

"Phil came to me for advice, and he's done everything I've suggested," Runyan said. "He has the type of swing that will hold up in competition. It's sound and compact. And he can hit the ball high, an asset that will help him considerably."

Besides his instruction, Runyan's golf connections were instrumental in developing players such as Rodgers and Courtney. Veteran professionals such as Olin Dutra and Lloyd Mangrum would regularly come to La Jolla to see Runyan and play golf. Runyan was eager to expose his young students to the game's best players. Rodgers recalled playing golf against Ralph Guldahl, Sam Snead, Byron Nelson, and Ben Hogan. The exposure to greatness that he received as a young golfer was almost unheard of, and it was mostly thanks to Paul Runyan.

In June 1957 Dutra and Guldahl joined Runyan and a local pro named Don Collett to help dedicate the South Course at Torrey Pines, a new public golf course along the Pacific Ocean, north of downtown San Diego and north of La Jolla Country Club. After the mayor cut the ribbon, they became the first foursome to play the course, and an estimated crowd of five hundred turned up to watch the exhibition. Runyan badly snap-hooked his drive and second shot on the opening hole, then holed a thirty-yard pitch shot for an unlikely birdie. That quintessential Runyan birdie helped the San Diego pros defeat Dutra and Guldahl in the four-ball match. Over the years Torrey Pines would become a regular stop on the PGA Tour, and the South Course, where Runyan recorded the first birdie, would become a U.S. Open site in the 2000s.

Phil Rodgers followed up his win at the LA Open with another win in 1962 at Tucson. At that summer's U.S. Open, he would have made the famous playoff between Jack Nicklaus and Arnold Palmer a three-way affair had it not been for an errant shot that became stuck in a spruce tree on the seventeenth hole. He finished in third place, a couple of shots out of the playoff. The following summer he went up against Bob Charles in a thirty-six-hole playoff for the Open Championship at the Royal Lytham & St. Annes Golf Club, only to come up short.

The only thing that could derail Rodgers, Runyan explained, was Rodgers himself. "If he'll just deny himself off the course, I see no reason why he shouldn't have a tremendous career on the tour."

Denying himself was the one area where Rodgers failed to follow his mentor's advice. Runyan tolerated Rodgers's arrogant attitude and even encouraged his cocky trash talk because he noticed that Rodgers played his best golf when he was bantering. But food was another story. Rodgers ate like there was no tomorrow. When Rodgers qualified for the 1956 U.S. Open as an eighteen-year-old amateur, Runyan offered to share a room to help Rodgers keep his expenses down. They ate dinner together every night, and Runyan was shocked to see what Rodgers put into his body. At each meal Rodgers's bill would be more than double Runyan's. Back in the hotel room, Runyan would hear Rodgers lie awake all night belching and wondering why he couldn't fall asleep.

12

Last Hurrah

In 1959, when memberships were selling for $1,200 apiece, members at La Jolla Country Club were asked to vote on a proposal to purchase 350 acres, at $1,000 per acre, in Carmel Valley, a then-desolate spot north and east of La Jolla. There, a new, longer course could be built, and the club would be moved. That would mean selling the valuable land where the club sat overlooking the Pacific Ocean.

It's true—that land could have fetched top dollar from the right developer. Any developer, really. But the move would have completely robbed the club of its identity.

The membership was polled on the matter, and the results indicated that there was some interest in relocating to Carmel Valley. The club's board of directors, clearly advocates for staying put, quashed the matter before it went any further. There would be no move to Carmel Valley or anywhere. La Jolla Country Club was staying put.

PAUL AND JOAN Runyan's home adjacent to La Jolla Country Club, with its contemporary exterior rooflines and cool-gray front door and entrance lanai with the startling black-and-white vinyl floor and Victorian rosewood furniture that led to three bedrooms with windows overlooking the Pacific Ocean, was enough to make a man take a look around and feel satisfied. That man could sit in one of the green-plaid chairs in the living room next to the soft-pink-painted brick fireplace and stare out at the ocean and conclude that his struggle was over, life was pretty good. And it was.

Paul Runyan was not that man. Not when it came to his golf.

No matter how nicely Joan decorated the house, he was not the type to curl up on a loveseat and get lost admiring his walnut kitchen cabinets in the adjoining room.

It's true that he and Joan had a great situation at La Jolla. They were adored by members of their club, surrounded by natural beauty, enriched by professional fulfillment, comforted by a nice home and a stable personal life. But what had all that work been for—all the wind sprints between lessons, constantly watching his diet, repetitively hitting chip shots and pitch shots—if not to compete? As Runyan cruised past his fiftieth birthday, his best days as a competitive golfer were in the rearview mirror, but he was not finished. And in the right situation, with favorable conditions, he could still play championship-level golf.

His journey to prove that point began in February 1961, which was a decade after his close call at the U.S. Open at Oakland Hills. At the PGA Seniors' Championship in Dunedin, Florida, that winter, Runyan's appearance prompted Associated Press writer Whitney Martin to describe him as a "worried-looking little man" as he battled Jimmy Demaret in the final round in front of three thousand people. Runyan began the day two strokes behind Clarence Dozer but caught him on the sixth hole and flipped the margin to a two-stroke advantage after the first nine holes. The "thimble sized sharpshooter who spoon feeds his opponents until they have had more than enough" shot a three-under-par 69, good enough for a three-stroke victory over Demaret.

Runyan's victory over 371 other senior members of the PGA in Dunedin earned him the right to represent the United States that summer in Fairhaven, England, at the World Seniors' Golf Championship. Paul and Joan decided to make the European trip a family affair, inviting their teenage boys and Joan's sister Jane, who was living in San Clemente. And, for the first time since 1933, Runyan committed to play in the Open Championship. He also added the French Open to his schedule.

Shortly before the Runyans departed for England, Paul earned some delayed recognition for tutoring Gene Littler, who had just won the U.S. Open at Oakland Hills. Littler could hardly stop telling the press about how Runyan had helped him, but Runyan felt a little embarrassed by the attention. A couple of years had passed since he had dispensed the advice that turned Littler's game around. He told sportswriter Red Smith that a simple grip change, which took only fifteen minutes, was the extent of his tutelage. Littler worked on the new grip for a couple of hours before returning to the golf shop to tell Runyan how solid his shots felt. The only problem was that everything was going right of his aim.

"Think about it," Runyan told him. "If you've been hooking shots for a year, then naturally you've been aiming to the right to compensate, whether you knew it or not. Now you're hitting the ball the way you want, so just live with it a few weeks and you'll unconsciously come around on the line."

Another San Diego golf prodigy was Mickey Wright, and she went out of her way to thank Runyan that summer after a putting tip she received from him over the telephone.

"Delighted to help," Runyan had told her when she called. "Because when I teach putting I simply tell the pupil what I want him to do and then walk away without watching him hit a ball."

He explained his technique to Wright, and she won two tournaments in a row. Suddenly Runyan had a lesson sheet full of players asking him to fix their stroke. Now they'd be waiting a few weeks until he returned from his European golf vacation.

FAIRHAVEN GOLF COURSE in England reminded Runyan of La Jolla. It was not overly long and in fine playing condition. Only the grass and the smaller British golf ball took some getting used to, but Runyan found that both added significant distance, sometimes as much as thirty or forty yards, to his drives.

His opponent in the thirty-six-hole world championship match was fifty-year-old Sam King from Kent, England, whom Runyan described as a "combination farmer–golf pro, very poised and congenial." That description may have undersold King's accomplishments as a player. He had to his credit nine top-ten finishes in the Open Championship and had been a part of three European Ryder Cup teams.

Both players broke par in the morning round, Runyan with a one-under-par 71 and King at two under with 70. King increased his lead to two up on the second hole of the afternoon round with a birdie, but Runyan gained it back a few holes later with a birdie of his own.

After trailing all day, Runyan finally squared the match on the ninth hole of the afternoon, a long par five. He then took the lead a hole later after a fairway wood to the 500-yard tenth hole finished eight feet from the cup, and he holed the putt for birdie. Once Runyan had the lead, he never let it go; he closed out King 3 and 1 to win the PGA World Seniors' Championship.

"This was about as good match play golf as I have ever turned in," Runyan said after the round.

Then it was on to the Open Championship at Royal Birkdale in Southport, where Runyan first had to qualify to even get into the championship field. He was one of just fifteen Americans who made the trip to England for the event; others included Frank Stranahan and the betting favorite, thirty-one-year-old Arnold Palmer. The field of more than 350 qualifiers would get whittled down to 108 championship contestants, and Runyan emerged from the qualifier with rounds of 74-71 at the Hillside and Birkdale courses to secure a spot in the championship.

Once the Open got under way, the conditions turned brutal. Heavy winds demolished the refreshment booths, wrecked tents, and overturned trailers. The overwhelming gusts gave way to twenty consecutive hours of torrential rain that saturated the course, halting play and postponing the final rounds. Only two Americans survived the thirty-six-hole cut: Palmer, who was one stroke back of the lead, and Runyan, who just squeaked in, one stroke in front of the cut line. Lamenting his play, Runyan (75-77) told someone he was playing "nice and easy, like a bum."

Runyan was playing the sixth hole in the third round when the weather turned so bad it stopped play. As the conditions worsened, his play improved, and he slowly climbed up the leaderboard. With volunteers stationed at every green with buckets and blankets to soak up water, players slogged along, and Runyan patched together decent scores. He shot 75-72 over the final two rounds, finishing in a tie for eighteenth place, fifteen strokes behind champion Arnold Palmer.

The Runyans concluded their European tour at the French Open at La Boulie, outside Paris. Paul felt tired, and it showed in his play. He made an eight on a par five, a seven on a par three, and he double-bogeyed three par fours. And he did all of that without hitting a ball out of bounds. He finished the week nineteen strokes adrift of champion Kel Nagle.

There was no rest for the weary. Back in California, Runyan had just two months to bask in the glow of his Fairhaven victory before he began qualifying all over again for the 1962 PGA Seniors' Championship. He survived the thirty-six-hole qualifier in Southern California, and in February 1962, just a few weeks after his student Phil Rodgers won the LA Open, Runyan found himself back in Dunedin, Florida, trying to deliver a repeat performance.

The par seventy-two course at Dunedin had been stretched out to more than seven thousand yards, but the fifty-three-year-old California club pro with the enviable trophy case back home remained unfazed. He shot under par in each of the first three rounds (71-69-68) yet still trailed by a few shots. On the final day he took control early. He birdied the first and third holes to grab the lead, birdied two more holes on the front nine, then dodged the challengers the rest of the way. He shot 70, and his ten-under-par total of 278, which equaled his total from 1961, was enough for a three-stroke victory over Dutch Harrison, Joe Brown, and Errie Ball.

He played that week (really, throughout this two-year stretch) with a relentless determination, his mind fixed on victory. The hit blues instrumental "Green Onions" was released that year by Booker T. and the MGs, and the certainty, the absoluteness of that song—which in the decades that followed would get used extensively in film and television—seemed to mirror Runyan's march toward victory in Dunedin. His title defense was a foregone conclusion.

"Ol' Paul Runyan Is Still a Tiger" read one newspaper headline. In what might have been a touch hyperbolic—only Runyan would know—he said, "This was the most significant thing I have ever done in golf. I wanted to win worse than anything."

Runyan had to wait five long months before traveling to Prestwick, Scotland, to try and repeat as World Seniors' champion, and Sam King once again would be his opponent. The Englishman began the rematch looking like a man determined to avenge his defeat. King won three of the first four holes, and Runyan appeared to be in serious trouble.

He reversed the momentum quickly, winning the eighth, ninth, and tenth holes to square the match. Both players traded leads on the back nine, with King ending the morning one up.

On the first hole of the afternoon round, Runyan pushed his drive out of bounds onto a railway line and lost the hole. The mistake seemed to settle him down, and he played steady golf the rest of the match, stringing together wins at the twenty-first, twenty-fifth, and twenty-sixth holes to gain a one-up lead. He arrived at the thirty-first hole with a two-up lead and faced a long, uphill chip shot over a ridge in the green. Using a six-iron, he holed the chip for a birdie to go three up. King would win just one hole the rest of the way, and Runyan closed out the match on the seventeenth (the day's thirty-fifth hole) for a 2-and-1 victory.

He had now accomplished a rare triple-double in golf: he was twice a PGA champion, twice a PGA Seniors' champion, and twice a World Seniors' champion.

13

High Heavenly Ground

Of all the test balloons on the fringes of golf that Paul Runyan sent up over the years, perhaps none was more far-fetched than his efforts to promote Throlf, a game invented by the Reverend Lawrence Waddy, headmaster of Santa Maria International Academy in Chula Vista, California. In April 1968 Runyan agreed to participate in the world-debut Throlf match, which pitted him against San Diego Chargers center Sam Gruneisen.

What was Throlf? Basically, it was golf, but players threw the ball with their arm instead of striking it with a club. In his match against Gruneisen, Runyan played conventionally, with golf clubs. Gruneisen, "throlfing," beat him by two strokes.

That summer Reverend Waddy dreamed up a fundraiser to benefit the Santa Maria school. More than one hundred spots were made available to "throw to beat the pro" at Presidio Hills—the same short course where Phil Rodgers had first learned the game—and anyone who signed up to play was entered in a drawing to win a $350 set of golf clubs.

And the pro who turned up to take on all comers at Presidio Hills? It was none other than two-time PGA *champion Paul Runyan.*

ON THE HEELS of his success in senior golf domestically and abroad, in 1962 Paul Runyan published a book, *Paul Runyan's Book for Senior Golfers*. It landed him on the cover of the August 6 issue of *Sports Illustrated*, where he was depicted (in a painting from the magazine's art department) stepping up to a drive and wearing a light blue sweater, his customary eyeglasses, and a posh green hunter hat that looked like it was lifted straight from Robin Hood's closet.

That same year, Sam Snead published his own book, *The Education of a Golfer*.

Runyan's book was 150 pages and included a foreword from Bobby Jones, who graciously wrote that he could think of "no one better qualified to write an authoritative book on golf instruction than Paul." In its pages, Runyan dispensed techniques to help cheat Father Time and continue to play successful golf into late middle age. For instance, he recommended a form of abdominal crunches to aid core strength and swinging a garden rake to help keep a golfer's hands and arms strong.

He cautioned, "Swing it out of sight somewhere, or in the dark, so your neighbors won't think you suddenly lost your mind."

Like Winnie the Pooh, he claimed his magic potion was honey, which he always carried in a jar in his golf bag and used to quell sudden hunger and calm his nerves. A discerning reader would recognize that roughly a quarter of Runyan's book was aimed directly at seniors; the rest of it was a golf instructional for all ages. He did little to hide this fact, even writing that players young and old could benefit from the book.

As he spun through middle age, his training regimen had clearly made a positive impact on his own game. He wrote that he was longer off the tee by ten to fifteen yards in his fifties than he had been during his prime, a fact that he brought up often around the Runyan household, at least until Joan scolded him for his vanity.

"You used to beat them by being straighter," she told him. "And by chipping and putting their eyes out."

One explanation for his increase in distance—besides swinging a rake around the house—was a change in his technique. In his younger days, whenever he saw his swing on film he was horrified by his lateral sway off the ball. The lateral shift had always been intentional; Runyan believed it would maximize his leverage. However, he was unaware just *how much* he swayed until he saw himself on film. As he aged, he ditched the sway, instead relying on his arms and hands and wrists to zip the club through the impact area.

In the second half of the 1960s, Runyan became a much-sought-after public speaker. He had a career's worth of accomplishments to trade on: a longtime, successful playing record; a recognizable profile as one of the United States' most well-regarded club professionals; independent, proven philosophies for full-swing and short-game techniques; and now a book to promote.

He warmed crowds with his remarks at dinners for the New York Golf Writers and the Boston Golf Writers. He spoke extemporaneously, telling his audience about the great characters, places, and incidents he had encountered over the course of his lengthy career in golf.

At a meeting of the San Diego Advertising and Sales Club before the 1968 Andy Williams–San Diego Open, Runyan kept the crowd engaged by describing what it was like to cross swords with traveling gambler Titanic Thompson, how it felt to trounce Sam Snead 8 and 7, and how every golf professional in the business owed a debt of gratitude to Walter Hagen for elevating the status of the profession. Prior to Hagen, golf professionals were treated like second-class citizens. With his flair for pomp and circumstance, Hagen helped change that outdated mind-set.

Runyan, by his figuring, would make ten or so appearances like this a year to talk about golf. He told one audience, "I'm just enough of a ham to want to talk whenever I can about golf or whatever else about which I know something."

Around this time Runyan, feeding his hunger for hamminess, concocted an idea: a rematch with Snead. He tried to reach out to the television producers of Shell's Wonderful World of Golf about it.

"Sam has lived with the memory of that defeat long enough," Runyan told the San Diego Advertising crowd. "He deserves a rematch."

The Shell television series, which began in 1961, showcased elite golf matches at courses around the world. Snead was featured in arguably the most famous Shell match of all time: a 1965 tilt against Ben Hogan at Houston Country Club. Among the matches that would be televised in the series in 1968 would be Snead taking on Roberto De Vicenzo at Congressional Country Club, while Runyan's student Phil Rodgers would play Dave Thomas at the Old Course at St. Andrews. But, it seemed, the television executives had little appetite for a Runyan-Snead rematch. The idea never progressed beyond his pitch.

In February 1968 Runyan traveled to Tacoma, Washington, to speak to members of the PGA Northwest Section over two days at the group's spring meeting. A crowd of 125 pros showed up to hear his two talks: "Experience in Teaching the Golf Swing" and "Hints on Putting and the Short Game." It was his first visit to the Pacific Northwest since his days as a jewelry sales rep, and his only memory of that trip was spending five hours in a Seattle hotel room.

A month later, Runyan would be in Atlanta to visit Rich's Department Store for its fifteenth annual Golf Jamboree, where he offered bunker lessons by appointment and gave a series of exhibitions over a long weekend. Did he drop in on Bobby Jones during this trip, as he had on other Atlanta stops? His window to see Jones was closing; Bobby would be dead by late 1971.

THAT VISIT TO Tacoma had been no accident. A few years before Runyan addressed the PGA Northwest Section, two golf clubs in the greater Seattle area decided their city needed another championship-level course. The two sides got together and began searching for a spot where they could build one. In early 1967 they found a parcel of land on the Sammamish Plateau, east of Redmond, Washington. There they would form Sahalee Country Club.

The eight-member committee that secured the land chose the name Sahalee, which meant "high heavenly ground," out of respect for the Chinook Indian Nation, whose heritage had been rooted in that region of the Pacific Northwest. The club organizers hired golf course architect Ted Robinson and charged him to create a course that could host major USGA or PGA golf events. Next, they retained the services of Louie Schmidt, a golf course superintendent, who would be in charge of construction and maintenance of the course. Finally, the committee sought a well-established golf professional who could get the club started out on the right foot. For advice, they reached out to Runyan.

Carl Johnson, part of that eight-member committee, called Runyan to ask him to serve as a consultant while they tested the market. The group paid Runyan a small fee and flew him up to Seattle to see the property. Runyan made a few follow-up trips and even passed along the names of some potential candidates for the job.

That summer, for the first time in sixteen years, Runyan entered the PGA Championship at Pecan Valley Golf Club in San Antonio,

Texas. At sixty years old he was clearly past his prime, and the course, which measured more than seven thousand yards, hardly favored his short-hitting style. He missed the cut after shooting rounds of 79-74, but there were still flashes of terrific play. On Friday of the tournament, while wearing a navy blue shirt, plaid pants, and a hat that looked like something a beekeeper might don for protection, Runyan played alongside Tom Weiskopf and Rex Baxter. On the sixteenth hole, Runyan watched Weiskopf tee off with an iron for position before selecting a driver himself because, quite frankly, he needed the distance. His drive went just past Weiskopf's lay-up off the tee. Then, after watching both players approach the green with irons, Runyan grabbed his four-wood and hit it within a yard of the hole, setting up a birdie. While he missed the cut by four shots, Runyan could take solace in the fact that he beat Baxter (by two strokes) and Weiskopf (by six)—not bad for an aging club pro with a jar of honey in his golf bag.

As his mind wandered back to Sahalee and the club's vast potential, he realized that maybe *he* would make a good prospect for the job of head pro. He had been at La Jolla for fourteen years and thought it might be time for a change.

At home he brought up the idea to Joan. She agreed that a change might do them some good. And, she told him, there could be the potential to make more money. Professional golf purses had taken a considerable bump since Runyan's days on the competitive circuit. In 1934 Runyan had been pro golf's leading money winner, earning a shade less than $7,000; in 1967, seven pros had earned more than $100,000 in prize money, with Jack Nicklaus and Arnold Palmer approaching the $200,000 level. While Runyan would not be competing regularly for prize money on the PGA Tour, golf purses had undergone massive inflation and a new job could be the couple's last best opportunity to cash in on their earning power. However, the thought of moving to Seattle and leaving behind La Jolla's beautiful weather did little to motivate Joan.

"You either have to be more satisfied with our current situation until something else comes along or we decide to go to the Northwest," Paul told her.

Regarding that "current situation," a few longtime La Jolla members suspected that some friction had developed between Runyan and one senior member of the club's leadership. While that squabble, whatever it was, was never aired publicly, it seems that Runyan may have expected this person eventually to try to force him out.

Paul and Joan talked it out for two days and nights. They decided that Paul would apply for the job, but when it came time to discuss his salary he would ask for the world, figuratively speaking. He drafted a letter stating his salary demands, declaring that in his estimation he was the best candidate for the job. The committee liked his pitch and didn't blink at the money. Both sides batted around some particulars, but when it was all settled Sahalee hired Paul Runyan as its first golf pro for an annual salary of $45,000.

"The beauty of the area captivated me, with all the evergreen trees and the mountains and the water," Runyan told the USGA's John Bodenhamer for a magazine profile in the 1990s. "It's just such beautiful country. I also knew Sahalee was going to be one heck of a golf course after seeing it during my visits."

Runyan began the new job on August 1, 1969. Despite the natural beauty that surrounded the golf course, the working conditions were spartan. There was no clubhouse, only a mobile home used as a temporary golf shop. The club erected a large tent that functioned like a makeshift locker room, where members could change their shoes before and after a round of golf. Eventually the club would get around to building the necessary infrastructure to make it an elite destination.

Runyan loved the people at Sahalee. Members from the committee that hired him soon became frequent playing companions and gambling buddies, including Carl Johnson, Harry Wilson, and Jack Wright. Runyan also blended easily with the down-to-earth Seattle community. He had never seen a club so diverse. "All kinds of people from every background were welcomed as members from the beginning, and decisions were made in a real democratic fashion," he told Bodenhamer.

The membership at Sahalee loved Runyan. Whether or not they had articulated it to him during the search process, the club wanted an old-school golf professional like Runyan. He addressed members as "Mr." or "Mrs." so-and-so and brought an element of dignity to the club. Every Sunday during the golf season, he would welcome kids to the practice tee and offer golf instruction for free, whether they were beginners or accomplished players. On Wednesdays he'd make it a habit to join up with the last group off the tee sheet, no matter who they were or how well he knew them.

For all the romancing that went on between the Sahalee members and their first club professional, Runyan's time at the club would be relatively brief. Joan quickly grew tired of the Seattle weather, and in early 1972 the couple began exploring other opportunities. They landed at Green Gables Country Club in Denver, Colorado.

Donald Brenner arrived in Denver the day after Super Bowl Sunday in 1974. The twenty-five-year-old attorney attended a party at Green Gables, and someone there told him he could join the club for just $500. That may have seemed like a rock-bottom price, but for a young attorney preparing for the bar exam it was a lot of money. Fortunately for Brenner, he had a doting grandmother who lent him the money, and he joined the club anyway, cash flow be damned.

He went to the club one day that spring to introduce himself to the staff. Among the people he met was the club's teaching professional, Paul Runyan. Brenner was a golf junkie, and that name got his attention.

"My gosh," he said to Runyan, "you're not the same famous Paul Runyan who won the PGA?"

Indeed he was. Runyan was equally surprised to learn that someone as young as Brenner would recognize him.

"I went out and played that day, I think with some of my dad's friends who are now deceased," Brenner said. "About a month later, Runyan called me."

"Can you do me a big favor?" Runyan asked over the telephone.

"What's that?" Brenner asked.

"We need a fourth for a pro-am."

Brenner was thrilled. He joined Runyan's group, and they won the pro-am, thanks to Brenner's eagle on the final hole. He was so excited that he broke into a somersault and hurt his wrist in the process.

"That wasn't real smart," Runyan told him, shaking his head.

Situated around Ward Lake on the west side of Denver, Green Gables presented only one problem, which was that it was a fifteen-minute-plus commute for most of the members. Brenner didn't mind. As far as he was concerned, beauty trumped drive time, and Green Gables was a gorgeous setting in which to play golf.

Brenner had grown up near Chicago, and he and his father had routinely driven more than thirty minutes to play golf when he was a kid. He had taken a few lessons back then from Johnny Revolta, one of Runyan's contemporaries from the 1930s. The fact that Brenner could talk golf like someone twice his age was part of the reason he and Runyan got along so well. Runyan gave him lessons, and they became frequent playing companions and pro-am partners. Almost always, even in pro-ams, Runyan walked and carried his own golf bag. Throughout his senior years he was an advocate for walking golf courses whenever possible.

Similar to their arrangements at other clubs, the Runyans came to Green Gables as a package deal. Paul spent most of his days on the lesson tee, and Joan (or "Joanie," as Brenner and other Green Gables members called her) looked after the merchandise in the golf shop.

"They ran a great pro shop," Brenner said.

The Runyans would be joined in Denver by their younger son, Jeff, who, after working in the construction industry in Texas, decided he wanted to give the golf business a try. He started by running the driving range and cart service at the club, and eventually he would enter the PGA apprentice program, hoping to follow in his father's footsteps.

Jack Taylor, Paul's right-hand man and golf-swing confidant from La Jolla, also followed Paul and Joan out to Denver and worked at Green Gables.

In August 1974 Runyan made his final appearance as a competitor at the PGA Championship, held that year at Tanglewood Park in North Carolina. The rough that week was especially gnarly—Tom Watson and Arnold Palmer both described it as some of the worst spinach they'd ever seen—and the course featured numerous forced carries of 235 yards or more over the tall grass. Runyan struggled with it. In his first-round 84 he had gotten down in two from 150 yards no fewer than four times. His drives simply couldn't carry far enough to reach the fairway, and on some holes he resorted to aiming his drives down the mown walking paths that connected to the fairways, just so he would have a playable second shot. He was paired that day with sixty-two-year-old Sam Snead, who could still hit the ball a reasonable distance and shot 69 to vault into contention. After the 84, Runyan quietly withdrew from the championship.

"Paul was having a little trouble making those greens," Snead said after the round. "In fact, he was having trouble getting to the fairways." Snead finished third that week, just three strokes behind winner Lee Trevino.

As the wrinkles mounted on his forehead and the signs of sun damage began appearing on his skin, Paul Runyan let his hair grow out over his ears. Perhaps he was just trying to fit in with the prevailing hairstyles of the 1970s. He hadn't turned into a full-blown hippie, but a few fellow golf professionals in Colorado wondered if he'd gone soft. Hardly. He still spent hours on the practice tee every day at Green Gables. Many of those hours were spent working with his students, but he logged plenty of time grinding over his own golf game.

While he maintained his soft touch with members, he could be gnarly when he wanted to get a point across.

Players continued to seek him out for lessons, including established tour players like Gene Littler and John Schroeder. In 1980 the University of Texas All-American Mark Brooks showed up at Denver Country Club for the Trans-Mississippi Amateur; he was the defending champion. Brooks liked to hang around the golf shop, and in advance of the tournament he had arranged a lesson with Runyan at Green Gables. The following day he was back in the golf shop at Denver Country Club, and one of the assistant professionals asked him how his lesson with Runyan had gone. Brooks, who would later represent the Hogan brand after turning professional, had been using a bag full of Hogan equipment, including his putter, during his lesson, and he explained that Runyan had watched him hit some putts.

"Well, what do you think?" Brooks had asked.

"For starters," Runyan had said, "you're using a bad putter that was made by a really bad putter."

When Brooks retold the story, the pros at Denver Country Club couldn't help but laugh.

That sort of verbal jab seems reflective of the tension that existed between Runyan and Hogan, said Donald Brenner. "Hogan thought that Runyan didn't play the game the way he thought it should be played. Hogan judged a player by how many greens he hit, not what score he shot. He didn't think it was fair that putting was so important. One time Runyan said to me, 'It's too bad that Hogan didn't have Arnold Palmer's personality, because golf could have become more popular in the forties.' Runyan told me he helped Hogan with his putting a bit, but Hogan didn't want to play that way because he thought it wasn't pure golf."

On the public speaking circuit, Runyan would tell a story that corroborates Brenner's account. One day during a preround warm-up, Runyan was chipping near the practice green when Hogan breezed by. Hogan eyed Runyan and without stopping said, "I know I could chip better doing it that way, but it looks so awkward I can't afford to do it." In retelling the story, Runyan would add that he purposely omitted the expletive Hogan used in making the statement. However, whenever Runyan was asked over the years to rank the game's all-time greatest players, he included Hogan right at the top, along with Bobby Jones, Jack Nicklaus, Sam Snead, and the other usual suspects.

MORE THAN FIFTEEN years after he had left La Jolla Country Club, it had not forgotten Paul Runyan or the impact he had made on generations of golfers and country club members in the community. In 1976 the club conferred honorary membership status upon Paul and Joan. The Runyans were moved by the gesture, and in January that year Paul wrote to club president George Delafield to accept the honor. In his letter he described how he and Joan had established deep roots in the La Jolla community and had enjoyed some of their happiest days at the club. "We can only hope that when we are put out to pasture, that it may be in the Jewel of Jewels," he wrote.

At the end of his letter, Runyan requested a copy of the club's constitution and bylaws "so I may live up to them."

PART 5

On the Tee until the Last

14

Author and Influencer

As he aged and came to terms with the realization that there was more of his life in the rearview mirror than there was road in front of him, Paul Runyan, like so many people of a certain age, became more introspective. He realized he had more questions than answers, and those answers maybe weren't as certain as he once thought—except, of course, in matters of short-game instruction. After all, some things are simply not up for discussion.

He thought of himself as a spiritual person, a man with a strong belief in a higher power, but he professed no specific religious affiliation. He respected opposing viewpoints. It mattered more to him that you were a decent person and kind to others than where you attended religious services, if you did at all.

When his boys were young, he tried taking the family to a nearby Presbyterian church on Sundays, hoping to expose them to organized religion. But for a golf professional, Sundays are sacred for an entirely different reason. He had groups to start off the first tee, members who needed a swing lesson, and tournaments to run.

His son Jeff inherited his father's spiritual outlook. Nowadays he laughs at the memory of his dad trying to scurry his family in and out of church on Sundays. With a shake of his head and a smile on his face, he says simply, "That didn't last very long."

GOLF HISTORY MOSTLY overlooked his role, but Paul Runyan had a hand in bringing the Golden Bear out of hibernation.

That episode began seventeen years after the publication of Runyan's first book and involved his collaboration with Dick Aultman and illustrator Anthony Ravielli to publish *The Short Way to Lower Scoring*. It was a *Golf Digest* book, which meant that the magazine giant owned by the *New York Times* was the publisher and held the copyright. Simon and Schuster distributed it as a trade book. The book was a short-game-specific instructional, whereas Runyan's earlier *Book for Senior Golfers* had been part-instructional, part-lifestyle guide, part-homespun tales from life on the road during the pork-and-beans days of early professional golf.

In his new book, Runyan outlined his entire short-game system with the specificity of a Russian novelist. Ravielli, who had famously illustrated Ben Hogan's best-selling *Five Lessons: The Modern Fundamentals of Golf*, aided Runyan's words with detailed drawings that helped readers follow along and see his technique in action. Sporting his new longer hairstyle that draped past his ears, the author appeared in a photograph on the front jacket cover of the book wearing a bright red mock turtleneck, red belt, his trademark plaid pants, and brown golf shoes. The image shows him hitting a pitch shot with perfect fundamentals, the loft of the club pointed toward the sky, his hands and arms directly in front of his fully rotated torso, and the ball gently knuckling toward the putting surface.

Golf Digest released excerpts of the book, and one of them caught the attention of Jack Nicklaus, the aforementioned Golden Bear, who, with apologies to Arnold Palmer, was by then the world's most popular, influential, and accomplished professional golfer. Nicklaus had spent the winter of 1979 laboring through some much-needed full-swing modifications with his longtime instructor Jack Grout, hoping to work his way out of a slump. According to longtime *Golf Digest* editor-in-chief Jerry Tarde, Nicklaus's game was in such dire straits at the time that his golf career appeared to be drifting toward sunset.

After sampling the excerpts, Nicklaus tracked down a copy of Runyan's book and read it cover to cover. Then he began playing around with Runyan's chipping technique. Surely, with his famous attention to detail, he found it impossible to overlook Runyan's blunt assessment on page 100, where the author wrote that Nicklaus chipped like an eight- to ten-handicap golfer who used too much wrist action. Like he had been as a player, Little Poison the author could be cutthroat when he deemed it necessary.

Nicklaus reached out to his old friend and rival Phil Rodgers—a known Runyan disciple—who by then had parlayed an uneven playing record into a second career as a club builder and instructor. Like his mentor Runyan, Rodgers was damn good at teaching golf, yet he was still awaiting a big break (or a noteworthy pupil) to help propel him into the upper echelon of golf instructors. He flew to Florida and spent a few weeks with Nicklaus, showing him a variety of shots, many of which had come directly from Runyan's arsenal. Nicklaus later said he hadn't worked so hard at his golf game since he was a teenager. Rodgers was more in awe of Nicklaus's lifestyle than his work ethic.

"I stayed at his house, which is like a seven-star hotel," he said. "They've got three or four or five boats in the backyard, a putting green, three tennis courts, all kinds of stuff. Barbara took really good care of everybody. Basically all I did was stimulate his interest a little bit."

The fruit of their labor showed that summer when Nicklaus won the 1980 U.S. Open at Baltusrol and the PGA Championship at Oak Hill. Nicklaus was back on top, and Rodgers had much to do with Jack's return to form. However, he was careful not to overstate his role. He knew from his days as a tour regular that credit and blame should always go to the player, not the coach. However, there was no denying the effect that Nicklaus had on Rodgers's career path as a golf coach. Rodgers was the first to acknowledge it.

Rodgers's work with Nicklaus gave a tremendous boost to his second career, and he morphed into a much sought-after coach and club designer. Over the years he would help countless top players with their short game and full swing.

"He made me, with his success and all that," Rodgers said of Nicklaus. "He did. I was just a regular guy teaching, trying to scrape off enough to eat and live on. I didn't have much to fall back on, and Jack got me started."

Runyan went mostly unheralded for the role he played in jump-starting Nicklaus. There was little hubbub at Green Gables over the new book or the Golden Bear's resurgence. Rodgers mentioned that his philosophies were rooted in what he had learned from Runyan, but most golf writers chose to focus on the chummy relationship between Nicklaus and Rodgers. That was fine with Runyan. He would have loved the recognition but was simply happy that a great player had recognized the merits of his system. He had long lamented that so few players adopted his methods around the green. On the other hand, he was grateful for this fact during his playing days. He was so confident in his short-game system, he believed it helped him win more than his fair share of golf tournaments.

Around the time of Nicklaus's resurgence, Paul and Joan began discussing the possibility of retirement, or at least scaling back. They were preparing to leave Denver for a People to People program golf trip when tragedy struck. Joan Runyan, seventy-two, died suddenly, two days before Thanksgiving 1981 after suffering a massive cerebral hemorrhage. When she failed to show up for work at Green Gables, friends and coworkers knew something was amiss. Every day, like clockwork, she would arrive shortly before noon, driving the couple's ragtop Continental that Runyan had received for winning the 1962 World Seniors' Championship. But on this day she never arrived. She lived for nine hours after the hemorrhage; Jeff Runyan, who was away in California, rushed back to Denver as soon as he heard the news, but he failed to arrive before his mom passed.

Paul was devastated. He and Joan had been married for fifty years. A small group of Green Gables members got together and helped him spread her ashes on Ward Lake adjacent to the fourteenth hole. Joan had always loved to walk around the lake, often accompanied by the family dog.

Shortly after Joan's death, Runyan, still heartbroken, disappeared from the club. Days turned to weeks, and soon it became almost a month. No Runyan. Don Brenner had been promoted to golf chairman at the club, and a few of the longtime members started nudging him to find out where Runyan was and when he would return to work. Brenner had Runyan's home telephone number but couldn't bring himself to call.

Finally, after nearly a month-long absence, Runyan returned to the club. Brenner heard he was in his office and worked up the nerve to talk to him.

"I walked in there, and I'm supposed to talk to Paul," he recalled. "I tried to get some of the older guys to do it, but they wouldn't. I was just a young guy, a hot-shot attorney, at least in my own mind. So I walked in, and I'm really going to give it to him for not calling me and not showing up for over a month."

When Brenner entered his office, Runyan looked up with tears in his eyes. Before Brenner could get a word out, Runyan said, "Donny, I can't tell ya. No golf chairman has ever been so kind as you, to give me a whole month off to grieve for the loss of my beloved wife."

Brenner was taken aback, speechless. It was all *he* could do to not cry. "What do you say?" he pondered years later. "What do you do?"

AFTER JOAN'S DEATH, Runyan saw no reason to stay in Denver. He announced to the members at Green Gables that he would be heading west for California before the next golf season. He left quickly, quietly. As an honorary lifetime member at La Jolla Country Club, he figured that would be the best place to hang his hat while he figured out his next move. He knew plenty of people there and had a comfort level with the community. He bought a midcentury house with a flat roof and a beautiful view over Pacific Beach, and Joan's sister Jane, who lived just blocks away, helped him remodel and decorate it. Paul Jr., still on the West Coast, assisted with the remodel and eventually moved in with his father. Under this arrangement, Runyan took a wide-angle look at his life and contemplated how he wanted to spend his remaining years.

"Dad was down in La Jolla, licking his wounds, so to speak, after my mom died," Jeff Runyan said. "But my dad wasn't one to roll over and follow someone into the grave. He had a lot to do. There wasn't a day he didn't get up, particularly when I was around him at the club, where he didn't say, 'You know, I think I'm really close to getting this right.'

"He just never quit."

Runyan the golfer, age seventy-three, emerged from mourning the following spring to play in the Vintage Invitational at the Vintage Club in Indian Wells. After an opening-round 77, he shot his age in the second round to make the cut at six over par. Bill Froloff from the *Desert Sun* profiled Runyan in the newspaper, introducing Little Poison to a new generation of readers who may have been unaware of his place in the game.

That December, after a one-under-par 71 in the opening round of the

PGA Senior Open Championship at PGA National Golf Club in Palm Beach Gardens, Florida, Runyan drew some headlines, and he tried to use the opportunity to focus attention on his difficulties gaining eligibility for professional senior golf. He sought an exemption onto the then-fledgling Senior PGA Tour, but the tour awarded just thirty exemptions for older players, and those were handed out based on lifetime earnings. His problem was that he had played so long ago. Purses in the 1930s were tiny compared to purses after World War II. His place on the lifetime earnings list, he felt, failed to accurately represent his accomplishments as a golfer. Even the PGA Senior Tour media guide left a blank spot next to Runyan's lifetime earnings. That number was impossible to calculate and a poor indicator of his play anyway.

"They only have me down for making $16,000 or some such figure," he told one journalist after his round. "But 30 years ago they gave me credit for $148,000. I finished tied for 19th in a senior event this year and won $8,300 just for that."

He was perplexed. But his game, amazingly, remained as solid as his sturdy body. He attacked par fours with fairway woods and relied on his short game to buoy his scores. Battling 25 mph winds at PGA National, Runyan, the field's oldest player, clipped Sam Snead that day by eight shots and tied Arnold Palmer, who said, "I think what Paul did today was magnificent. I just hope I'm here when I'm seventy-four."

Later that month, Runyan traveled to Australia, where he had arranged six weeks' worth of lessons and clinics. As an instructor, arguably he had never been in higher demand. He had become a member of the *Golf Digest* instructional staff, which offered him the opportunity to travel and teach at different *Golf Digest* golf schools around the United States.

"These started out as five-day schools," said Dick Drager, who was a young, up-and-coming instructor when his longtime mentor, legendary golf instructor Bob Toski, helped arrange for Drager to come work for the *Golf Digest* schools as an assistant director.

"By Wednesday, most of the students would be wiped out," Drager said. "So we changed the format and started doing three-day schools. It was probably the best staff ever assembled in golf. They had a series of schools down in Florida, then out west in Tucson, Arizona. I'd walk out on the tee to help get things set up, and I still can't believe it, because out would come Mr. Toski, then Jim Flick, Davis Love, Pete Kostis, Paul Runyan, Chuck Cook, Jack Lumpkin. These guys were all Teachers of the Year, and five of them are in the Hall of Fame.

"Paul generally taught the short game. He was always dressed immaculately and always had a pep in his step. I remember early on seeing him walking around the practice tee with a sledgehammer. I'm going, 'Paul, what purpose does the sledgehammer serve?' And he said, 'I'm going to keep my wrists and hands and forearms strong.'"

Off the golf course, Runyan became reacquainted with Berniece Harbers, whose late husband Hienie Harbers had made a small fortune inventing and patenting mobile stadium seating in the 1960s. Hienie and Berniece had been members at Annandale Golf Club in Pasadena since the days Runyan had been the golf pro, and for years they had been bridge partners with Joan and Paul. Both now widowed, Paul and Berniece—who was "Bea" to her close friends—found solace in each other's company.

"They kind of gravitated together," said Jeff Runyan. "The whole time my mom and dad were at Annandale, they had been traveling companions. Whenever Dad went to a tournament, Hienie and Berniece would go. Hienie Harbers was actually my godfather. He had passed away about four or five years before my mother. So Berniece was swinging in the wind, and she loved to travel and loved golf. And loved my dad."

Nobody had a better firsthand account of Paul and Bea's late-in-life romance than Patti Brugman, a Harbers family friend. At the time she was Patti Wilson, a newly minted teacher fresh out of graduate school who was looking for a cheap place to live.

"Bea knew my mom really well, and she was just a good friend of the family," Brugman said. "She was such a lively, fun person. Bea was short and stocky but always cute and silly and golden. She wanted me to live with her, and I was sort of homeless at the time, so I moved in and lived on the third floor.

"She was traveling extensively and dating as much as she could. As a matter of fact, her license plate was FOXYBEA, so she was definitely on the hunt. She reported back to me that there were a couple of guys she was looking at for a second marriage. One of them was a golfer, so of course I immediately pitched for whoever that was, because I was a golfer, too. Paul had such a fabulous reputation. Everywhere they went, people knew him."

Energized by their new romance, Paul and Bea decided to get married. First, though, Paul wanted to square the plan with his sons.

"When it got more serious, he decided that he would like our approval to marry Berniece," Jeff Runyan recalled. "This was just before he left to go play in the first Legends of Golf tournament, which was truly the legends of golf, at Onion Creek Country Club in Austin. I caddied for Dad in those tournaments. We were at dinner in Austin, and Berniece was with us. We were all chatting. They were getting kind of lovey-dovey then, which was cool. He said, 'Jeffy, I want to ask you something.' He always called me Jeffy. I said, 'What's that, Dad?' He said, 'Would you mind or be angry if I told you I would like your approval to marry Berniece?'

"I looked at Berniece, and she had a big grin on her face. I said, 'I'm so happy for you, Dad. To have someone you've known for so long that you've spent so much time with, and she's been alone and you've been alone. To me, it's the perfect match. You're a lucky man.'"

Their wedding on July 2, 1983, took place in Santa Cruz, California, about 350 miles up the coast from Pasadena. Bea's specially designed wedding ring failed to arrive from the jeweler before Paul and Bea left Pasadena for the wedding, so Bea dispatched her houseguest Patti Wilson to wait on the ring and personally fly it up to the Monterey Peninsula in time for the ceremony. Wilson and the $25,000 ring both arrived safely and on time.

After the wedding, the couple lived in Bea's house on South San Rafael Avenue in Pasadena. It was a large home on two gorgeous acres of property, surrounded by pine trees and azaleas. Patti extended her stay on the third floor for a few more years. Paul and Bea made sure to include her at every meal, like a surrogate daughter. Whenever they went out for dinner, they invited Patti along and liked to treat her at fancy places. At the dinner table Paul would inevitably start sharing stories about his golfing past, at least until Bea decided the conversation needed a refresh, and she would change the subject. Around the household, Patti's main responsibilities were to keep an eye on the house when they were away and make sure the sprinklers were running on schedule.

"Bea would do all the cooking, and I would just be another person at the table," she said. "Every meal was a golf lesson. It was delightful."

Paul did his best to make himself at home. There was an odd-shaped, oversized laundry room adjacent to the kitchen of the old Victorian house, which mostly went unused because a housekeeper took the couple's clothes out to be laundered. Paul filled the room floor to ceiling with golf clubs. He and Bea shared a bedroom, but he used one side of the house on the second floor to store his personal effects. Late one night he was looking for something in one of the spare rooms when Patti came jogging down the stairs from the third floor. As Paul turned the corner and Patti reached the bottom of the stairs they collided, scaring Patti half to death. He caught her before she fell to the ground, and once their excitement died down they shared a relieved laugh.

"I screamed bloody murder," she said. "It was very funny. He was a great guy, so insistent, and he always had a twinkle in his eye. I just loved that man."

A few months after the wedding, Jeff Runyan, then living in the Palm Springs area, where he worked in the golf course construction business, came up to Pasadena to visit his father. Paul had something on his mind and pulled his son aside.

"Jeffy, there's something that's been bothering me," he said.

"What's that?" Jeff asked.

"Do you think I've sinned if I've been in love with or have loved two women in my lifetime? Do you think your mother would be disappointed?"

"Dad, I think you're the luckiest man in the world because you've had two women that loved you enough to put up with your ornery self. Mother would probably be happy. She's waiting for you to get up there so you can all play bridge together."

Runyan smiled.

"I feel better," he said, patting his son on the shoulder.

RUNYAN NEEDED A place to give golf lessons and settled on Arroyo Seco, a par-three course located just below the 110 Freeway in South Pasadena and within walking distance of home. He had passed on an ownership stake in the golf course shortly after it opened in the 1950s, but now here he was again. However, he played most of his golf at Annandale, where he had become something of a living legend. When his body felt up to it—which was most days—he would hit a small bucket of balls, then play eighteen holes. On days when he chose not to play, he'd still hit balls, sometimes for two or three hours.

One day golf journalist Al Barkow showed up at Runyan's door to conduct an interview for his book *Gettin' to the Dance Floor: An Oral History of American Golf*, which would be published in 1986. Barkow was impressed by the house, his host's hospitality, and his willingness to sit for an interview. They spent nearly a whole day together, part of the time at Arroyo Seco, where Barkow watched him give a few lessons. At some point during their conversation they veered off topic. Runyan asked Barkow where he'd be staying that night.

"I'm actually not sure yet," Barkow said, having not yet booked a hotel room.

"Well, you can stay here," Runyan told him.

Barkow laughed it off, but after Runyan's insistence he took him up on the offer.

"Put me up in his house," Barkow recalled with a chuckle. "Very generous. He was a very nice man, very accommodating. Just a good guy, you know."

WITH HIS MIND still sharp, Runyan kept his eye out for good business opportunities. He and Bea still maintained a heavy travel schedule, mostly to accommodate the People to People golf trips he led on behalf of the U.S. State Department and its People to People sports program, which dated back to Dwight Eisenhower's presidential administration. Those trips typically took the couple abroad for at least two months every year—sometimes much more. They visited China, Australia, and many points in Europe. Whenever Runyan visited Scotland, the members of his group naturally wanted to play a round at the Old Course at St. Andrews. While it's true he might have been underwhelmed by the Old Course when he first played it in 1933, he grew to appreciate its charm and challenge on subsequent visits.

One business opportunity came in the early 1980s, when Ely Callaway sold his winery for millions and decided to enter the golf business. The businessman bought a stake in Hickory Sticks USA, a club manufacturer that built throwback-looking clubs with hickory-covered shafts. He rebranded the company with his own name and continued manufacturing Hickory Stick clubs; after a few years he bought the rest of the company and moved its operations to Carlsbad, California.

Callaway needed a pitchman, and Runyan was one of the few surviving professional golfers from the hickory shaft era with any marketability. Callaway brought him on to help market the company's clubs and serve as a sort of vintage design consultant. The company even created a line of Little Poison Hickory Stick putters. If you know where to look, you can still find some today, floating around for sale on the internet. Before the company moved its operations to Carlsbad, Runyan was regularly traveling down to Temecula, California, to meet with representatives from Callaway. He often came back with prototype clubs, and most of those would end up in his already crowded laundry room–turned–club storage area. He was on the Callaway payroll, so Bea tolerated the clutter.

Callaway's meteoric rise in the golf business would be almost unprecedented. After the Big Bertha driver launched in the early 1990s there was no looking back; Callaway became an industry leader and has stayed that way ever since. Runyan had some input on the development of the Big Bertha, but much of his time was spent in consultation with club designer Richard Helmstetter, a onetime pool cue designer who became Callaway's chief of new products, on wedge design.

Paul Runyan helped Callaway Golf get off the ground, and while there's no metric to quantify Callaway's assistance to Runyan, it helped the longtime golfer stay relevant. So did his 1990 induction into the World Golf Hall of Fame. That year's inductees included eighty-two-year-old Runyan, the late Horton Smith, two-time U.S. Amateur champion Bill Campbell, and longtime friend and PGA Tour star Gene Littler.

"I'm very proud of my record, but not just for myself," Runyan said at the time of his induction. "It proves that golf gives the good little men a chance to beat the good big men. There are a couple other games that do that . . . badminton, ping-pong. But not many."

A YEAR AFTER his World Golf Hall of Fame induction, Runyan caught wind of an over-eighty Super Seniors event at Canoa Hills Golf Course in Tucson, Arizona. He called up the tournament committee and asked for a spot in the field. He showed up and won the one-day event, carding a round of six-over-par 78, becoming the first player in the three-year history of the event to break his age. When informed of his feat, Runyan explained that he became mad any time he failed to break his age.

Runyan battled for the title with eighty-one-year-old George Sinderson of Tucson, who kept pace with Runyan for most of the round but stumbled down the stretch, on his way to shooting 82. Sinderson's downfall came on the greens, where he suffered four three-putts and one four-putt.

Following the round, after they had shaken hands and signed their scorecards and Runyan had accepted congratulations for his victory, he pulled Sinderson aside. He told him he couldn't stand watching his putting, and if he had a few minutes he thought he could help. So the pair walked over to the practice putting green, and Runyan gave his fellow competitor a putting lesson.

"He makes no secret of the fact that he wants to prove himself the best over-80 player in the world," wrote Tom Foust in the *Arizona Daily Star*.

The competitive fire still burned. But his kindness and willingness to help another player never wavered.

15

"The Legend Never Really Died"

Fargo Country Club in Fargo, North Dakota, hosted the 1995 U.S. Junior Amateur Championship, and in the months leading up to the tournament organizers tracked down Paul Runyan and invited him to be a part of the championship. Eager to see what had become of the club where he had worked more than seventy years earlier, Runyan accepted the invitation—and brought Bea with him. The Runyans arrived a few days early, and the tournament committee showed him around the golf course so he could see the changes that had taken place since the 1920s. He even played a few holes under the hot summer sun, although, to be fair, a hot summer day in North Dakota is a far cry from the stifling California desert or the thick Arkansas humidity he had known in his childhood.

For two days before the championship, Runyan hung out near the putting green and talked to the junior golfers as they came through, sometimes offering instruction, other times just meeting the kids and asking where they were from. At the tournament banquet the contestants and their parents—and as many club members as could be crammed in—watched a short film that showed Runyan winning the 1938 PGA Championship. Then Runyan took the microphone and spoke to the crowd. He talked about how golfers should conduct themselves and how the game helps build character. The crowd hung on his every word.

After a long day holding court on the putting green, Paul and Bea boarded a shuttle bus to transport them back to their hotel. The driver had stepped off the bus to talk to his supervisor and failed to notice the Runyans. They sat there by themselves for close to fifteen minutes while the driver stood outside, looking for anyone who might need a ride. When he got back on the bus, he looked toward the back and saw the older couple in their late eighties and immediately started apologizing for making them wait.

"No, that's okay," Runyan told the driver. "We're in no hurry. We know you were waiting to see if others needed a ride, and that's the right thing to do."

SIXTY YEARS AFTER Paul Runyan's triumph at Shawnee-on-the-Delaware, the PGA Championship arrived at Sahalee Country Club in Seattle, on the opposite side of the country. Runyan would play a significant role in the prechampionship festivities because PGA officials had chosen to present him with the organization's Distinguished Service Award. Inaugurated a decade prior, the award honored outstanding individuals who displayed leadership and humanitarian qualities, including integrity, sportsmanship, and enthusiasm for golf. Past recipients included Bob Hope, Gerald Ford, Gene Sarazen, Arnold Palmer, and George H. W. Bush.

On Monday of tournament week, hard-of-hearing Runyan played Sahalee's back nine alone. He shot 42. Among his goals, he was curious to see if the maintenance staff had found a way to grow thick rough underneath the hundred-foot-tall trees that lined each fairway. He must have seen enough lush grass to pass inspection, because at his Tuesday press conference, to which he arrived wearing a green Callaway golf shirt and pants of peach-and-green plaid, he told the press that long hitters should beware—Sahalee was not their course if they failed to hit it straight. He answered questions about the course setup, the state of the game, and his favorites to win the championship. During tournament week, he predicted that the winner would be David Duval, who had, in Runyan's words, "more guts than a government mule." Earlier that spring, while being interviewed for a magazine article, he had said that Nick Price, Greg Norman, and Vijay Singh would stand the best chance at Sahalee. As luck would have it, Singh won that week in 1998, capturing his first major championship.

The following spring, Paul and Bea were in Augusta, Georgia, for the Masters, where he would play in the Par-3 Contest. In the weeks leading up to the tournament he had trouble communicating with officials from Augusta National, so when he arrived that Wednesday at the wrong gate outside the club, golf bag in hand, tournament organizers panicked for just a moment while they figured out where to slot him in the contest.

Before he teed off, Runyan was approached by a middle-aged man wearing glasses. The man was Runyan's godson, John Fischer, son of 1936 U.S. Amateur champion Johnny Fischer. Like his father, Fischer was a lawyer. And he loved golf. Naturally it helped that he had grown up in the company of his old man's posse, which included notable players like Tommy Bolt, George Dunlap, and Runyan, his dad's old buddy from their navy days in Norfolk, Virginia.

Fischer and Runyan spent a few minutes catching up near the practice putting green. They hadn't seen each other in decades, not since Runyan had left for the West Coast when Fischer was just a boy. Fischer's father had died in 1984, which Runyan remembered. He asked Fischer how his mother was doing and marveled at how much John had grown since childhood.

"Last time I saw you," he kidded as he put his hand up to his chest, "you were just this high." Runyan, of course, stood just 5 feet 6.

Then, suddenly, Runyan told Fischer he had to get changed into his golf shoes. Fischer followed along, expecting Runyan to head into the clubhouse. Instead, Runyan walked into a bag room and changed his shoes next to a group of caddies getting ready to go out.

"What are you doing in here?" Fischer asked, humored and perplexed.

Runyan confessed that he'd always felt more at home around bag rooms and caddie yards than locker rooms. That's the way he'd grown up, and not all the southern hospitality in the world could change who he was at his core.

Fischer stayed close that day as his godfather played alongside Tom Watson and that year's Ryder Cup captain, Ben Crenshaw. He walked along, following every shot.

"I say 'walked' sort of loosely," Fischer remembered. "He practically ran, he walked so fast. Everything I've read about him said that he was always running someplace. Always in a hurry, always going at a clip."

Afterward, Runyan gave some interviews and thanked many of the patrons who had watched him play. Then he slowed down long enough for a late afternoon nap at his hotel. That evening, he and Bea returned to the club for dinner.

This time, Augusta National left nothing to chance. The club sent a private car to pick them up and drop them off at the front door.

BEA RUNYAN DIED on August 29, 2000. There was a small funeral at a church in nearby La Cañada, and afterward friends and family gathered at Paul and Bea's house in Pasadena. Pattie Wilson was there, and she found Paul sitting alone in the breakfast room, surrounded by African violets, Bea's favorite flower. She was now Patti Brugman, and her husband John, who had gotten to know the Runyans while he and Pattie dated, was at her side. Patti and John could tell Paul was feeling down, unsure what his future might hold.

"I've got to move out in two weeks," he said.

The Harbers kids had made plans to sell the house, which legally had belonged to Bea and now belonged to them, and Paul's son Jeff figured a change of scenery would be good for him anyway. Plus, the old Victorian house, beautiful though it was, had lots of stairs, which had made Jeff worry about the potential of a fall.

"He wanted to stay in Pasadena and keep giving lessons at Arroyo Seco," Jeff Runyan said. "I kept trying to convince him that he didn't want to live in the kinds of places that he'd probably wind up. I took him around to a few of the nicer retirement homes. Then I told him that I had a house with plenty of room, and he decided that was probably a good idea, so he agreed to move down to Palm Desert with me."

Now twice a widower, Paul packed light. He moved in with Jeff in Palm Desert and began combing the Coachella Valley looking for a place to teach. He found the Golf Center at Palm Desert, a practice facility adjoining a nine-hole, par-three course near Jeff's house. Runyan walked into the golf shop one day and found Joe Simonds, the general manager. This was not the first time he'd walked into a golf shop unannounced to ask for a job.

"Mr. Simonds, I was hoping you could help me out," he said. "And I think I can help you."

Simonds studied Runyan for a moment, uncertain what the old

man could possibly want. He was mildly aware of who Paul Runyan was but didn't know he lived in town.

"What would you like to do?" Simonds asked.

Runyan proposed teaching at the Golf Center, and Simonds decided he'd be a fool to turn him down, so they arranged for Runyan to give lessons. Typically, he would teach for two hours each morning, then he'd drive his golf cart to Jeff's house and take a nap before returning in the afternoon for two more hours. Only then would he call it a day.

Runyan became friendly with Simonds, who was grateful to have the aging pro around, even if the majority of golfers that came through the facility had no clue that the little old man giving lessons on the practice tee was a two-time major champion who had walked the fairways with Jones, Hagen, Sarazen, Hogan, Snead, and other greats. Or that he had beaten those greats his fair share of times and had a closet full of trophies to prove it. Simonds appreciated Runyan's soft spot for young golfers. If Runyan saw a kid struggling, he would whistle from his golf cart and wave the kid over. Then he'd offer a suggestion to fix a faulty grip or other swing flaw.

Whenever he had a spare moment, Runyan would apologize to Simonds for not pulling his weight. Simonds would hear none of it.

"Paul, you don't know how lucky we are to have you," he'd say.

As the months dragged on, Runyan was beset by a series of small health problems that started to add up. His stability became shaky. He fell off a ladder. He broke his hip. After that he never seemed quite the same. Then he developed pneumonia and spent a month in the hospital. That stay was prolonged by silver dollar–sized bedsores on the backs of his ankles and the balls of his feet.

"They just never healed," Jeff Runyan said, "and all the skin grafts and painful operations in the world didn't help him."

Jeff took a more active role in managing his father's affairs as the old pro's health declined. He helped look after the money. He made sure to get him up each day and into special boots he wore to help his feet. If he needed to travel, Jeff was the one pushing the wheelchair through the airport.

They were in Colorado, visiting Jeff's son Gentry, on September 11,

2001, when the United States was attacked by terrorists. Runyan came down the stairs and saw the events unfolding on the television. He stared at the newscast.

Jeff apologized that his dad had to see it. "It's the world we live in now."

Paul just shook his head and muttered, "It's not my world anymore."

Yet, somehow, Paul Runyan's spirit, his zest for life, remained intact. Golf had much to do with it. A lesson book full of appointments gave him purpose. In 2001 Runyan gave what is believed to be his last formal interview, to PGA of America's Bob Denney, who later retired with the title of PGA historian emeritus. Denney showed up at the Runyan house and spent an afternoon talking with Paul, then watched him give a lesson.

"He had a tremendous historical background, and that set the table for me trying to learn a little more about him," Denney said.

Denney had been at Sahalee in 1998 when Runyan received the Distinguished Service Award from the PGA. Something about Runyan—the depth of his passion for golf, for teaching—stuck with Denney, and he wanted to see it again in person for himself.

"There were a lot of changes over the years with the winners of that award, but Paul was certainly one that I thought stood out because of his connection to the location and his contributions to the game," Denney said. "There were a lot of people that he inspired. There were a lot of pros who looked up to him and listened to him. He really made the profession stand out.

"The legend never really died."

Of all the stories Runyan shared with Denney that day, he got most excited reliving the exploits of Titanic Thompson from his earliest days as a golf pro.

"That guy," Runyan told Denney, "he could get up and down from anywhere."

So could Runyan, Denney thought.

FOR HIS FINAL act as a golf instructor, Paul Runyan gave a joint lesson to Alona McFarland-Hudgens and Roxanne Davis, longtime friends and retired flight attendants from Northwest Airlines.

"Stewardesses," Davis corrected. "That's what we were called back then."

It was an early March day in 2002 at the Golf Center in Palm Desert, and the pair that had spent hundreds of hours together cruising at high altitudes decided that a couple of hours on the lesson tee with the legendary pro would do them some good. Despite having had opportunities to play abroad while working for Northwest—in Japan, South Korea, and other faraway places—golf was a hobby that seemed better suited to retirement because, McFarland-Hudgens said, "Golf is really difficult when you're flying because your time zones are all goofed up. It's much more pleasurable when you're on a regular schedule."

Surely Paul Runyan, who had traversed the globe during his eight decades playing and teaching the game professionally, could agree with that.

The two flight attendants had latched onto Runyan through a referral of sorts. They had lived in Seattle while flying for Northwest, and McFarland-Hudgens's late husband, Ron McFarland, had been a member at Sahalee when Runyan was the head pro. The whole time, McFarland had bragged to his wife about how lucky the Sahalee members were to have such a distinguished instructor.

"Ron thought Mr. Runyan was a master teacher and always encouraged me to get lessons," McFarland-Hudgens said. "So when I moved down to the Palm Springs area in 2000 I found out he was at a public golf course. He was an excellent teacher, a patient teacher. But he labored a bit. You could tell he wasn't feeling well."

Through his chesty cough and apparent weakness, Runyan, like he had thousands of times before, did his shtick. Despite the pleasant weather, he wore a windbreaker to stay warm. He suggested a minor grip change for McFarland-Hudgens and implored both players to chip with a variety of clubs for greater versatility. At the start of the lesson, Runyan sat in his golf cart. After a few minutes he stood up to offer hands-on instruction, then sat down again. No matter. His pupils were still impressed.

"You know, here we were, two women in their fifties," said McFarland-Hudgens. "You might wonder how someone like him would relate to us. I think he related well to everyone. He was very kind."

When the lesson ended, Runyan was upbeat and asked when they might come back. That would never happen. Shortly after the lesson, Runyan's health took a downward turn; he had pneumonia in both lungs. His son Jeff got him admitted at the Eisenhower Medical Center in Palm Springs three days later.

On Sunday, March 17, 2002, St. Patrick's Day, Paul Runyan, the lifelong golf professional who had authored one of the game's most unlikely victories and owned one of the greatest short games—maybe *the* greatest—in the history of the sport, died at age ninety-three.

A few days later McFarland-Hudgens and Davis read about Runyan's death in the newspaper. They were stunned, and one of them called the other to make sure she had seen the news. Two decades later, neither could recall who picked up the telephone first.

"It was sad," said McFarland-Hudgens. "We wanted to take more lessons. But it was his time, and we realize that."

As word of his death spread and his obituary started popping up in newspapers around the country—including the *New York Times* and the *Los Angeles Times*—condolences emerged from the world of golf. Among those expressing their admiration for Runyan were Arnold Palmer, who was hosting that week's Bay Hill Invitational at his Bay Hill Club and Lodge, and Tiger Woods, who won Palmer's event that Sunday by four strokes. Woods recalled how fun it was to watch Runyan drive the ball straight as a string during his pretournament nine-hole round at Sahalee in 1998.

Gene Littler gushed over Runyan's boundless energy for golf. Hootie Johnson, then chairman of Augusta National Golf Club, said, "Paul's longevity and competitive spirit will long be remembered." It seemed every obituary saved a line to acknowledge Runyan's greatest professional triumph, his 1938 upset of Sam Snead. Snead, of course, had gone on to win more than eighty PGA Tour events and seven major championships.

Jeff Runyan said his father had still had a lot he wanted to do, including attend the Masters that April.

Sam Snead made it to Augusta that April, although those close to him thought—perhaps even knew—that he wasn't up to it. A series of small strokes had taken their toll on Snead, who suffered through frustrating mental lapses and forgetfulness. On Thursday of the Masters, Snead showed up on the first tee at Augusta National to carry out his duties as the sole honorary starter. He made solid contact, but the shot sailed toward the patrons right of the fairway, striking a man in the head and breaking his glasses. That was the last golf ball Sam Snead ever hit. He died at age eighty-nine on May 23, 2002, sixty-seven days after Runyan had died in Palm Springs. There was special significance in that number. Recall that Runyan had thrown a near-flawless 67 at Snead in the morning round at Shawnee in 1938 to take a five-up advantage to lunch. Now he had beaten Snead to the hereafter by a margin that equaled his score.

ON AN EARLY spring afternoon in the California desert, Jeff Runyan uncovered in storage outside his house a trunk that had belonged to his dad. After half a century in the desert, Jeff, now a man in his seventies, longed to be closer to his son and grandson and decided it was time for a change of venue, so he put his house in La Quinta Cove on the market and made preparations to move. His older brother Paul, a California sculpture artist of some prominence, who loved surfing and yoga, had died the previous year.

Jeff's moving preparations included deciding what to keep and what to throw out. His dad's trunk—a sturdily built, olive-drab tank of a case that looked like it could have been recovered from the wreckage of the *Titanic*—had followed him around for years. With only a vague idea of its contents, he remained unsure what to do with it.

He opened the lid and began rummaging around. He was worried that all the years sitting untouched in the hot, dry desert might have damaged the items inside. Rather, everything was pristine, albeit old and fragile. He found handwritten letters from his parents' earliest days as a couple, scrapbooks, golf photos, family photos, Western Union telegrams, news clippings, and enough historic golf scorecards and ticket stubs to make a collector drool. There was a brochure from Paul's days as a consultant with Bristol, the club manufacturer that had released a line of "Little Poison" putters. There was a congratulatory letter from Spalding after he had won the 1938 PGA Championship. Jeff even dug out a small envelope that contained correspondence between his father's commanding officers when he had sought a commission in the navy.

It had been two decades since his father's death, but Jeff had sometimes caught himself preserving his father's memory through his own behavior. He shaved with the same Norelco electric razor. ("He wasn't a soap and water guy," Jeff said of his father.) He used some of his dad's tools. He owned a bottle of the same cologne. He even played golf with some of his dad's mannerisms, such as forgoing a glove and chipping with the heel of his club off the ground, stroking the ball like a putt. But the olive-drab trunk had dogged him. He knew he couldn't throw it away, even though he joked to himself about having a private bonfire, just to be done with the whole thing. For some unknown reason, he never struck the match.

"I've been carrying Dad around with me for a long time since he died," he said as he flipped through a stack of letters as brittle as a Wheat Thin.

Carrying his dad around had a double meaning.

"Where's your dad buried?" a friend asked.

There had been no burial per se, Jeff explained, only a memorial service at Annandale Golf Club in Pasadena in early April 2002, a few weeks after Paul died. Countless longtime friends had turned out to pay their respects, including two of the best players he ever taught, Phil Rodgers and Chuck Courtney.

"It was just heartwarming," Jeff Runyan said of the memorial. "There were so many people there who had come from so far away."

Like his first wife, Joan, Paul had been cremated.

"I have his ashes," Jeff said. "And one day I'm going to take him back to Arkansas and sprinkle him on his mother and father's grave."

Those graves are at Greenwood Cemetery in Hot Springs, beneath the shadow of Hot Springs National Park, not far from the Oaklawn Racetrack and Casino, about two miles as the crow flies from the long-gone family dairy farm where Runyan learned how to put in an honest day's work and the adjacent country club where he found his future. If the wind coming off the Ouachitas is right, some of those ashes could catch a gust and head south and east and find a landing spot on one of the narrow Bermuda fairways where Paul Runyan, then a tiny caddie, became a man, where he learned to play golf, and where he learned the most valuable golf lesson of his lifetime: that how many would always trump how mighty. It's uncertain how true that lesson remains today, in an era when golf, especially professional golf, seems irreversibly intent on rewarding brawn. Experts today in golf metrics will tell you that long hitting is disproportionately rewarded, compared to other skills like putting, approach play, and scrambling. It was his wish, Runyan said late in life, to be remembered "as the best of the truly light hitters." With each passing year, that spot seems more secure.

Acknowledgments

This book formally got its start in 2020, during the earliest days of the pandemic, although it would be unfair to call it a pandemic project. The process of assessing the story of Paul Runyan's life and his 1938 victory over Sam Snead began a year or so earlier, while I was writing a magazine profile about Phil Rodgers, his student. I was lucky enough to interview Phil a few times before he passed away, and he impressed upon me how important Runyan had been in his life. I remembered reading a little bit about "Little Poison" when I was a kid but knew very little beyond a basic sketch of his golf accomplishments. Sometime after I finished my profile of Rodgers, I decided to dive headfirst into Runyan. When I discovered that he had learned to play on a golf course with sand greens, I was all in. That's because I too had learned to play on a sand-green golf course.

This coincidence became more than a coincidence in my own mind. It hooked me and became fuel to track down his story, as well as passion to finish the job. Various other "coincidences" throughout the course of my research reminded me of something that I learned when I wrote *Scoreless* in 2016: the best stories come looking for us, not the other way around. The trick is noticing when the story spits in your face and asks to be written.

To really know a subject, I believe you have to go out and find it in its natural habitat. In my case, writing about events that mostly occurred decades before I was born, I needed to see the places where Paul and Joan Runyan spent their lives. So I traveled to Shawnee-on-the-Delaware, Pennsylvania, and Hot Springs, Arkansas, and La Jolla, California, and other stops in between. I tried to learn as much about these places as I did the people I was writing about, to better understand how the former may have affected the latter.

I also believe that talking to people is imperative to gathering a story. I was lucky that many people agreed to be interviewed for this book. They were Al Barkow, Joseph Bausch, Don Brenner, John Brugman, Patti Brugman, Chuck Courtney, Ben Crenshaw, Roxanne Davis, Bob Denman, Bob Denney, Dick Drager, John Fischer, Jay Fox, Barry Howard, Rob Howell, Mark Johnson, Ginny Kirkwood, Jon Kirkwood, Tom Kirkwood, Sidney Matthew, Alona McFarland-Hudgens, Frank Merhar, J. J. Obstronski, Mungo Park, Randy Reed, Roger Reierson, Phil Rodgers, Jeff Runyan, Cliff Schrock, Steve Taggart, Skip Tredway, Peter Trenham, Dr. Faith Vilas, Gordon Way, Guy Yocom, and Phil Young.

Meeting Jeff Runyan, Paul and Joan's younger son, was tremendously helpful to my research. I had tried for a year to track him down, to no avail, then one day he answered my call. By the time we met in person, I was fairly far along in the book, and he was able to provide answers that had been eluding me for months. Suddenly so many things became clearer. Jeff and I became friends (I hope he would agree), and I'm grateful for his support of this project. I'd also like to think that his old man would have been pleased with the book or at least would have appreciated the hustle.

During my visit to the Shawnee Inn and Golf Resort, every member of the Kirkwood family that I talked to or spent time with was supportive and helpful. I had a delightful conversation on the veranda of the Shawnee Inn with Ginny Kirkwood, which reinforced how important family was to her and her husband. I received two marvelous tours of the grounds at Shawnee: one from Jon Kirkwood and the other from Steve Taggart, the director of golf.

Chuck Courtney and Frank Merhar, who have been fixtures on the grounds of La Jolla Country Club since they were young boys under the tutelage of Paul Runyan, showed me around the club one chilly, sun-filled, early spring day. It's a beautiful spot for golf, and I can see why the Runyans felt at home there for so many years.

Charles Kelly, Michael Towle, and Jody Kahn gave me feedback on my book proposal when I was just getting started, and their collective guidance helped steer me in the right direction. Thanks to Rick

Dooling for talking me through some of the procedural aspects of the publishing process.

I was fortunate to connect early on with two revered golf journalists, Guy Yocom and Al Barkow, who, it turned out, were not only knowledgeable about Paul Runyan and Sam Snead but had spent time with them personally. Guy graciously shared some highlights from his own reporting, and I can't imagine doing without that information as background. Al performed a similar function. Both men could sense how badly I wanted to tell this story and responded with the utmost courtesy.

After reading Jay Revell's profile of Bobby Jones historian Sidney Matthew that preceded a story with my own byline in the spring 2021 issue of the *Golfer's Journal*, I asked Jay for an introduction to Matthew, thinking maybe, just maybe, somewhere in his extensive Jones collection, he might have some information on Runyan. It turned out that Sidney had interviewed Runyan in the early 1990s, and that interview, which had been video recorded, was available as part of his Bobby Jones collection at Emory University in Atlanta. It became a great source for my research, and any time I reached out to Sidney with a golf history question, he either had the answer or knew where to look for it. His enthusiasm for golf history is unmatched, and I'm grateful he took an interest in my work.

Liz Robbins, executive director of the Garland County Historical Society in Hot Springs, Arkansas, was delightful and helpful during my trip and helped me track down photographs, news clippings, and a few old Hot Springs city directories. Other staff and volunteers who assisted Liz were just as eager to help me.

During a visit to Hot Springs Country Club, its general manager, Barry Howard, showed me around the club and shared some of his own memories of Paul Runyan. He also introduced me to Jay Fox, Randy Reed, and Tyler Meyl from the Arkansas State Golf Association, who by chance were on site that day officiating a college event. They were all willing to help, and Jay even introduced me to Brian McRae, the club president, who knew a lot about the club's history and took an interest in my project.

Janet Tilden read my manuscript as it neared completion and gave me some much-needed guidance to help make it better. Maureen Bemko was tireless in her review of my prose, carefully editing my work and offering many helpful suggestions.

Rob Taylor, my editor from the University of Nebraska Press, liked my idea from the start and kept me within the boundary stakes as I approached my submission deadline. Somewhere along the way, we discovered that we shared some golf history: his high school golf coach was my college golf coach.

My usual playing companions at the Players Club at Deer Creek in Omaha—who include Tony Roth, James Kinney, Carl Heine, and Tim Riha—often asked how I was coming on the book, and I found that talking through it with friends was a great benefit as I structured the story. The same goes for my Muirfield Village crew: Kevin Shepherd, Mike Emery, and David Howser. I can't imagine a better group in the world to sit around with at a dinner table and debate swing theory while holding butter knives in our hands. Thanks, gentlemen. Your interest in my work kept me motivated.

Don Germer and Skip Tredway, a couple of old-school (but young at heart) club professionals in Omaha, are probably the ones to thank for the initial spark that became this book. They encouraged me to write about Phil Rodgers, and that led me to Runyan. Thanks pro, pro.

Finally, special thanks go to my wife, Laura, and my kids—Joe, Emma, Ben, and Zack—for their support these past few years. Laura can tell when I'm working on a new book, because every time I leave the house in the morning or return at day's end, I'm dragging around an extra tote bag or banker's box filled with my book files. Just like my golf clubs on a road trip, they go where I go.

If my kids are ever compelled to sit down and read this book, I hope they glean from Paul Runyan's story the same thing that I did: it's not the size of the dog in the fight that matters, but the size of the fight in the dog. It's cliché but true. Nobody knew that better than Paul Runyan.

Bibliographic Essay

What follows is my guided tour through the research and production of this book. I can't say why exactly, but I've always preferred to read an author's notes this way, in prose form. My apologies if you are someone who enjoys a more traditional system of bibliography and citation. I have attempted to cite the key sources that I used to piece together the story of Paul Runyan's life and his 1938 victory over Sam Snead at the PGA Championship. In many spots you'll notice that I have pulled bits and pieces—sometimes the smallest of fragments—from various sources (newspapers, photos, interviews), thrown them into a blender, and churned out what I hope is the smoothest and most accurate version of the story in question. You're sure to notice wide variety in the sources I've drawn from, especially with newspapers. A single anecdote may have been compiled from newspapers in California, Arkansas, New York, and North Dakota. I sometimes wish it was simpler, but as an author I accept the responsibility of connecting these sometimes disparate pieces for the reader's benefit.

Prologue

The scene that dominates the prologue was first described to me by Paul Runyan's godson John Fischer during a telephone interview. Fischer attended the Masters in 1999 and provided an important first-hand recollection of Runyan's involvement in the Par-3 Contest. He also guided me toward a story in the *South Florida Sun Sentinel* (then known simply as the *Sun Sentinel*) by Michael Mayo, originally published on April 8, 1999, that profiled Runyan at the Masters.

The anecdotal information included in the second paragraph comes from my own observations of the Masters, as I have been keenly aware of the event for more than twenty-five years as of this writing.

Ben Crenshaw graciously recounted his experience playing with Runyan that day in an interview, and he provided helpful background information about Hot Springs Country Club, where Runyan played the game as a boy.

1. Something in the Water

I sourced much of the information about the thermal springs in Arkansas that precedes chapter 1 from the National Park Service website (www.nps.gov). The site includes helpful images and illustrations about the geology of Hot Springs. I found additional supporting information during my visit to the Hot Springs National Park Visitor Center, located in the former Fordyce Bathhouse in Hot Springs.

The census information at the start of the chapter comes from the Fourteenth Census of the United States, which I located for Garland County, Arkansas. Former *Golf Digest* senior writer Guy Yocom interviewed Paul Runyan various times over the years, and Yocom graciously provided his recollections of those conversations to me as background for this book. Runyan's place of birth (19 Baker Street) was included in that information, and I visited the address during my time in Hot Springs.

I was able to reconstruct much of Runyan's early life in this chapter through two books: *Gettin' to the Dance Floor: An Oral History of American Golf*, by Al Barkow (New York: Atheneum, 1986), and *The Short Way to Lower Scoring*, by Paul Runyan (Norwalk CT: Golf Digest, 1979). A three-part 1993 interview with Runyan that lawyer and golf historian Sidney Matthew conducted in Sea Island, Georgia, helped fill in additional gaps in Runyan's early years. That interview is housed in the Manuscript, Archives, and Rare Book Library at Emory University in Atlanta, Georgia. I traced Walter and Mamie Runyan's employment history through Hot Springs city directories that were on file at the Garland County Historical Society.

Hot Springs Country Club has a great appreciation for its history, and much of the background information on the formation and early years came from the club's own archive, which included postcards, survey documentation, an early club stock certificate, and Martin Eisele's writings—all compiled in the club's privately published history book, *Hot Springs Country Club: The First 100 Years, 1898–1998*. I found additional information on Eisele and his association with Charles Walgreen through the Garland County Historical Society. Andrew Carnegie's visit to Hot Springs was chronicled in the March 15, 1912, edition of the *Hot Springs New Era*. David Hill's 2012 article "The Invaders" in *Grantland* provided some general background for me on the colorful underworld history of Hot Springs; so did his book *The Vapors* (New York: Farrar, Straus and Giroux, 2020).

The announcement of the Arkansas State Golf Association's state tournament was published in the *Hot Springs New Era* on April 15, 1916. Through a series of email exchanges, architect and golf historian Mungo Park, great-nephew of Willie Park Jr., helped me place Hot Springs Country Club in the chronology of Park's design work. A short news article in the June 30, 1913, edition of the *Hot Springs New Era* provided information about the land purchase that preceded the building of the club. A *New Era* article published on November 19, 1919, titled "Banner Season for Golf Enthusiasts," recapped Willie Park's contributions to the golf course and the growing enthusiasm for the club.

Babe Ruth's annual visits to Hot Springs were well chronicled in the New York and Hot Springs newspapers, including two helpful articles in the *Hot Springs New Era*, one from February 25, 1921, and the other from February 16, 1923. Additional background on Babe's travels through Hot Springs was available from the Hot Springs Historic Baseball Trail.

The city of Hot Springs has information about the Majestic Hotel on its website (www.cityhs.net), and I located some articles in the *Hot Springs New Era* about the hotel's farm, including one from October 30, 1920, that detailed its profitability. I found additional background on the Majestic in an article titled "Majestic Hotel: The History of a Grande Dame," by Isabel Burton Anthony, which was published in the forty-ninth edition of *The Record*, on file in the Garland County Historical Society. While I acknowledge that much about Walter

Runyan's relationship with the Majestic farm remains unknown, the clearest version of that story came from unpublished segments of Guy Yocom's 1994 interview with Runyan for *Golf Digest*. The 1934 newspaper profile that is referenced more than once in this chapter was published in various newspapers across the country, but I found it in the April 6, 1934, edition of the *Pensacola News Journal*, where it was headlined "Paul Runyan Proves That Milking Cows Is Good Exercise for Future Golf Wars." A lengthier version of the same story appeared in the *Arkansas Democrat* on Sunday, March 25, 1934; that version included the anecdote about the Runyan boys' failed attempt at swimming.

Longtime Garland County historian Alta Smith had a hand in tracking Runyan's story over the years. There's a file (File 13, Box 19) in the Chamber of Commerce Collection at the Garland County Historical Society that houses Smith's research on Runyan, including a 1934 "Note to the Sports Editor" of the local newspaper and her own handwritten notes.

I first learned that Runyan had grown up playing on sand greens in Hot Springs when I watched a video of his 1988 speech at the PGA Teaching Summit. Later, I corroborated this fact in the Hot Springs Country Club centennial history book and in Runyan's own books, where he explains developing his short-game technique based on course conditions. The final section of the chapter, where I explain the intricacies of playing on sand, is based on my own experience, having grown up playing on a golf course in Kansas—that remains open for play—with sand greens.

2. Six Hundred Balls a Day

The bit about the young player climbing a mountain that precedes the chapter was my own summation of the colossal task Paul Runyan undertook in going from an unknown club professional "teaching ladies" and repairing clubs to one of pro golf's best players.

I first read about Jimmy Norton's advice to "teach the ladies . . . and grow a mustache" in the article from the *Pensacola News Journal* (April 6, 1934) that I referenced in the previous chapter. During my visit to the Garland County Historical Society, I found an article Runyan wrote about his early years in golf. Headlined "Paul Runyan: The Leading Prize Winner of the Winter Circuit Tells His Story," the article, which appears to have been published in 1934, is two full pages and a jump, but unfortunately the name of the publication is missing. However, it includes more details about the mustache, such as its "ragged" look and "red wisp."

Garland County historian Alta Smith's "Note to the Sports Editor" included some details about Runyan's short stint in Fargo, North Dakota. Some of those details were corroborated in Runyan's own writing from the first-person story I referenced in the previous paragraph. My interviews with Roger Reierson and Mark W. Johnson helped me better understand Runyan's time in Fargo and the general history of the club. The club's website (www.fargocc.com) includes a timeline with historic dates in the club's history. Additional background came from an article in the *Bismarck Tribune* of August 2, 1924.

The story about "Wild Bill" Mehlhorn's club repairs was shared by Guy Yocom, who was *Golf Digest*'s technical editor at the time of his interview.

Runyan's employment at Concordia Country Club in Little Rock is detailed in Al Barkow's book *Gettin' to the Dance Floor*. In that same book, Runyan explains to Barkow his relationship with Harry Tenenbaum. It's safe to say I had as much fun tracking down Harry Tenenbaum's story as any in this book. For starters I visited the Tenenbaum Recycling Group (TRG) website (www.trg.net), which included some valuable company history, such as a description of the sign outside Abraham Tenenbaum's business. An *Arkansas Gazette* story from August 21, 1921, explains most of the details surrounding Harry Tenenbaum's questionable marriage. Other pieces of that story and Tenenbaum's background came to light through my examination of U.S. Census records from 1910, 1920, and 1940; articles in the *Arkansas Gazette* (June 30, 1929, and May 10, 1952); an article in the March 12, 1960, *Omaha World-Herald*, headlined "TV Tycoon's Gift Turkeys to FCC Were in 'Bad Taste'"; and an article in the January 15, 1965, edition of the *St. Louis Post-Dispatch* that explained how Tenenbaum's estate would get divided after his death.

Harry Tenenbaum's exploits as a club golfer were recounted in the

Arkansas Gazette on October 30, 1927, and October 14, 1928. The story of Tenenbaum's hole in one came from the April 15, 1929, issue of the *Arkansas Gazette*. The matches between the Arkansas club professionals and their efforts to start a PGA section were followed in the *Arkansas Gazette* on October 30, 1927, and October 14, 1928, just beneath the stories about Tenenbaum.

Runyan's victories in the Arkansas Open were recounted in various places, including in his own words in the article headlined "Paul Runyan: The Leading Prize Winner of the Winter Circuit Tells His Story." I found Runyan's scores from the 1926 South Central Open in the *Tennessean*, published February 3–4, 1926. The article "Western Open Draws Nation's Leading Golfers," from the September 4, 1927, edition of the *Chicago Tribune*, referenced the "Who's Who" of golf. The *Tribune* offered daily recaps and scores on September 9 and 10, 1927.

I first learned of Runyan's money match at Willow Beach with Titanic Thompson, Dutch Harrison, and Julius Ackerbloom while reading "Dusty Relics of Arkansas History" in Little Rock's *Daily Record*, which was published online the week of February 3–9, 2020. I interviewed Bob Denman, the article's author, for more information, and he pointed me to Harrison's biography, *Mr. Dutch: The Arkansas Traveler*, by Beach Leighton (Champaign IL: Sagamore, 1991), which includes Harrison's version of the story. Denman told me that he learned to play golf on what he described as "an old, run-down, weather-beaten nine-holer" called Rock Creek Golf Course, which sat on the same ground where Concordia Country Club once stood. Denman explained that today the property is used by First Tee of Arkansas, and none of the original holes remain. However, he explained that the original clubhouse is still standing, deep in the woods of the property, near a Methodist church and the remnants of an old (hidden) smoking and drinking pavilion from the Concordia Country Club days. *Golf Digest*'s Dave Kindred wrote an article, "The Myths of Titanic," that was published in the magazine's May 1996 issue, and it includes a brief description of the match. Guy Yocom helped fill in a few additional details about Thompson from his notes.

The Arnold Rothstein murder was well covered in the New York newspapers, and I used articles from the *New York Daily News* (November 6 and 25, 1928) and *Brooklyn Daily Eagle* (November 9 and 18, 1928) as background. The *Edmonton Journal* in the Canadian province of Alberta published a December 4, 1928, article on Titanic's $13,000 bet at Grassy Sprain Country Club.

Gene Littler's take on Paul Runyan's bump-in with his future wife Joan comes from the foreword to Runyan's book *The Short Way to Lower Scoring*. Runyan's quotes about feeling dizzy around Joan came from the 1934 story he authored, which I found at the Garland County Historical Society. Jeff Runyan provided background on his mother's family. I tracked the family's whereabouts through U.S. Census records from 1930 and 1940.

Runyan described taking the job with Craig Wood at Forest Hill in *Gettin' to the Dance Floor*; in that same text he also explained the high-stakes gambling that took place at the club. His reservations about taking the job—specifically, being too young—were revealed in an article in the March 29, 1930, *Dayton Herald*, headlined "Youthful Paul Runyan Victor in Open Meet." For additional coverage of the 1930 North and South Open, I located the following news articles: "21-Year-Old Assistant Pro from New Jersey Shoots Near Perfect for 2 Rounds," by Dillon Graham, in the *Asheville Citizen-Times* on March 29, 1930; "Runyan Leader in Pinehurst Meet," from the *Charlotte News* on March 27, 1930; "Runyan Pays Debt with Golf Money," from the *Bismarck Tribune* on March 29, 1930; "Smith Trailing in 1st Round of Play at Pinehurst," from the *Charlotte Observer* on March 28, 1930; "Runyan Winner in Open Tourney" from the *Charlotte News* on March 29, 1930; and "Jersey Pro Wins Pinehurst Event," by Dillon Graham in Raleigh's *News and Observer* on March 29, 1930. I found additional supporting information about Pinehurst on the resort's website (www.pinehurst.com), and Lori Wright from the Tufts Archives at Pinehurst shared various pieces of Pinehurst history, including an article, "Runyan Wins the North and South," from the *Pinehurst Outlook* on March 29, 1930, which detailed his win. The article "It Was a Fun Time in the Thirties," by Dan Jenkins, from the April 4, 1966, issue of *Sports Illustrated* was a helpful source throughout my work on this book, and in that story was Jenkins's line about the Masters eventually out-southerning the North and South.

The story of Johnny Dawson from Spalding handing Runyan a half dozen Spalding Dots between rounds at Pinehurst was compiled from two sources: *Paul Runyan's Book for Senior Golfers* (New York: Dodd, Mead, 1962) and an article, "He Cut 'Em All Down to His Size," that was published in the PGA *Book of Golf: 1978*, which was shared with me by USGA senior historian Victoria Nenno via email.

While I have inklings about who the creditors were in the story of Runyan's debt, I never solved that riddle. While chasing the story, I tracked down Jack Vilas's 1929 autobiography, *My Life to My Children* (1929; repr. Rustic Books, 2007). His granddaughter Dr. Faith Vilas agreed to an interview, and she provided some anecdotes about her grandfather and his personality. *The Record* (1999), published by the Garland County Historical Society in Hot Springs, contained information about Vilas's stint as the town's deputy sheriff. *The Record* (1986) provided background information on the Vilas family. I found news articles about Vilas in the following publications: the *Hot Springs Sentinel-Record* on December 27, 1913, February 3, 1914, and May 26, 1914; the *Chicago Daily News* on February 11, 1929; the *Chicago Daily Times* on September 27, 1939; and the *Arkansas Gazette* on June 5, 1927, January 17, 1930, and June 10, 1932. In his 1988 presentation to the PGA Teaching and Coaching Summit, which I found on YouTube, Runyan mentioned Jack Vilas's influence and his putting grip.

The story of Frank Walsh's telegram to Craig Wood after the 1930 North and South came from Runyan's *Book for Senior Golfers*. Runyan's own telegram to his fiancée, Joan, was in a trunk full of letters, photos, and memorabilia that Paul's son Jeff Runyan shared with me. As I explained in the main text, I found the note Runyan had written to the fan named Sharon during a general internet search. Just out of curiosity I sent that note and a couple other samples of Runyan's handwriting to Susan Westenbroek, a certified professional graphologist (handwriting expert) in Texas. I will spare you her full analysis, but in her description of Runyan she described him as very organized, extremely loyal, tasteful, intelligent, honest, and someone whose "enthusiasm can be contagious and difficult to resist." She also mentioned an understanding of numbers; more on that later.

I located the cover of the May 1930 issue of *Golfers Magazine* on the internet in an expired listing on a golf auction site. I found a recap of the 1930 sports scene in an article in the *Dothan (AL) Eagle*, published on January 1, 1931.

Runyan's account of his time at Forest Hill came from *Gettin' to the Dance Floor* and the article in the PGA *Book of Golf: 1978*. Runyan's course record bet with Craig Wood was a small news item in the *Asbury Park Press* on August 9, 1930. His victory at the New Jersey State Open was recapped in that same publication from August 14–16, 1930. The Associated Press announcement of Runyan's engagement ran in the *Jersey Journal* on February 19, 1931; his own retelling of the engagement, including the run-in with Gerald Rosenberger, was in the PGA *Book of Golf: 1978*. Other details about the wedding came from the *Arkansas Gazette* on March 22, 1931.

3. Samuel Jackson

The comparison between Chuck Berry's "Johnny B. Goode" and Sam Snead's upbringing is my own concoction, which came to me after hearing the song one day and reflecting on the idea of nurturing talent in relative obscurity and coming out of nowhere to take on the world. Many of the stories that are part of the Snead lore were included in Al Barkow's book *Sam: The One and Only Sam Snead* (Lanham MD: Taylor Trade, 2010), which I read as a follow-up to my telephone interview and email exchanges with Barkow. My other main sources for Snead anecdotes were Barkow's *Gettin' to the Dance Floor*; *Herbert Warren Wind's Golf Book* (New York: Simon and Schuster, 1948); "The Ride of Sam Snead's Life," a 1999 *Golf Digest* story by Guy Yocom; and "It's Time to Remember Sam Snead," a 2019 *Golf Digest* story also by Yocom.

I found the history of the Omni Homestead and the Snead family's ties to the area in various places, including Guy Yocom's aforementioned 2019 *Golf Digest* article, Jerry Vondas's 2006 article "Man Was Part of a Great Golfing Family" on a Pittsburgh media site (www.triblive.com), and the history section of the Omni Homestead website.

To avoid unnecessary repetition, I'll point out that all the stories about Sam Snead's upbringing in the first half of this chapter came from three books: Barkow's *Sam* and *Gettin' to the Dance Floor* and Wind's *Golf Book*. Having stated that, I'll include a few notable highlights. Barkow's *Sam* explained how Snead's middle name was given to honor Stonewall Jackson. The stories about Snead's mother teaching him to sew and knit and about trapping animals and catching fish with his bare hands are included in Wind's *Golf Book*. Both of Barkow's books explain the love/hate relationship Snead seems to have had with Freddie Gleim and Nelson Long. The story of Snead's impromptu lesson with the "big-busted woman" comes from *Gettin' to the Dance Floor* and is recounted in *Sam*.

My assessment of Snead's golf swing was formed through years of seeing his swing on video and in books. Swing instructor Mike Emery spent significant time explaining to me certain traits in Snead's swing, such as his upper body extension, left-heel lift, and squatting move on the downswing. Dick Drager, a golf instructor and former Snead colleague at the Golf Digest instructional schools, told me stories about Snead's participation in golf clinics and his talent for hitting shots on command.

I found an article about Snead's practice round with Chandler Harper for the Middle Atlantic Golf Championship in the *Newport (VA) Daily Press*, published on July 24, 1934. Other news articles about that event were printed in the *Richmond Times-Dispatch* on July 24, 1934, and the *Danville (VA) Bee* on July 25, 1934.

The story of Snead's trip to the 1935 Miami Biltmore Open and the club he borrowed from Freddie Gleim is included in *Gettin' to the Dance Floor*. The tournament and Snead's actual winnings were recapped in the *Miami Herald* on December 18, 1935. A footnote in that same article indicated that most players would travel to Nassau on the SS *Northland*.

Barkow details the story of the 1935 Cascades Open at length in *Sam*. Snead's opening rounds were well reported in the September 21, 1935, *Richmond Times-Dispatch*. The *Bluefield (WV) Daily Telegraph* published a short recap of the final round.

In *Gettin' to the Dance Floor* Snead gave an account of his return to Miami in 1936, which included his deal with Dunlop. Al Barkow spelled out in *Sam* how Snead's deal with Freddie Martin and the Greenbrier came about; he also included the Lew Keller story about Snead's money matches in New York. Snead's 1936 Miami Open winnings were posted in the *Miami News* on December 9, 1936. The story that closes out the chapter—about Snead speaking with Craig Wood and Henry Picard and then heading for California with Johnny Bulla—comes from *Gettin' to the Dance Floor*.

4. White Plains

Before the main text of chapter 4, I attempt to set the scene for readers about what life was like for a golf professional in the 1930s, because very few, if any, of today's top touring professionals also have club jobs. The information about Runyan turning Metropolis Country Club into his own training ground was gathered from Al Barkow's *Gettin' to the Dance Floor*, the PGA *Book of Golf: 1978*, and my interview with Dick Drager. I found that Runyan's hourly lesson fee was $4 in an article titled "Paul Runyan Taught Golf at 17" in the *Capital Times* of Madison, Wisconsin, published on April 11, 1933. The final two paragraphs, where I likened Runyan's play to a magician's act, constituted my own synopsis after reading countless articles about Runyan from the early 1930s mentioning that he left spectators and fellow competitors mystified by his success.

Runyan described his golf trip to Pinehurst in 1931 in "Paul Runyan: The Leading Prize Winner of the Winter Circuit Tells His Story." (He described the trip as a honeymoon, noting that the beauty of Pinehurst in March, with "birds chirping, the grass and trees a gay green, the flowers bright and beautiful and not a cloud in the blue sky," distracted him from his golf.) Details of the tournament were reported in the *Raleigh News and Observer* on March 26, 1931; the *Klamath News* of Klamath Falls, Oregon, on March 29, 1931; and the *Asheville Citizen-Times* on March 29, 1931. The first two rounds of the Southeastern Open were covered in that same edition of the Asheville newspaper. The *Orlando Sentinel* reported the final results on April 1, 1931. The Rockne plane crash was in newspapers all over the country that same day, overshadowing all other sports news.

Patti Brugman told me about Runyan's affinity for Craig Wood in our interview, and various interviews Runyan gave over the years corroborated that account. The scene at Gerald Rosenberger's house, where Runyan was interviewed by members from Metropolis Country

Club, comes from *Gettin' to the Dance Floor*. The story about the Forest Hill members asking Runyan to reconsider after Wood decided to take another job came from the PGA *Book of Golf: 1978*. Background information on Metropolis Country Club was available on the club's website (www.metropoliscc.org).

Runyan described Edmund Waterman as like a "czar" in *Gettin' to the Dance Floor* and the PGA *Golf Book: 1978*; both books include other details about Waterman's personality. (Curiously, Waterman's given name is sometimes spelled Edwin; in telegrams, he signed his name as Edmund or Ed, so I chose Edmund as the preferred usage in the main text.) While I found it hard to believe, I read in the profile of Runyan that was published in the *Arkansas Democrat* on March 25, 1934, that there were 1,600 members at Metropolis Country Club. Runyan explained his teetotaling ways to Guy Yocom in their 1994 interview; he also told Yocom about how his West Coast trip in 1929 failed because he went to bed too early.

Jeff Runyan shared the letters between Paul and Joan Runyan during their first summer in New York. The "Mother Harris" letter Runyan wrote to Joan's mother was also included in that private family archive.

I found stories about Runyan's play at the 1931 Westchester Open and the Metropolitan PGA Championship in the following newspapers: the *Glen Falls (NY) Post-Star* on October 1, 1931; *Brooklyn Daily Eagle* (October 2, 5, 6, 8, 11); *Rochester Democrat and Chronicle* on October 5, 1931; *The Tennessean* on October 5, 1931; and *Charlotte News* on November 20, 1931. These stories included the anecdotes about Sarazen's sometimes strained relationship with sportswriters and fellow competitors. The Lou Niss column was published in the *Brooklyn Times Union* on October 1, 1931. The congratulatory notes Runyan received after his victory over Sarazen were courtesy of Jeff Runyan's archive. Runyan's praise of Sarazen, in which he describes him as "the only player who ever intimidated me," came from *Gettin' to the Dance Floor*. I studied Runyan's so-called jerky swing in video clips I found online. Ralph Trost's description of Runyan's swing came from his column in the *Brooklyn Daily Eagle* on October 2, 1931.

Runyan explained his relationship with Jesse Jelenko (and the story of their back-nine bet) in his 1993 interview with Sidney Matthew.

Jeff Runyan provided me with numerous telegrams, and Jelenko's relationship with Runyan was revealed in some of those messages. I pieced together the financing of Runyan's winter golf tour from his own account in *Gettin' to the Dance Floor* and in a letter from Mannie Dias to Runyan that was in Jeff Runyan's archive. The account of the touring lifestyle in the 1930s was developed based on my examination of the topic in *Gettin' to the Dance Floor* and Dan Jenkins's "It Was a Fun Time in the Thirties," a 1966 *Sports Illustrated* article. I pulled a few other details, such as the checking of golf balls for the proper compression, from Guy Yocom's 1994 interview with Runyan. Cyril Walker's slow-play antics were covered in the *Los Angeles Evening Express* on January 14 and 15, 1929.

Jeff Runyan told me about his parents' love of dancing. Guy Yocom told me that Runyan described dancing as a stress reliever in their interview. Various news accounts from the 1930s mention that the Runyans loved to dance. An article in the *Richmond Times-Dispatch* from July 19, 1938, rated the Runyans' dancing (and table tennis) skills against other pro golf couples.

Runyan's golf results from the winter of 1931–32 were covered in the following newspapers: the *Fort Worth Star-Telegram* on January 25 and February 22, 1932; *Charlotte News* on January 31, 1932; *Tampa Tribune* on February 24, 1932; and *Brooklyn Daily Eagle* on February 23, 1932. Ralph Trost called Runyan "soft-spoken" and "angelic-looking" in his March 26, 1932, column in the *Brooklyn Daily Eagle*. Al Barkow recapped Runyan's winter tour and the story of the Metropolis members letting him keep their share of the profits in *Gettin' to the Dance Floor*.

5. "I Don't Know How He Does It"

In my own mind, it's sometimes hard to distinguish between the parts of the Bobby Jones story that I've absorbed through books and media during my nearly three decades of interest in golf and the parts that I've gathered specifically while researching this book. I found Runyan's interactions with Jones to be critical to the story. They add context and help place Runyan among the many legendary golfers of the early twentieth century.

Before I began my research I was unaware how often Jones and

Runyan crossed paths, beyond their pairing at the inaugural Masters Tournament in 1934. Jones historian Sidney Matthew conducted an extensive interview with Runyan in 1993 for his work on a documentary film about Jones, and that interview was critical to this chapter and the short narrative that precedes it. In that interview, Runyan described the matches he and Horton Smith played against Jones and Ed Dudley. The anecdote about Jones hitting a soft fairway wood off a downslope came from Guy Yocom's 1994 interview with Runyan; that shot came on the second hole at Augusta National. I'm not sure when Grantland Rice first nicknamed him "Runyan of the five spoons," but I found that phrase in his column in the *Philadelphia Inquirer* on June 7, 1934. My friend Lee Millward suggested that "Little Poison" sounded like the name of a hip-hop artist. I liked his line so much I decided to use it in my book.

The details of Runyan's agreement with Spalding and Bobby Jones's collaboration with J. Victor East came from Sidney Matthew's 1993 interview with Runyan. Additional background on Spalding's contributions to other sports came from the company's website (www.spalding.com). I found an article on Spalding equipment from January 1933 titled "Spalding Announces Important Refinements in Spalding ROB'T T. JONES, JR. Golf Clubs!" which was published in *Golfdom*. I also relied on Spalding advertisements from 1932 and 1933 that were published in the following newspapers: the *Chattanooga Daily Times*, *Kansas City Star*, *Minneapolis Star*, *Quad-City* (IA) *Times*, and the *Evening Star* of Washington DC. Those clips provided important details about the price of golf equipment in the Jones/Runyan era; the clip from the *Quad-City Times* contained the nugget about eighteen of twenty U.S. Open winners playing a Spalding ball.

The story of Runyan's first encounter with Jones in 1928 (and his subsequent visits with Jones in Atlanta) came from the Sidney Matthew interview. Although he recalled the wrong year, Runyan also described the 1930 Southeastern Open (sometimes called the Augusta Open) to Matthew. That tournament was well covered by the *Atlanta Constitution* on March 31 and April 2, 1930.

Shav Glick was the *Los Angeles Times* reporter who called Runyan the hottest golfer on tour between 1933 and 1935 in a story published on April 8, 1997. Runyan's victory in the Agua Caliente Open was described in the *San Bernardino Daily Sun* and the *Lincoln (NE) Star* on January 15, 1933. Runyan's own handwritten notes on the rear side of a photo from the trophy ceremony filled in a few details about the winner's purse from the event. The *Hutchinson News* detailed the Runyans' trip to Kansas in articles published on January 17 and January 27, 1933. Runyan's victory with Horton Smith at the International Four-Ball was reported in the *Brooklyn Daily Eagle* on March 14, 1933. Dan Jenkins's *Sports Illustrated* story "It Was a Fun Time in the Thirties" contained the anecdote about the tournaments that sounded like they belonged on a billiards circuit. Because of its unique format—utilizing oversized cups—the 1933 Florida All-Year-Round Open at the Miami Biltmore got a lot of ink in the newspapers. I relied on clips from the *Miami Daily News* on March 6–7, 1933, and the *Daily Record* (of Long Branch, New Jersey) on March 6.

Ralph Trost's column about Runyan's attitudes toward equipment, headlined "Runyan's Wood Shaft Jigger Scores Plenty," came from the March 14, 1933, edition of the *Brooklyn Daily Eagle*. Runyan explained the subtle differences between hickory and steel shafts in his interviews with Sidney Matthew and Guy Yocom.

Uncovering the origin of Runyan's nickname was harder than I expected. Trost's column gave the reader "Little Poison" but failed to reveal its origin. From articles in the *Tacoma News Tribune* on February 28, 1968, and the *Palm Springs Desert Sun* on March 13, 1982, I learned that the nickname came from sportswriter Lawrence Robinson.

The Ryder Cup dinner at Auby's Lagoon was reported in the *Miami News* on March 3, 1933. The Billy Burke controversy was widely reported in the sports sections of newspapers in 1933; I relied on stories from the *Reading (PA) Times* on April 10, 1933, *Sioux City Journal* on April 16, 1933, and *Jacksonville Daily Journal* on June 13, 1933. Red Cole's "Talk of the Times" column in the *Tampa Times* on June 13, 1933, was a helpful recap of the whole scene, including the effect of Johnny Goodman's U.S. Open victory. The controversy over scheduling after the Ryder Cup (so players could play in the PGA Championship) was reported by the *Miami Herald* on July 22, 1933. The tune-up match against New York amateurs was reported in the *Meriden (CT) Record* on June 13, 1933, and the *Kansas City Times* on June 14. Jeff Runyan shared a program from a testimonial dinner for the Ryder Cup team that was held on the evening of June 14 at the Hotel Roosevelt, and it contained supporting information about the matches. Jeff's bundle of research material included letters, postcards, scorecards, programs, and telegrams from the 1933 European trip. There was even an oversized map of the SS *Aquitania*.

The website for Southport and Ainsdale Golf Club (www.sandagolfclub.co.uk), which contains wonderful aerial video footage of the golf course, included important pieces of club history, course layout, and a recap of the two Ryder Cups it has hosted. The club embedded a three-minute highlight reel from YouTube that showcases the large sand dunes that surrounded the putting greens and the massive crowds that turned up to watch the competition. The *Boston Globe* (June 28, 1933) and the *Brooklyn Daily Eagle* (June 29, 1933) published lengthy recaps of each day's play. Bernard Darwin's reporting was published in the *Boston Globe* on June 28. Runyan recalled some details from his match against Percy Allis in the *PGA Book of Golf: 1978*.

I used Sidney Matthew's interview with Runyan for his memories of his first trip to St. Andrews and the 1933 Open Championship. Qualifying scores for the Open were published in *The Guardian* (of Manchester, England) on July 7, 1933. I was able to peg Paul and Joan's return date to the United States after locating their names on a passenger manifest for the SS *Washington*. I found results of Runyan's play at the 1933 PGA Championship in the *Brooklyn Times Union* from August 10 and the *New York Daily News* from August 12. Runyan's victory at the Pasadena Open was covered in the *Pasadena Post* on December 25, 1933. The original congratulatory telegrams Runyan received after the victory were in Jeff Runyan's archive.

The grand opening of Augusta National Golf Club was covered in the *Atlanta Constitution* on January 16, 1933. In addition to relying on Paul Runyan's own memories of the first Masters from his interview with Guy Yocom—much of which was published in *Golf Digest* in April 2016—I reconstructed the tournament through news articles from the following publications: the *Atlanta Constitution* (March 20,

24, 26, and 27, 1934), *Miami News* on March 19 and 25, *Green Bay Press Gazette* on March 22, and *Charlotte Observer* on March 24.

I found a lengthy summary of Runyan's victory in the West Coast Open in the March 3, 1934, edition of the *Miami Herald*. The *Miami News* covered the outcome of the International Four-Ball on March 8, 1934. Runyan's superb play at the Charleston Open was recapped in the *Fort Worth Star-Telegram* and the *Montgomery Advertiser* on March 18.

Runyan's thoughts on Augusta National's beauty and its difficulty (particularly in comparison to Forest Hills–Ricker and Augusta Country Club) came from his 1993 interview with Sidney Matthew. He further explained his feelings on Augusta's difficulty for short hitters, the clambake-like atmosphere of the first Masters, and the pretournament Calcutta in his interview with Guy Yocom. I found the story of Horton Smith using one of Runyan's drivers to win the Masters in Ralph Trost's column, headlined "Midget Runyan's Wood Drives Horton to 284 and Big Augusta Prize," in the *Brooklyn Daily Eagle* on March 25, 1934.

I found extensive coverage of Runyan's win at the Cavalier Open in the *Virginian-Pilot* and the *Norfolk Landmark* on April 3, 1934. The background on Runyan assessing the wet conditions and giving himself a pep talk came from Charles Houston's column in the April 8, 1934, edition of the *Richmond Times-Dispatch*.

Grantland Rice's description of Runyan being "as cool as a slice of cucumber on ice" came from his column ("The Sportlight") in the *Philadelphia Inquirer* on June 7, 1934. Jack Doyle's odds for the 1934 U.S. Open were published in the *Inquirer* on June 3, along with a lengthy preview of the championship. For the rest of the section on the Open at Merion, I relied heavily on the extensive coverage of the *Inquirer* from June 1 to June 4. During their 1993 interview Sidney Matthew asked Runyan point-blank if he had pitched to a forward tee box on the eighteenth hole at Merion so he could clear the quarry, and Runyan dispelled the notion without hesitation.

In researching Runyan's first major championship victory—the 1934 PGA Championship—I used articles from the following newspapers: the *Brooklyn Times-Union* (July 28), *Brooklyn Daily Eagle* (July

30), *New York Daily News* (July 29, 30, 31), *Burlington Free Press* (July 30), *Binghamton (NY) Press and Sun-Bulletin* (July 27), *Tampa Times* (July 30), *Richmond Times-Dispatch* (July 30), and *Blytheville (AR) Courier News* (August 3). A telegram to Runyan from the "Big Three" of Waterman, Rosenberger, and Jelenko was part of Jeff Runyan's archive. Runyan's interviews with Guy Yocom and Sidney Matthew provided additional context and Runyan's own memories of the championship, including his feelings that everything was conspiring against him that week. The decision to include the probability of Runyan holing his eight-foot putt was inspired by my study of golf analytics, including Mark Broadie's landmark book *Every Shot Counts* (New York: Gotham Books, 2014). I would also like to thank golf strategist Scott Fawcett for hammering Broadie's data points into my psyche.

6. A Code of His Own

The scene that precedes chapter 6—Runyan and Olin Dutra meeting up for a friendly match at Metropolis Country Club—came from Ralph Trost's column, headlined "'David' and 'Goliath' Meet Again, and Once More David Is Victor," from the *Brooklyn Daily Eagle* on August 6, 1934. The story of Runyan purchasing the five-acre Arkansas farm for his parents came from "Fear of Tuberculosis Led Runyan into Golf," in the *Blytheville Courier News* on September 3, 1934. The Garland County Historical Society in Hot Springs had a file (File 13, Box 19) on Runyan in the Chamber of Commerce Collection that included two photos of the farmhouse and a pair of news clips about the purchase, both from unnamed newspapers.

The first paragraph of the main text is my own summation of the collective opinion of the leading sportswriters of the 1930s, whose fascination with Runyan centered on his knack for beating bigger, stronger opponents in spite of his supposed shortcomings. The Jimmy Powers column ("They Laughed!—Then Runyan Went Out and Won Pro Title") in the *New York Daily News* was published on July 31, 1934. Tommy Armour's comments about Runyan's popularity were included in that column. Ralph Trost's interview with Craig Wood was published in the *Brooklyn Daily Eagle* on August 4, 1934.

I read about plans for Paul Runyan's testimonial dinner at the Hotel Commodore in the September 4, 1934, edition of the *Bronxville Press.*

Runyan's contract with the Miami Biltmore was detailed in the *Miami Daily News* on October 9, 1934. Dan Jenkins's *Sports Illustrated* article "It Was a Fun Time in the Thirties" provided a few anecdotes about the relationship between pro golfers and hotel owners in Miami. The *Miami News* article from October 9 also previewed Runyan's trip to Australia, as did the *Louisville Courier-Journal* on October 8 and 13.

I pieced together the Australia trip through articles in the *Los Angeles Times* (October 10, 18, 19, 22, 1934, and January 4, 5, 1935), *Los Angeles Post* (January 4, 1935), and *Pomona (CA) Progress Bulletin* (January 4, 1935). The trip was well covered in the Australian newspapers, and I used articles from the *Melbourne Age* (November 7, 1934) and *Sydney Morning Herald* (November 6, 8, 9, 1934, and December 4, 1934). I found a passenger manifest for the group's return trip on the SS *Monterey*, which arrived in the port of Honolulu, Hawaii, on December 27, 1934. Jeff Runyan's archive contained numerous telegrams from the Australia trip, a passenger list for the SS *Mariposa*, a personalized program of the trip from the Victorian Golf Association, and a scrapbook that appears to have been a gift to Paul and Joan Runyan from an Australian journalist. And of course, he shared with me the photo of his father with Spencer and Carroll Tracy and the captain of the *Mariposa*. The scrapbook had some Australian news articles pasted inside, including one with Runyan's line about being a plugger and exercising good judgment. I found the same quotes in a June 9, 1934, article by Joseph Glass titled "Paul Runyan Prepared for His First National Title," published in *Literary Digest.*

For the 1935 North and South Open, Lori Wright from the Tufts Archives shared a booklet titled *A Message from Donald Ross*, in which Ross explained the course changes in his own words. The *Pinehurst Outlook* from March 1935 included a recap of the tournament. The rest of my description of Runyan's victory came from the *Charlotte Observer* on March 28, 1935; *Columbia Record* on March 30, 1935; and *Atlanta Constitution* on March 30, 1935. A *Charlotte News* story from October 27, 1935, noted that Pinehurst had been awarded the 1936 PGA Championship.

I found recaps of Runyan's victory in the 1935 Westchester Open in the *New York Daily News* and *Yonkers Herald Statesman* on August 24, 1935. I relied on the October 14, 1935, edition of the *Louisville Courier-Journal* for coverage of his win in the Grand Slam Open. The exhibition match that Runyan played with Frank Strafaci, Tommy Goodwin, and Babe Ruth was covered by the *Brooklyn Times Union* on August 13, 1935.

The John Pelley incident, which closes out the chapter—and is one of my favorite anecdotes about Runyan, period—made news in the *Brooklyn Citizen* and the *Miami News* on December 11, 1936. I wrote the story's postscript—about the Western Union telegram Runyan received at the 1937 PGA Championship—when I came across the telegram from Early and Butcher in Jeff Runyan's archived materials.

7. A Talent Nonpareil

The story that precedes this chapter—about Sam Snead's underappreciated knowledge of swing technique—came from my telephone interview with Al Barkow on February 11, 2021.

The story of Snead acquiring a new driver and putter on the eve of the 1937 LA Open came from Barkow's books *Gettin' to the Dance Floor* and *Sam*. I found Snead's tournament results from that event in the *Los Angeles Times* from January 12, 1937. The story of Snead inadvertently hustling Dutch Harrison and Bob Hamilton came from Dan Jenkins's *Sports Illustrated* article "It Was a Fun Time in the Thirties." Snead's victory in the Oakland Open was covered in the *Sacramento Bee* on January 18, 1937.

The oft-repeated anecdote about Snead hearing his picture would be in the *New York Times*, which has become part of the Snead lore, came from Barkow's *Sam*. I found recaps of Snead's victory at the Bing Crosby Pro-Am in the *San Francisco Examiner* and *San Mateo Times* from February 8, 1937.

Fred Corcoran's impact on Snead's career was described in Barkow's *Sam*. Sports agent Hughes Norton discussed Corcoran while reflecting on the impact of legendary agent Mark McCormack during his February 15, 2022, appearance on the *No Laying Up* podcast, episode 522. John J. Romano wrote a column titled "Young Sam Snead Hailed as New Sensation of Golf," which appeared in the *Miami Herald* on

February 15, 1937, and described Snead's rapid ascent in the golf world. Grantland Rice proffered his high opinion of Snead, which most sports fans probably viewed as a special seal of approval, in a column he wrote that I found in the *Louisville Courier-Journal* of February 13, 1937.

Snead's victory in the St. Paul Open was covered in the *Minneapolis Star Tribune* on August 2, 1937. I found recaps of his victories in the Nassau Open and the Miami Open in the *Miami Herald* from December 21 and 26, 1937. I found the Wilson HOL-HI K-28 advertisement in the same newspaper (December 26). The praise that Snead received from spectators and others after his win in Miami was reported in the *Pittsburgh Sun-Telegraph* on January 2, 1938, in an article headlined "Sam Snead Seen as Greater than Jones and Hagen."

I tracked Runyan's 1937 results in the same newspapers in which I followed Snead. The May 22, 1936, edition of the *Scarsdale Inquirer* ran a story about the Runyans buying a house on Malvern Road. Sidney Matthew prompted Runyan to explain his relationship with Spalding and J. Victor East in their 1993 interview, and that conversation included Runyan's description of his new set of irons and the process of getting used to them. Runyan's solid play in the opening round of the 1937 PGA Championship was covered in the *Pittsburgh Press* on May 25, 1937. That same newspaper included the story of Snead's rules snafu. In a column I found in the *Oshkosh (WI) Northwestern*, sports columnist Dillon Graham tracked the play of potential Ryder Cup members Runyan, Snead, and Byron Nelson.

In reading weekly golf coverage in newspapers from 1938, it's clear that most every sportswriter in the business considered Sam Snead to be the game's best player; it seemed that it was only a matter of time before that became a given. The *Daily Times* of Mamaroneck, New York, on September 28, 1938, ran a story under the headline "Snead Acclaimed as Nation's Greatest Golfer" after he had captured the Westchester 108-Hole Open.

Runyan's feelings about formalizing a pro golf tour were made known in newspapers around the country; I zeroed in on two clips in particular, both from January 3, 1938: one from the *Racine (WI) Journal Times* and one from the *Zanesville (OH) Signal*. The *Pittsburgh Sun-Telegraph* published a story on January 14, 1938, headlined "14-Club

Ruling Fails to Affect Golf Scoring," which detailed the effects of the change in the rules.

Results from the 1938 Los Angeles Open were carried daily in the *Los Angeles Times*, January 7–11, 1938. Highlights from Snead's repeat victory at the Crosby came from the *South Bend Tribune* on January 16; a final-round recap under the headline "Snead Repeats Win in Crosby Tourney" ran in the *San Bernardino County Sun* on January 17, 1938.

First-round results from the Pasadena Open were published in the *Hartford Courant* and the *Los Angeles Times* on January 22, 1938. The *Times* also recapped the tournament on January 25. The Jim Braddock victory over Tommy Farr was discussed at length in the sports pages of the *Brooklyn Daily Eagle* on January 25, 1938, and a story about Braddock's subsequent retirement was published in the *Oakland Tribune* on January 31.

Snead's victory at Greensboro, including his run-in with the rules of golf, Runyan's involvement, and columnist Jake Wade's assessment of the situation, was covered in the *Charlotte Observer*, March 26–29, 1938. I also relied on Ralph Trost's column, headlined "Snead Suffering from Top-Flight Golf Jitters," that ran in the *Brooklyn Daily Eagle* on March 19.

8. "Lawdy, the Man Ain't Human"

The description of the Shawnee Inn and Golf Resort that precedes chapter 8 was inspired by my visit to the resort in May 2021 and my tour of the grounds with Steve Taggart and Jon Kirkwood. Others who helped me get my bearings at Shawnee were Ginny Kirkwood, Gordon Way, Rob Howell, and J. J. Obstronski. Tom Kirkwood, Peter Trenham, and Joseph Bausch helped me understand what I could expect to see in advance of my trip. The rift between Gene Sarazen and the PGA that I allude to was described in the *Pottstown (PA) Mercury* on April 6, 1938.

Prior to my visit, author and historian Phil Young graciously shared with me some of the research he used as background for his own writing about Shawnee. That information included old photos of the property, maps of the golf course at different iterations of the routing, and a description of the golf course by A. W. Tillinghast himself, titled "The Golf Course of the Shawnee Country Club: Briefly Described by

Mr. A.W. Tillinghast, under whose supervision the course was planned and developed." I found additional background information about Tillinghast on the Baltusrol website (www.baltusrol.org). All that information helped me understand and describe the "golf capital of America."

Jon Kirkwood told me C. C. Worthington's backstory, and I supplemented that with Phil Young's unpublished writing on Worthington and his father, who had invented the direct-acting steam pump.

Tillinghast's quote about the conditions of the property being "most unusual" came from his description of the golf course that Phil Young shared with me. I found news clippings about the opening days of the Buckwood Inn scattered in Pennsylvania newspapers, including the *Wilkes-Barre Record* (May 24, 1911), *Allentown Leader* (June 22, 1911), and *Scranton Times-Tribune* (June 30, 1911). Through conversations with Steve Taggart and Jon Kirkwood I came to understand that Shawnee became a testing ground for Tillinghast to experiment with different course design ideas. From everything I gathered from Taggart and Kirkwood and information the club has on file, it seems that Tillinghast had carte blanche to modify the course as he wished—a testament to the strength of his relationship with Worthington.

The story of the Shawnee Open is told, to some extent, through displays and trophy cases in the golf shop at the Shawnee Inn and Golf Resort today. I found additional information about the tournament in Phil Young's unpublished writing, including John McDermott's regrettable comments about European players in 1913. The story of C. C. Worthington's efforts to help form the PGA of America was included in Harry Grayson's column in the *Greenville (OH) Daily Advocate* on July 11, 1938.

I first learned of the heat wave that factored into the 1938 PGA Championship from reading Al Barkow's *Gettin' to the Dance Floor*. After learning from Guy Yocom that Runyan emphasized the hot conditions in their interview, I dug into the newspapers to find out more. The *Allentown Morning Call* printed the story about Reverend Buettner, who was overcome by heat exhaustion twice that week. On July 11 the same newspaper reported about the tremendous crowds who sought relief at local swimming pools.

I nearly missed the story of Paul Runyan preparing for the heat at a training resort. At first it seemed like a throwaway line in his interview with Guy Yocom, but I followed the trail until I found more information about Bill Brown's Health Farm in Garrison, New York, which is now long gone. Cassie Ward, executive director of the Putnam History Museum in Cold Spring, New York, shared information on the Brown facility from the museum's files and pointed me toward some related articles. The brochure I referenced in the chapter was among the things she provided to me, and it included a vivid description of the resort's amenities. Guy Yocom's interview with Runyan that was published in the August 1994 issue of *Golf Digest* included Runyan's tactics for battling the heat. As a testament to how involved a person can get while working on a project like this, one night I dreamed that Runyan walked from the Brown Health Farm to Shawnee Country Club, then went out and won the PGA. Just to humor myself, I looked it up the next day, and it's about eighty-five miles from Garrison to Shawnee. No, Runyan did not walk to work that week.

I learned about the PGA Championship kickoff festivities that took place in the Buckwood Inn from a story in the *Allentown Morning Call* that was published on July 9, 1938. Associated Press sportswriter Paul Mickelson's column in the *Reading (PA) Times* on July 13 noted that the players were charged $8 per night for their hotel rooms at the Buckwood Inn. I narrowed down the list of favorites by examining pretournament sports columns in the *Miami Herald*, *Brooklyn Citizen*, *Lancaster (PA) New Era*, *Elmira (NY) Star-Gazette*, and *Allentown Morning Call*.

Sam Snead's victory with Vic Ghezzi at the Inverness Four-Ball was recounted in the *Cincinnati Enquirer* on May 30, 1938. The *Akron Beacon Journal* carried news of Snead's victory at the Goodall Round Robin with a large headline, "Sam Snead Beats Sarazen in Playoff for Top Money at Cincinnati," on June 27, 1938. Snead's victories at the West Virginia PGA and the West Virginia Pro-Am (where, interestingly, Snead's amateur teammate, Billy Campbell, was just fifteen years old) made news in the *Hinton (WV) Daily News* on July 8 and 9.

You could read about Howard Hughes's globetrotting just about everywhere in early July 1938, but I stuck with a story from the *Allen-*

town Morning Call on July 11 that included a photograph of Hughes and his four-person crew posing in front of an airplane. The headline "Hitler Attacks Futuristic Art" in that same edition of the *Morning Call* caught my attention, so I used information from the story in my narrative.

Qualifying results were published in the *Palm Beach Post* on July 11, 1938. Snead's play and his chances to win after his first-round 69 were the focus of an article in the *Lancaster New Era* on July 11.

Runyan told Al Barkow about bookmaker Jack Doyle in his interview for *Gettin' to the Dance Floor*, and the story made it into print. Tracking down information on Doyle took some work; while he was often mentioned or quoted in the newspaper, he was rarely the main focus of a story. He always seemed to be lurking in the shadows, being quoted in one story, laying odds in another, always in sight but never in focus. My description of Doyle was based on Walter McCallum's story "No Money in Golf for Bookmakers" from the *Evening Star* (Washington DC) on July 27, 1938. I learned about Doyle's background as a bookmaker and pool hall owner (and his decision to sell the pool hall in 1937) from articles in the *Brooklyn Daily Eagle* and *Rochester (NY) Democrat and Chronicle* from December 6, 1937. Doyle's 1938 predictions were from the *Brooklyn Daily Eagle* on December 28, 1937. An article from Henry McLemore that was published in the *Davenport (IA) Democrat and Leader* on May 20, 1938, detailed Doyle's decision to offer pari-mutuel betting on golf. Runyan's quote about Levi Lynch came from *Gettin' to the Dance Floor*. Walter McCallum's story from the *Evening Star* on July 27 included the description of Doyle hanging around Shawnee in a pair of broadcloth pants.

The comparison between Tony Manero and Cesar Romero was my own doing; after seeing photos of Manero, I compared him side by side with Romero and couldn't help but notice a resemblance. Interestingly, there were other similarities. For instance, they were both born in New York City, just two years apart. The story of Manero betting on himself at the 1936 U.S. Open came from *Gettin' to the Dance Floor*. In my interview with Guy Yocom, he recalled Runyan telling him the same story.

I followed the results from the week's play at Shawnee in various newspapers, including the *Brooklyn Citizen* (July 12), *New York Daily News* (July 13, 16), *Harrisburg Telegraph* (July 15), *Philadelphia Inquirer* (July 14, 16), and *Rochester Democrat and Chronicle* (July 16). Byron Nelson's comment, in which he says it wasn't his turn to win, came from an interview that was published in the *Reading (PA) Times* on July 15.

My reference to the famous photograph of Ben Hogan that was taken by Hy Peskin at the 1950 U.S. Open comes from my own memory. The brutally hot conditions that day at Shawnee were evident to me when I came across an Associated Press photo that ran in the *Philadelphia Inquirer* showing Gene Sarazen carrying an umbrella for shade. The story about heavyweight fighter Tony Galento relocating his training session came from the *Harrisburg Telegraph* on July 15. Runyan's quote about being smarter than the rest of the field—and the subsequent details about his wife drawing a cool bath—came from Barkow's *Gettin' to the Dance Floor*. Other details about his routine, such as avoiding ham and Coca-Cola, came from Guy Yocom's interview with Runyan.

I checked numerous New York newspapers for coverage of Howard Hughes's landing in New York but relied primarily on that of the *Brooklyn Citizen* from July 14 and the *New York Daily News* from July 15. The Snead-Foulis and Runyan-Smith matches were covered in the *Harrisburg Telegraph* on July 15. Bob Brumby's description of the Snead-Hines match was published in the *New York Daily News* on July 16; Brumby also reported on the Runyan-Picard match. Runyan's quote about Picard getting ruffled came from *Gettin' to the Dance Floor*. I found a reference to "Chocolate Soldier" Picard in the *Elmira (NY) Star-Gazette* from July 16.

Bob Brumby's line "David tees off against Goliath" came from the same July 16 story in the *New York Daily News* referenced above. Grantland Rice's preview of the match, in which he describes it as "the old battle between a hard puncher and a boxer," ran in the *Boston Globe* on July 16. Based on my knowledge of the two players, I attempted to explain for the reader the ways Snead and Runyan were similar and different.

Walter McCallum reported the story about the Shawnee locker room attendant carrying the $1,000 bet in the *Washington Evening*

Star on July 27. Bill Boni reported that Runyan was a 2-to-1 underdog to Snead in the *Evening Star* on July 18, two days after the match. Ultimately—as I allude to in the main text—nothing that's been published disputes Runyan's account of the odds that Jack Doyle put out. Without question, Runyan was the underdog; Doyle's odds seem to be somewhere between 2-to-1 and 10-to-1. In the paragraph where I describe the possibility of Runyan eating breakfast and descending the stairs of the Buckwood Inn to find Jack Doyle, I hope it's clear—notice that in the text I used the word "maybe"—that this scene was possible, maybe even likely to have occurred. However, I've used my artistic license to describe this scenario, based on my knowledge of Runyan and Doyle. Some of the minor details of the Buckwood Inn, such as the number of stairs at the main entrance, were based on my visit there in 2021.

The scene on the first tee of Shawnee Country Club before the start of play was based mostly on press photos I found while researching the Runyan-Snead match. Those photos revealed some of the small details, such as the stitching on Runyan's right collar. If you're wondering how I put together his color scheme, I didn't; it was reported in the newspapers. Henry McLemore, in the *Blackwell (OK) Daily Journal* on July 17, described Runyan's attire as "pastel shaded haberdashery." Ralph Trost, in the *Brooklyn Daily Eagle* on July 17, noted that Runyan wore a light blue hat and dark blue trousers. Earlier in the same story, he described Runyan as "a tough little man masquerading in baby blue." In the photograph where the two players shake hands, Runyan is holding his hat and the unidentified object (which looks like a small tin) in his left hand. Reports of the crowd size that day varied slightly, but most newspapers pegged the turnout between 2,500 and 3,000 people. The *Philadelphia Inquirer* reported 3,000. Seabiscuit's triumph at the Hollywood Gold Cup was reported in the *Allentown Morning Call* on July 17.

I found the Movietone News footage embedded in a video tribute to Runyan created for his 2011 induction by the Colorado Golf Hall of Fame (accessed at www.coloradogolfhalloffame.org). The *Philadelphia Inquirer* reported that Joan Runyan was on the tee to watch her husband begin his round.

Reconstructing the action from the final match was a tall order, but thankfully the *Brooklyn Daily Eagle* published a hole-by-hole description of the action on July 17. I relied heavily on these descriptions throughout this part of the narrative. I also read coverage of the match in the following newspapers: the *Philadelphia Inquirer* (July 17), *Ithaca Journal* (July 18), *Washington Evening Star* (July 18), *Blackwell Daily Journal* (July 17), *Arkansas Gazette* (July 17), and *Allentown Morning Call* (July 17). I found Henry McLemore's column on the stymie in the *Elmira (NY) Star-Gazette*, published July 16. The Movietone News reel showed Runyan chipping his ball over Snead's and grabbing it out of the cup as he marched off the green.

Jeff Runyan's archive contained numerous congratulatory telegrams from his father's friends around the country, and many of those people indicated they had followed the action on the radio.

I based the line "I can win" on various interviews and accounts Runyan gave over the years in which he explained that he coped with pressure by telling himself that his opponent was feeling just as much strain as he was and he needed to simply remain focused on the business at hand. Snead's quote, "This isn't golf, it's magic," and his thought that he couldn't make a putt in a bathtub came from his book *The Education of a Golfer* (New York: Simon and Schuster, 1962).

The scene of Runyan and Snead crossing the bridge over the Binniekill was inspired by an International News press photo. Snead's quote about being unable to match Runyan and Runyan's response that his luck was holding out came from Bob Brumby's story in the *New York Daily News* on July 17. Henry McLemore's line about Runyan spending the intermission in a Turkish bath came from his story in the *Blackwell Daily Journal* on July 17. McLemore was also the writer who described Runyan as "merciless as an executioner." Ralph Trost's description of Snead's despondency was included in his recap of the match in the *Brooklyn Daily Eagle* on July 17.

During my visit to Shawnee, its general manager, Rob Howell, guided me to the Shawnee archive room. That collection included a souvenir program from the 1938 PGA Championship, and Jack Patroni's hole description was included in that document. Steve Taggart took me out to the site of the former teeing ground of the eleventh hole, and we drove the length of the hole in a golf cart before getting out to examine what's left of the old green site. The match recap in the *Philadelphia Inquirer* included the scene where Snead's ball was stepped on and his joke that he was going to win. Snead's reaction ("Lawdy, the man ain't human") after the final putt had been holed came from Henry McLemore's write-up in the *Blackwell Daily Journal*. I relied on Movietone News footage to describe the melee of spectators rushing onto the green after Runyan clinched the match.

9. No Days Off

As I allude to in the main text, the section that precedes this chapter was influenced by the "Little Poison" article published in *Time* magazine on July 25, 1938. Runyan's quote about taking pleasure out of beating bigger players came from Al Barkow's *Gettin' to the Dance Floor*, although Runyan repeated some version of that line more than once.

The first three paragraphs of this chapter about the walk back to the clubhouse were inspired by a photograph of Runyan carrying the RUNYAN 8 UP sign as a throng of happy spectators gathered around him. My visit to Shawnee had helped me get familiar with the property, so I used Google Earth to plot the most likely route Runyan and others took back to the clubhouse and came up with a reasonable estimate of the distance. Then I contrasted Runyan's joy with the disappointment and shock Snead must have been feeling in those moments.

Walter McCallum's article "No Money in Golf for Bookmakers," which ran in the *Washington Evening Star* on July 27, inspired me to close out the Jack Doyle story. When I came across the telegram Doyle had sent to Runyan on the day of the finals in Jeff Runyan's archive, I had the cherry on top.

Yet again, it was a photograph that helped me set a scene; technically, it was two photos—one of Paul Runyan planting a kiss on Joan and another one where he grabs her in a bear hug and hoists her off the ground. As an aside, if you have the time and look in the right spots you will find more than just these two photos of Runyan embracing his wife after golf victories. I'm sure the press loved it for their newspapers, but it's noteworthy that on numerous occasions Runyan's first act after winning a golf tournament was to find his beloved wife and share the joy. Brumby's line about Runyan's pretty wife Joan came from his write-up in the *New York Daily News* on July 17. Charles Bartlett's column in the *Chicago Tribune* ran on July 17.

The details of the trophy presentation came from Fred Corcoran's article "Paul Runyan Gains PGA Title" in the August 1938 edition (vol. 19, no. 3) of *Professional Golfer of America*, the "official organ" of the PGA. Runyan's comments about not believing the outcome of the match were published in nearly every newspaper that covered the match. His comments to Al Barkow decades later were from *Gettin' to the Dance Floor*. I asked Al Barkow in our interview about how Snead coped with the loss, and his explanation is in the text.

Associated Press sportswriter Bill Boni reported in the *Washington Evening Star* on July 18, 1938, that Runyan returned to work at Metropolis Country Club the day after his PGA Championship victory. The *Arkansas Gazette* described on July 17 the reaction in Runyan's home state. The rest of the telegrams I mention in this chapter—and there were many more that I failed to mention—were part of Jeff Runyan's archive. I simply put them in chronological order based on the timestamp. Milton B. Reach's congratulations reached Runyan in a letter, dated July 18, 1938, on A. G. Spalding & Bros. stationery. The best part of the letter was Runyan's response, handwritten in pencil in the margins of the Reach letter. However, I'm unsure if the response was ever typed and mailed. Runyan wrote, "I cannot praise my new irons highly enough as they were entirely responsible for the good putting I was able to do." Presumably, he's saying that the irons allowed him to hit the ball close enough to have makeable putts.

I found Charles Bartlett's coverage of Sam Snead's triumph at the Chicago Open the following week in the *Chicago Tribune* from July 25, 1938.

10. "Whatever Became of Paul Runyan?"

Alan Shipnuck's August 13, 2020, article for *Golf* magazine, "The Great Escape: Soldiers Turning to Golf amid WWII Provides a Lesson in Playing through Tough Times," got me thinking about framing this chapter not just through the movements of Paul Runyan but through the context of the entire sport of golf and the war's impact. I tried to convey that idea in the three paragraphs before the chapter formally begins.

The South American trip that Runyan made with Jug McSpaden in the fall of 1938 was covered by the *Atlanta Constitution* and the *New York Daily News* on October 1, 1938. The *San Bernardino Sun* published a short article about Runyan's victory at the Argentine Open on October 31. That same day the *Brooklyn Daily Eagle* explained the fracas caused by Orson Welles's "War of the Worlds."

David Bloom's profile of Runyan in the *Memphis Commercial Appeal* included a recap of Runyan's play in South America and his feelings about the Snead victory at Shawnee.

I tracked Runyan's play from 1939 to 1941 in a variety of newspapers. His victory at the Goodall Round Robin in 1941 (and a preview of his qualifying round for the U.S. Open) was covered in the *Elmira (NY) Star-Gazette* on May 26, 1941. Jeff Runyan's archive included a tournament program from the Goodall championship, a Bristol brochure, and dozens of congratulatory telegrams that his father's friends sent after the victory (including messages from Craig and Jackie Wood, Mannie Dias, Harry Tenenbaum, and others). I found more information on the paddle-grip putter and Runyan's play at the 1941 U.S. Open in the *Dallas Morning News* from June 7, 1941, and the *Arkansas Gazette* from June 8, 1941.

From a clip in the *Richmond (VA) News Leader* of December 17, 1943, I learned that Runyan and Harry Cooper were on a golf course in Miami when they learned of the attack on Pearl Harbor. The Hank Greenberg and Bob Feller news was reported in the *Brooklyn Daily Eagle* on December 10 and 28, 1941, respectively.

Golf historian John Fischer was a great source for information about golf during the war; so was the Alan Shipnuck article referenced above. An article in the *Paterson (NJ) Morning Call* on November 11, 1942, "Professional Golfers Are Undecided about '43 Season," described just how indefinite tournament plans were at the outset of the war. Runyan's tournament results at the 1942 Masters and the compilation of his good play at the event since 1934 were neatly compiled in the letter from Augusta chairman Clifford Roberts that was in Jeff Runyan's archive. When you see something written on Augusta National letterhead, it gets your attention. An article I found in the *Danville (VA) Bee* from April 14, 1943, described the drastic changes at Augusta National since the 1942 Masters had been played.

It might have been underappreciated at the time, but Fred Corcoran's role in promoting golf during the war was well documented in the newspapers. For that section—including modifications to the professional tournament schedule in the early days of the war—I researched stories in the following newspapers: the *Oakland Tribune* (January 16, 1942), *Salt Lake Tribune* (January 2, 1942), *Fort Worth Star-Telegram* (March 18, 1942), *Asheville Citizen-Times* (May 30, 1942), and *Richmond Times-Dispatch* (March 23, 1944). The results of the 1942 Hale America National Open (and the story of Runyan's disgust with his play) were published in the *Miami News* on June 22, 1942.

Runyan's enlistment in the navy made news in the *Northwest Arkansas Times* on December 12, 1942. His pro-am partnership with Gene Tunney was mentioned in Dan Jenkins's article "It Was a Fun Time in the Thirties." Jeff Runyan told me what he knew about his uncle's navy career. I found more information about it through various articles in the *Hot Springs Sentinel-Record* and the *Arkansas Gazette* (namely, the article "Tells of Heroism of Wasp Crew" from October 28, 1942). There was a lengthy feature on Elmo Runyan in the *Arkansas Gazette* on December 13, 1942, titled "Back from the Solomons." I found a History.com article by Erin Blakemore, titled "WWII Wreck Found of USS Wasp, Where 176 Died after Torpedo Attack," that explained how the *Wasp* had been found in 2019.

The photo of Runyan demonstrating artificial respiration was in the *Asheville Citizen-Times* on January 30, 1944. I was able to place the start of Runyan's time in Norfolk through a story in the *Pittsburgh Press* on October 4, 1945. Ralph Trost's article in the *Brooklyn Daily Eagle* on June 15, 1944, provided some background on Runyan's day-to-day routine in the service. Trost also reported in the *Daily Eagle* on June 23, 1944, that Joan Runyan was working at a Norfolk book shop. An article from the *Richmond Times-Dispatch* of July 8, 1944, described the sports-crazed atmosphere in Norfolk and supplemented what John Fischer told me in our interview. Al Barkow told the story of Sam Snead's induction into the navy in *Gettin' to the Dance Floor*.

The background on Johnny Fischer came from his son John, whom I quote in the main text. I learned about Runyan's stint as a traffic cop in the *Binghamton (NY) Press and Sun-Bulletin* of April 24, 1944. Again it was Ralph Trost who tracked down Runyan while on leave to learn about his driving range at Norfolk and the hours he spent battling the sun; that article ran in the *Brooklyn Daily Eagle* on June 15, 1944. The results of the match between the Norfolk and Bainbridge golf teams were from the *Newport News Daily Press* on May 24, 1944, which followed up in May 1945 with the results of the match at the James River Country Club. The Red Cross Open was covered in that same publication on June 15, 1944, and in the *Brooklyn Daily Eagle* on June 15 and 19.

It was alarming and sad to come across rumors of Runyan's demise as a golfer, although those reports proved to be both premature and inaccurate. I gathered the bulk of that story from an article in the *San Francisco Examiner* from December 8, 1944. Ralph Trost had alluded to a slip in Runyan's play in the *Brooklyn Daily Eagle* on June 17, 1944.

Sam Snead's discharge from the navy was covered in the *St. Petersburg Times* on September 13, 1944. Runyan's win at the 1945 Virginia Open was mentioned in the *Los Angeles Times* on December 14, 1945, but the *Richmond News Leader* and the *Newport News Daily Press* published more complete recaps on July 17, 1945.

Jeff Runyan verified his older brother's birthdate, and an article in the *Pittsburgh Press* on October 4, 1945, provided the date of Runyan's discharge from the navy. That same article reported that Runyan would be quitting golf to enter private business.

11. La Jolla

The segment that precedes the chapter is a direct quote from my interview with Jeff Runyan on March 2, 2022.

I was shocked the first time I learned that Paul Runyan left golf for five years to work as a jewelry sales rep. It baffled me; in some respects it still does. However, his son Jeff helped me better understand the decision by describing how his father was between country club jobs, and with the war behind him the timing was right for a fresh start. Yet I wonder if Paul Runyan had one or two more major championships up his sleeve that he never realized because of the partial career detour. We will never know.

I found a photograph of Runyan making a jewelry sales call in the May 26, 1946, edition of the *Des Moines Register*, under the headline "Paul Runyan Sells Jewelry." The *San Bernardino County Sun* published a brief article, headlined "Salesman Runyan," on July 1, 1946, that reported his $30,000 salary. During Runyan's five-year stint in the jewelry business, almost every time he was mentioned in a golf article, the writer noted that he was a part-time golfer, full-time jewelry salesman. Runyan's opinion of the job—including his eventual disdain for it—came from his interview in the PGA *Book of Golf: 1978*.

I learned about Pasadena's history, particularly its postwar growth, from the city's website (www.cityofpasadena.net). Chuck Courtney and Jeff Runyan described for me why the city appealed to Runyan, including the proximity of the California Institute of Technology and the Jet Propulsion Lab and the smart people who worked there. Ralph Trost's column in the *Brooklyn Daily Eagle* on June 18, 1946, reported on the side hustles of professional golfers such as Jug McSpaden and Vic Ghezzi. Guy Butler of the *Miami News* had written a similar column that appeared in print on March 10, 1946. Byron "Umbrella Man" Nelson's side business was reported in the *Wilkes-Barre Times Leader* on July 11, 1945, and in the *Knoxville News-Sentinel* on August 24, 1945.

The 1946 U.S. Open at Canterbury was covered in the *Brooklyn Daily Eagle* on June 11, 1946, and the *Rochester Democrat and Chronicle* on June 16, 1946. I found coverage of Runyan's runner-up finish to Ben Hogan that fall at the Dallas Open in the *Chattanooga Daily Times* and the *Pasadena Star-News* from September 30. Al Barkow told me about the 1947 U.S. Open at St. Louis Country Club and the unfortunate result for Sam Snead. I found additional coverage of the event in the *St. Louis Star and Times* from June 12, 1947.

Runyan's victory at the 1947 Southern California PGA Championship was covered in the *Los Angeles Times* on August 10 and 11, 1947. For background information on Annandale Golf Club, I turned to the club's website (www.annandalegolf.com). Although he would have been just a young boy, Jeff Runyan had some memories of the family's Victorian house in Pasadena and Gertye Harris taking care of the boys.

Information about Runyan's dissatisfaction with the jewelry job came from the PGA *Book of Golf: 1978*. Runyan's quote about polishing up his sales talk after getting drubbed by Ben Hogan was from the *Los Angeles Times* on October 18, 1948.

Jeff Runyan's birth was announced in the *Los Angeles Times* on February 4, 1948, under the headline "Golfer Paul Runyan Proud Father Again." Walter Runyan's death was reported in the *Arkansas Democrat* on March 20, 1949. I obtained a copy of his death certificate from the Arkansas State Board of Health. During my 2022 visit to Hot Springs, Arkansas, I visited Greenwood Cemetery to see the graves of Walter and Mamie (she died in 1976). Elmo "Dick" Runyan's appointment as manager of the Hot Springs Convention Auditorium was reported in the *Hot Springs Sentinel-Record* on March 14, 1967. His other civic responsibilities were reported by the *Sentinel-Record* after his death on November 7, 1971, and then on October 14, 1973.

Runyan's evening golf clinics at the Wilshire Driving Range were reported by Charles Curtis in the *Los Angeles Times* on June 12, 1949. Harry Brooks's sudden death and the events that sent Runyan to Annandale as golf pro came from the *Pasadena Independent* (October 26 and November 18, 1949) and the *Los Angeles Times* (November 18, 1949).

You might recall from my notes on chapter 2 how handwriting expert Susan Westenbroek recognized in Paul Runyan's handwriting a fascination with numbers. That seemed to jibe with what I had read in Runyan's books, where he would frequently reference odds and numbers to help make a point. Both Guy Yocom and Al Barkow told me that Runyan had a head for numbers. That's all true, said Chuck Courtney, who is the former student referenced in this chapter. Courtney explained to me how Runyan used numbers and science in his teaching; he also told me how he blended those rigorous disciplines with Ernest Jones's philosophies. Runyan's line about being overly specific in his instruction comes from the introduction to his book *The Short Way to Lower Scoring*. The story about Byron Nelson's 66 at Augusta National came from Runyan's 1988 speech at the PGA Coaching Summit.

I traced Runyan's qualification and march through the 1951 U.S. Open at Oakland Hills in the following newspapers: the *Los Angeles*

Times (June 5 and 17, 1951), *Nashville Banner* (June 15, 1951), and *Rock Island (IL) Argus* (June 16, 1951). The story of Runyan's malfunctioning putter that he took off the rack at Annandale for the U.S. Open came from Guy Yocom's interview with Runyan. All the telegrams Runyan received during the tournament were in Jeff Runyan's archive.

Runyan described Annandale as "the best job I've ever had" in an interview with the *Pasadena Independent* on October 22, 1954. That article included the family's reasons for moving out of Pasadena, the smog being the primary one. I found the description of Rose Bowl revelers in the January 1, 1955, edition of the *Los Angeles Times*.

My description of La Jolla Country Club was formed through my interview with Chuck Courtney, who has been associated with the club for his entire life, and my own tour of the property in early 2022, which was guided by Courtney and Frank Merhar. Courtney directed me to the club's history book, *La Jolla Country Club: Celebrating Eighty Years of Prestige, Perseverance, and Benevolence* (Virginia Beach VA: Donning, 2006), by Marc Figueroa. Jeff Runyan's description of La Jolla as "Camelot" helps explain just how much the Runyans loved La Jolla—and how loved they were by members of the club. Chuck Courtney shared the story of the Southern California Golf Association officials at the club. Jeff Runyan told me about his father's affinity for caddies, even if it meant bailing them out of jail. Courtney and Runyan both described to me how Paul and Joan ran the golf shop and how Jack Taylor became such a trusted assistant.

I was fortunate enough to have interviewed Phil Rodgers a few times before his 2018 death. I had hoped to write a book about his career, but what emerged from those conversations was an article I wrote about my interviews with Rodgers and his up-and-down golf career; it was published in the *Golfer's Journal* in March 2021. Rodgers also guided me toward Runyan, and that ultimately led to this book. Rodgers's quote about accepting Runyan's advice came from his book *Play Lower Handicap Golf* (Trumbull CT: Golf Digest, 1986). I found the story of the one-club match between Rodgers and Runyan in the La Jolla Country Club history book by Marc Figueroa. The story of Runyan offering Rodgers advice on the morning of his victory at the 1962 Los Angeles Open came from the *Los Angeles Times* on January

9, 1962. Runyan's quote about Rodgers doing everything he asked of him came from the *Pasadena Independent* on January 12, 1962. The tales of legendary pro golfers coming to practice with Runyan at La Jolla Country Club were told to me by Chuck Courtney and Phil Rodgers.

On the USGA's website I found a 2008 story by David Shefter about opening day at Torrey Pines in 1957 and Runyan's involvement. Just to be sure I had thoroughly "researched" the property, when I visited La Jolla in 2022 I played a dozen or so holes at Torrey Pines (carrying my bag, at twilight rate) before darkness, and a sudden rain shower sent me inside. Runyan's comments about Rodgers needing to deny himself off the course came from the story in the *Pasadena Independent* on January 12, 1962.

12. Last Hurrah

The story of the near sale of La Jolla Country Club that precedes the chapter comes mainly from Tod Leonard's article "Legendary Links: La Jolla Country Club Set to Host the 119th SCGA Amateur Championship," published in *FORE* magazine on April 26, 2018. A few other details in those three paragraphs came from *La Jolla Country Club: Celebrating Eighty Years of Prestige, Perseverance, and Benevolence*.

Most of the details of the Runyan home near La Jolla Country Club came from a January 22, 1956, edition of the *Los Angeles Times*, where Maxine Bartlett showcased the interior design. After I mentioned the article to Jeff Runyan, he explained that his mother and his aunt Jane shared a passion for what we today commonly call "flipping" houses. Jane (Harris) Schwinn was apparently a well-known interior designer along the California coast, and Jeff said that she and Joan were "constantly driving my dad crazy" by buying up properties and renovating them. Jeff also explained to me that his dad was not the sort of guy to sit around and be proud of his accomplishments when there was work to be done (or golf to be played).

I followed the Runyan buzz saw through competitive senior golf in 1961–62 in the *Tampa Tribune* (July 7, 9, 1961, and February 20, 1962), *Los Angeles Times* (September 17, 1961), *Sacramento Bee* (February 20, 1961), *Oakland Tribune* (June 25, 1961), *Somerset (PA) Daily American* (February 20, 1961), *York (PA) Daily Record* (July 7, 1962), *Charlotte News* (February

20, 1962), *Colton (CA) Courier* (July 14, 1961), *Arizona Republic* (July 12, 1961), *Raleigh News and Observer* (July 16, 1961), *San Diego Union* (July 22, 1961), and *Birmingham (England) Post & Birmingham Gazette* (July 7 and 10, 1961). Jeff Runyan told me about traveling to Europe and watching his dad play—all positive memories.

In writing these scenes I sometimes think of the action like a movie montage. I doubt that translates onto the page, but it helps me sort out the cadence in my head. As I pictured Runyan steamrolling through the Senior PGA Championship and traveling to England to play in the PGA World Seniors' Championship, I kept hearing "Green Onions" in my head. When I discovered that it had been released in 1962, I decided to celebrate the coincidence by weaving it into the narrative.

13. High Heavenly Ground

At the time of this writing, I had been playing golf for about twenty-five years and had never heard of Throlf, so when I read about the game and Runyan's involvement in promoting it, I figured using the story would help reveal something about Runyan's character. I suppose that "something" would be his enthusiasm for golf and outdoor recreation, no matter how far afield it was from the traditional golf that he played. The Throlf news articles appeared in the *Chula Vista Star-News* on May 31, 1968, and the *Imperial Beach (CA) Star-News* on May 30, 1968.

For my research I tracked down copies of *Paul Runyan's Book for Senior Golfers* (New York: Dodd, Mead, 1962) and Snead's *The Education of a Golfer*. In Runyan's book I found his tips, such as swinging a garden rake and eating honey to calm his nerves.

Runyan's speeches to the Boston Golf Writers and New York Golf Writers were covered in the *Boston Herald* on October 13, 1963. His talk to the San Diego Advertising and Sales Club made news in the *Venice (CA) Vanguard* on February 3, 1968. His 1968 speeches to the Northwest Section of the PGA were previewed in the *Tacoma News Tribune* on February 4 and recapped on February 28. I found an advertisement for Rich's Golf Jamboree in the *Atlanta Constitution* from March 28, 1968.

I found background information on the formation of Sahalee Country Club on the club's website (www.sahalee.com). Runyan's 1998 interview with John Bodenhamer in *Pacific Northwest Golfer* magazine described how he had come to work there. The April 5, 1969, edition of the *Times Recorder* of Zanesville, Ohio, carried a brief article about Runyan's decision to leave La Jolla for Sahalee.

The *San Antonio Express* on July 20, 1968, ran a story about Runyan's appearance at the PGA Championship. A photo of Runyan wearing plaid pants and an oversized hat accompanied the story.

John Bodenhamer's *Pacific Northwest Golfer* article described the conversations Paul and Joan had while deciding whether to move to Washington. Runyan also told Bodenhamer about the spartan conditions while the club was being built.

The article headlined "Paul Runyan Leaves Rain" in the *Tacoma News Tribune* on January 21, 1972, explained that the dreary Seattle weather was the primary reason for moving to Green Gables in Denver. The Tacoma newspaper ran another story the following day that included the news of Runyan's departure.

I interviewed longtime Green Gables member Don Brenner twice by telephone in 2020, and he provided tremendous insight into Runyan's time at the club. Jeff Runyan lived in Denver for a portion of the time his parents lived there and worked for his father at the club, and he had much to share about those years.

Considering how well Runyan had played into late middle age (and even his senior years), it was a bit of a sad ending for him at the PGA Championship. He simply couldn't hit the ball far enough to handle the course setup. I used two stories to help describe the scene at Tanglewood Park: one from the *Raleigh News and Observer* and one from the *Charlotte Observer* on August 9, 1974. Runyan made light of his final PGA Championship in his remarks at the 1988 PGA Teaching and Coaching Summit. He said, "I withdrew from the tournament after taking 84 from the first round when I had gotten down in two from 150 yards four times. And still shot 84. Because I couldn't reach the fairways. They let the grass grow to 235 yards. I'm trying to hit the walking path going down it to get it in the fairway." His comments elicited laughter from the crowd.

Longtime PGA member Skip Tredway described how Runyan let his hair grow out as he aged. Skip also told me the Mark Brooks story from the 1980 Trans-Mississippi Amateur. Don Brenner told me about Runyan's relationship with Ben Hogan; the topic also came up in Guy Yocom's interview with Runyan. Runyan shared the story about Hogan watching Runyan chip at the 1988 PGA Teaching and Coaching Summit. The letter that Runyan wrote to La Jolla Country Club president George Delafield accepting honorary membership at the club in 1976 was included as a foreword to the club's history book.

14. Author and Influencer

My interviews with Jeff Runyan and Patti and John Brugman helped me understand how Runyan evolved as a thinker. I wanted to initiate that topic before this chapter formally began because it's a recurring theme throughout the main text. Jeff Runyan told me about his father's attempts at taking the family to church when they lived in La Jolla.

Early on in my Runyan research I purchased a used copy of *The Short Way to Lower Scoring*. I've owned a copy of Ben Hogan's *Five Lessons* since I was a teenager; it contains Anthony Ravielli's illustrations.

It's widely known among serious golfers and golf professionals (of a certain age) that Phil Rodgers helped Jack Nicklaus resurrect his career, and part of my intent in the early part of this chapter was to explain Runyan's involvement. It started with Runyan's book, which Nicklaus purchased for himself, according to his own book, *My Story* (New York: Simon and Schuster, 1997). Rodgers explained to me his involvement with Nicklaus, which has been well documented over the years. I asked Don Brenner if there was much hoopla at Green Gables over Runyan's book or Nicklaus's revival, and he told me the reaction was subdued.

Jeff Runyan described the circumstances of his mother's sudden death, and Brenner explained his role in reaching out to Runyan to see when he would resume teaching at the club.

In my interviews with Jeff Runyan we spent the majority of our time discussing his father as an old man; Jeff described for me how his father dealt with Joan's passing and his decision to leave Denver and move in with Paul Jr. in La Jolla. That conversation was solemn until Jeff recalled his dad's ability to bounce back and keep fighting.

Bill Froloff described Runyan's play at the Vintage Club in 1982 and shared numerous Runyan anecdotes in his article in the *Palm Springs Desert Sun* on March 13, 1982. Runyan's play at the 1982 PGA Seniors' Championship and his battle to get exemptions from qualifying for senior golf tournaments came from articles in the *Palm Beach Post* and the *Fort Lauderdale News* on December 3, 1982. I learned about Runyan's Australia trip from the *Melbourne Age* piece that was published on December 30, 1982. Dick Drager and I spent a few hours together in late 2020, and he happily shared stories from his days working with Runyan in the Golf Digest schools.

Jeff Runyan and Patti Brugman recounted how Paul got together with longtime friend Berniece Harbers. Patti told me the story about the $25,000 wedding ring and her efforts to get it to the ceremony on time. When she told me that story, I hadn't learned that Runyan spent five years in the jewelry business; after learning that, the story of the wedding ring made more sense.

In my interview with Al Barkow, he told me about Runyan asking if he wanted to stay the night. Patti Brugman told me about Runyan's involvement in the State Department's People to People sports program, and a few news stories mentioned it as an aside. She and Jeff Runyan also told me how Runyan got involved with Callaway Golf, the Hickory Stick putter, and longtime club designer Richard Helmstetter. From everything Jeff Runyan told me, it appeared that Callaway had treated Runyan and his family in a first-class manner.

Runyan's 1990 induction into the World Golf Hall of Fame was a small news item in the November 4, 1990, edition of the *Corpus Christi Caller-Times*. Seeking more information, I visited Runyan's entry on the World Golf Hall of Fame website (www.worldgolfhalloffame.org). The *Tucson Citizen* covered Runyan's victory at the 1991 Super-Seniors Golf Tournament at Canoa Hills in an article published on April 30, 1991. The following day, the *Arizona Daily Star* ran a story about Runyan's appearance in the tournament.

15. "The Legend Never Really Died"

I never made it to Fargo. However, I spoke by telephone with Fargo businessman Roger Reierson in November 2020. Reierson met Paul Runyan during the 1995 U.S. Junior Amateur Championship and helped escort him around the club during the week. Reierson recounted the whole experience to me and steered me in the right direction as I probed for more details about Runyan's time in Fargo during the 1920s. The scene from that week precedes the final chapter and is straight from Reierson's memory.

I can't believe I've made it this far without mentioning Bob Denney. I came across a story about Denney's retirement from the PGA, where he had served as historian emeritus. I reached out to him by email and he agreed to a telephone interview. It turned out he had written an article about Runyan in July 2020 ("Paul Runyan Was 'Little Poison' in Competition, but a Gem on the Lesson Tee to Generations of Players") as one of his last assignments for the PGA before easing into retirement. Denney had been the last journalist to interview Runyan before he died, and I asked him what attracted him to Runyan. Why had he visited Palm Springs for an interview with an aging golf pro? Among the reasons Denney recalled was the feeling he got watching Runyan receive the PGA's Distinguished Service Award at Sahalee in 1998. Confirming Denney's memory, I found an article about the occasion in the *Tacoma News Tribune* (August 12, 1998) and other mentions in Runyan's obituaries. Jeff Runyan shared some memories (and photographs) of that trip. The magazine article I referenced where Runyan predicted Vijay Singh and others to factor into the championship was John Bodenhamer's piece from *Pacific Northwest Golfer*.

Runyan's godson John Fischer told me about the day he spent with Runyan at the Masters Par-3 Contest in 1999. Ben Crenshaw also recounted that day for me—which, if you're paying close attention, was the same Masters Par-3 Contest from the prologue. Other sources I consulted on the topic were Michael Mayo's article in the *South Florida Sun Sentinel*, Paul Newberry's Associated Press story that I located in the *Indiana (PA) Gazette*, and a story from *Florida Today*, all published on April 8, 1999. One final note on John Fischer: his article "In Match Play, It's Anyone's Game," from March 24, 2020, recounts Runyan's victory over Snead and is a fun read for anyone who enjoys the match-play format. It was published on *Sports Illustrated*'s Morning Read: Golf at a Glance website (www.morningread.com).

Patti Brugman recounted Bea Runyan's funeral and the scene in the breakfast room with Paul. Jeff Runyan filled in some details for me in our interview and explained how his dad wound up moving in with him in Palm Desert. Larry Bohannan, who is something of a legendary golf writer in the Palm Springs community, had a piece titled "Runyan Taught Good Game" published in the *Palm Springs Desert Sun* on March 19, 2002; it explained how Runyan went about asking Joe Simonds to teach at the Golf Center.

Jeff Runyan told me about his father's many health problems as he aged and recalled the moment that Paul came down the stairs and saw the news of the September 11, 2001, terrorist attacks.

In Bob Denney's 2020 article, he wrote about the last lesson Runyan gave before his death in 2002. I started combing the internet for clues on how to track down the retired flight attendants who took that lesson, and somehow I found them. Alona McFarland-Hudgens and Roxanne Davis remembered that day well, especially considering it was two decades in the past, and they shared details from the lesson.

Jeff Runyan recalled his father's final days for me, and I tracked the rest of it through newspapers. I read dozens of Paul Runyan obituaries, but the ones that stuck out were from the *New York Times*, *Los Angeles Times*, and *Hot Springs Sentinel-Record*. Jeff Runyan and Chuck Courtney recalled the memorial service at Annandale. Sam Snead's last appearance at the Masters was detailed in Al Barkow's *Sam*.

I was privileged to be present for the final scene at Jeff Runyan's house with the olive-colored trunk. Only Jeff would know, but I would wager that he found the experience of rummaging through that trunk—which, as I wrote, had dogged him for years—with someone who was genuinely interested in every photograph, news clipping, scrapbook, and old scorecard or telegram he pulled out of it a bit more tolerable than doing it alone with a burn barrel at his side. That day in La Quinta was a special moment in the production of this book; so was the day a month or so later in Hot Springs when I spent an afternoon at Hot Springs Country Club and Greenwood Cemetery. In caddie parlance, I had made a loop with the story of Paul Runyan's golfing life. I had taken the story from its roots out to the farthest point from home and then brought it back to where it began, on the narrow Bermuda fairways adjacent to an old dairy farm in Arkansas.